CHURCH, THE FALLING EMPIRE

Why they are so weak and strategies to save the church or die with them.

Death and life in the pulpit!

By Stewart Marshall Gulley
© November 2019 Revised
Revelation 2000

P.O. Box 2063
Los Angeles, California 90078

ISBN 1-928561-03-9

FREE DOWNLOAD
The 5 Things You Can Do Now
to Save the Church
Web: stewartmarshallgulley.com

MISSION STATEMENT
Self-actualization and realization:
Everything you need is already in you: I am
helping you to bring it out!

*Get your pen and get ready to take notes;
there's a lot of useful information throughout this
book. Take your time to read it.*

*Take note: If you find any contrasts in the book, it is the
beginning of a positive change: It implies that you're reading
it, and your life is about to change for the better. If there are
any mistakes, we'll have to catch them on the next printing
because this book needs to be in print now! It has been 20
years in the making. Souls are eager, and time is of the
essence!*

Useful information is only good if you use it.
However, the choice is up to you, but the
revelation is from God.
Food for thought*: 10 billion people globally, so*
why would any of them choose your church?

ANYONE CAN PREACH A MESSAGE, BUT IT TAKES A SPECIAL PERSON TO DO THE WORK!

Luke 11;28- Blessed are all who hear the word of God and put it into practice.

Definition of terms
Empire definition:

A group of nations or peoples ruled over by an emperor, empress, or other powerful sovereign or government: usually a territory of greater extent than a kingdom: Such as the former British Empire, French Empire, Russian Empire, Byzantine Empire, or Roman Empire.

When the church does what it's supposed to do, it will be worth going; otherwise, you're on your own! The coronavirus now makes churches think, being that they don't have crowds like they use to.
TAKE YOUR TIME TO READ THIS BOOK, EVEN IF IT'S ONLY 10 PAGES PER DAY.

Disclaimer
(I would dare not to finish this book)

You will not find any church names or pastor's names in this book. If so, the name was overlooked. This book does not aim to point the finger at anyone because we all have been hypnotized to a certain extent, where we wake up and find ourselves struggling to undo what we thought was right as a result of manipulation by others. You either realize who you are or know of some church with these problems but continue their habits.

Warning: This book is not about the rapture. However, many churches have stopped talking about it. Do they still believe it? It should be at least a five-minute message every Sunday for those who trust and believe and a prayer for those who don't!

Preliminaries

I've been to so many churches to the point that it was hard to understand the meaning of love with all the obligations and bickering going on. Some years ago, I asked God to show me how to love people. He told me that He would, but I would have to be hurt first. Besides, whatever people would do to me, I would not do it to anyone to know how the pain felt. However, He told me not to be worried about what they would do or say because he would strengthen me.

Before you read this book, this message is for those who assume to know everything and can't listen to anyone for any advice. Many people have studied in the best schools and taught by using the best books. They hung around prestigious people and focus on building churches and organizations but have overlooked the basics of life.

Ecclesiastes 9:13-16. I saw this example of wisdom under the sun, and it greatly impressed me: There was once a small city with only a few people in it, and a powerful king came to the city, surrounded it, and built huge siege-works against it. There lived a poor man in that city, but wise, and he saved the city by his wisdom. However, nobody recognized or remembered that poor man. **So I said, "Wisdom is better than strength."** despite the poor man's wisdom being despised, and his words no longer heeded.

Ecclesiastes 7:19. Wisdom makes one wise person more powerful than ten rulers in a city.

"There's a way which seems right to man, but the end is the way of death." —Proverbs 14:12

Power of wisdom. I want to help you save your church with the divine knowledge and creativity given to me. I am an example of that man that sat on the hill to provide you with divine wisdom.

Dedication

I dedicate this book to all who left their first love. Revelation 2

These are the words of him who holds the seven stars in his right hand and walks among the seven golden lampstands. [2] I know your deeds, your hard work, and your perseverance. I know that you cannot tolerate wicked people, that you have tested those who claim to be apostles but are not, and have found them false. [3] You have persevered and have endured hardships for my name, and have not grown weary.

[4] Yet I hold this against you: You have forsaken the love you had at first. [5] Consider how far you have fallen! Repent and do the things you did at first. If you do not repent, I will come to you and remove your lampstand from its place.

Hello, my friend,

I am so glad you decided to read this book, and I guarantee you that it will open your eyes. It has information that you will not hear from most of your famous leaders, and it is also very scriptural. I wrote this book over 20 years ago but not led to release it.

After writing approximately 20 other books, it came to my Spirit and me that it is about time I release the book. I've gained much wisdom over the 20 years and still learning. I've added a few things that were spiritually revealed to me since the beginning of this writing. However, the changes make up to 20%, 80% is still the same content I wrote 20 years ago. When you look at things differently, it makes you wonder why you didn't see it from the beginning: It's called **revelation.**

Don't stop reading this book; you will learn something that will give you revelation. I can only mention or suggest things, but God has to lead you, and upon your revelation, he will guide you.

Table of Rich Contents

Wise Quotes

Ecclesiastes 7:10 - Do not say, "Why were the former days better than these?" For you do not inquire wisely concerning this.

Ecclesiastes 7:11 -Wisdom, like an inheritance, is good, and it benefits those who see the sun.

The doors of the church are OPEN, but the hearts are CLOSED after entering!

Stewart Marshall Gulley

People admire children that can name all of the

books in the Bible, but I'd instead respect the children that know and understand what's in them!

Stewart Marshall Gulley

Don't let the wrong type of favoritism tear up your church. People are watching you closer than you think! A little leaven levels the whole lump!

If I Can Help Somebody

If I can help somebody as I pass along,
If I can cheer somebody with a word or song,
If I can show somebody he is trav'ling wrong,
Then my living shall not be in vain.
Then my living shall not be in vain,
Then my living shall not be in vain;
If I can help somebody as I pass along,
Then my living shall not be in vain.
If I can do my duty as a Christian ought,
If I can bring back beauty to a world up-wrought,
If I can spread love's message that the Master taught,
Then my living shall not be in vain.
Then my living shall not be in vain,
Then my living shall not be in vain;
If I can help somebody as I pass along,
Then my living shall not be in vain.

Alma was a black pianist, songwriter and lyricist who composed the famous "If I Can Help Somebody", a song written for the National Tuberculosis Society. According to the 1940 Census, Alma Bazel Androzzo was 27 and married to Andre Androzzo. Alma married Royal Thompson 1957

The song made famous by Dr. Martin Luther King, "If I Can Help Somebody as I Pass Along, then My Living Will Not be in Vain." written in 1945 by Alma Bazel Androzzo, made famous by Mahalia Jackson, a hit in 1951 for Irish tenor Joseph Locke.

To Be Mature-Paul Exhorts Unity -Ephesians 4: 1 -17

4 As a prisoner -for the Lord, then, I urge you to live a life worthy of the calling you have received. **²** Be completely humble and gentle; be patient, bearing with one another in love. **³** Make every effort to keep the unity of the Spirit through the bond of peace. **⁴** There is one body and one Spirit, just as you were called to one hope when you were called; **⁵** one Lord, one faith, one baptism; **⁶** one God and Father of all, who is over all and through all and in all.

⁷ But to each one of us, grace has been given as Christ apportioned it. **⁸** That is why it says: "When he ascended on high, he took many captives and gave gifts to his people."

⁹ (What does "he ascended" mean, besides the fact that He descended down to earth? **¹⁰** He who descended is the very one who ascended higher than all the heavens, in order to fill the entire universe.) **¹¹** So Christ himself appointed the apostles, prophets, evangelist, the pastors, and teachers**¹²** to equip his people for works of service, so that the body of Christ may be built up **¹³** until we all reach unity in the faith and the knowledge of the Son of God and become mature, attaining to the whole measure of the fullness of Christ.

¹⁴ Then we will no longer be infants, tossed back and forth by the waves, and blown here and there by every wind of teaching and by the cunning and craftiness of people in their deceitful scheming.

[15] Instead, speaking the truth in love, we will grow to become in every respect the mature body of him who is the head, that is, Christ. [16] From Him, the whole body joined and held together by every supporting ligament, grows and builds itself up in love, as each part does its work.

The Old Way Has to Go

ROMANS 12:2

And do not get conformed to this world, but be transformed by the **renewal of your mind,** that you may prove what [is] the good and acceptable and perfect as per the will of God.

Whenever someone meets you or goes to your church, the value of who you are is initially 100%. It's what you do that lowers your percentage of who you are, which eventually may go down to 50% of your trust. At 50%, a person may feel less about you, and it will not matter if you do or don't care, depending on the trust and care you've shown.

Ephesians 4: 17-32

[17] So I tell you this, and insist it in the name of the Lord, that you must no longer live as the Gentiles do, in the futility of their thinking. [18] They are darkened in their understanding and separated from the life of God because of the ignorance that is in

them due to the hardening of their hearts. [19] Having lost all sensitivity, they have given themselves over to sensuality to indulge in every kind of impurity, and **they are full of greed.**

[20] However, it is not the way of life you learned [21] when you heard about Christ, and the truth of Jesus Christ taught you. [22] You were taught, about your former way of life, to put off your old self, which is being corrupted by its deceitful desires; [23] to be made new in the attitude of your minds; [24] and to put on the new self, created to be like God in true righteousness and holiness. [25] Therefore, each of you must put off falsehood and speak truthfully to your neighbor, for we are all members of one body. [26] "In your anger do not sin": Do not let the sun go down while you are still angry, [27] and do not give the Devil a foothold. [28] Anyone who has been stealing must steal no longer but must work, doing something useful with their hands, that they may have something to share with those in need.

[29] Do not let any unwholesome talk come out of your mouth, but only what helps in building others according to their needs, that it may benefit those who listen. [30] And do not grieve the Holy Spirit of God, with whom you were sealed for the day of redemption. [31] Get rid of all bitterness, rage, and anger, brawling and slander, along with every form of malice. [32] Be kind and compassionate to one another, forgiving each other, just like how Christ forgave you.

Wake Up from Your Sleep

5 ¹⁻² Watch what God does, and then do it, like children who learn proper behavior from their parents. Mostly, God loves you. Keep company with Him and <u>learn to live</u> a life of love. Observe how Christ loved us. His love was not cautious but extravagant. He didn't love to get something from us but to give everything that He had to us. Love is like that.

³⁻⁴ Don't allow love to turn into lust, setting off a downhill slide into sexual promiscuity, filthy practices, or bullying greed. Though some tongues just love the taste of gossip, those who follow Jesus have better use in whatever they say than that. Don't talk dirty or silly. That kind of talk doesn't fit our style. Thanksgiving is our dialect.

⁵ You can be sure that using people, religion, or things just for what you can get out of them—the usual variations on idolatry—will get you nowhere, and certainly nowhere near the kingdom of Christ, the kingdom of God.

⁶⁻⁷ Don't let yourselves get taken away by the smooth religious talks. God gets furious with people who are full of religious sales talk but want nothing to do with Him. Don't even hang around people like that.

⁸⁻¹⁰ You groped your way through that murk once, but no longer. You're out in the open now. The

bright light of Christ makes your way plain. So no more stumbling around. Get on with it! The good, the right, the truth—these are the actions that are appropriate for daylight hours. <u>Figure out what will please Christ, and do it.</u> **John 9:4-**As long as it is day, we must do the works of him who sent me. The night is coming when no one can work.

11-16 Don't waste your time on useless work, mere busywork; it is just a barren pursuit of darkness. Expose these things to the shame that they are. It's a scandal when people waste their lives on things they do in the dark where no one will see. Rip off the cover of those frauds and see how attractive they look in the light of Christ.

Wake up from your sleep,
Climb out of your coffins;
Christ will show you the light!

So watch your step. Use your head. Make the most of every chance you get. These are desperate times!

17 Don't live carelessly, unthinkingly. Make sure you understand what the Master wants.

18-20 Don't drink too much wine. That cheapens your life. Drink the Spirit of God, huge draughts of him. Sing hymns instead of drinking songs! Sing songs from your heart to Christ. Sing praises over everything, any excuse for a song to God the Father in the name of our Master, Jesus Christ.

Chapter 1
Introduction

There may seem to be many myths in the Bible, over 20,000 different denominations, and 1600 versions of the Bible arranged from those written before King James Version. Some versions leave you asking the question, such as, "What is going on, and what is the truth? Who's report will you believe? We must come to the reality that people are not going for the Okie Doke, and they are getting revelation themselves of what they read in the Bible that they have not seen publicly.

One man esteems one day above another: and another esteems every day alike. Let every man be fully persuaded in his mind (Rom.14:5).

Does your mind lead you to Jesus Christ? Comparisons: *Chrisna* was born of a chaste virgin called Devaki. *Jesus* was born of an innocent virgin named Mary. *Buddha* was born of a virgin named Maya.

"I believe in the Lord Jesus for revelation."

As mentioned earlier, there are about 10 billion people on earth. Have you ever thought about God's process of elimination? What if he said he doesn't want more than 10 billion people on earth? Would that be why people are born every day and die every day just to keep that number? Who knows?

However, you have a choice to do the best you can while you're here. No matter how great you are or are not, death has no magic number, and we will finally leave here. Even your beauty has a deadline.

All this information pertains to me as well because no one is exempt. But this is another thought about death and primarily due to diseases. Should you get a condition, know that God can heal you. If you do not live for some reason, you have the confidence of knowing you will be with God and away from all of the misery here on earth.

I truly believe God knows any and everything. I recall thinking about the Tsunami where 230,000 people were killed on December 26, 2004, in over 14 countries, which was started by a 9.1 earthquake in Indonesia—making it one of the deadliest disasters in modern history. I decided to ask God about it, and He told me that He knew it was going to happen, but we didn't, and for me not to worry about it and go on and do what He called me to do.

Church the Falling Empire and Why They Are So Weak

It said that most people who purchase a book might only read the first chapter, and that's it. **The next thing that is said, if you want to hide something from a person, you should hide it in a book because many people do not read.** You will be doing yourself an injustice if you do not finish this book, which is an honest and fair warning. If you should get tired anywhere, put it down and pick it up later and continue. Read it a little more, whether you agree or not. We often don't agree with something, and then later in life, we get a new revelation and hate we waited too long to act to it.

This book will be like a fish dinner. You eat the meat and spit out the bones, referring to what you may disagree with, but you will hopefully do what is right. I like how most people have curious thoughts about the Bible and how it came about. However, there are some useful nuggets in it, but what astonished me was the scripture; Let God be true and every man a liar (Romans 3:4). Well, if a man got hold of the Bible, do you think he can make a few twists and turns in it? I've picked out the best of what I thought, and you can be persuaded by your mind (Romans 14:5).

Which way is your church going?

Do the best you can and: Do what is right and good in the LORD's sight, so that it may go well with you and you may go in and take over the good land that the LORD promised on oath to your ancestors, Deuteronomy. 6:18

Ecclesiastes 9:1--Whatsoever thy hand finds to do, do it with thy might; for there is no work, nor device, nor knowledge, nor wisdom in the grave where you will eventually end up.

This chapter strictly focuses on the scriptures from the Bible. Even though they are from the Old Testament, which was under the law, they still have meaning. Although, Bible scholars will spend time trying to dissect different verses instead of spending time helping humankind: rather than trying to prove who's right or wrong or see who's the wisest. The second chapter explains the insight concerning things in the Bible but is not taught, which I found surprising. For example, it's like a recipe; if some ingredients are missing, you're guaranteed a catastrophe in the kitchen. Same as what has happened to the church.

The Bible is so prejudiced, and yet it is meaningful. Men had to print the Black Heritage Bible to let people know who the blacks were in the Bible. Same as our United States History, where Blacks are excluded for their great works. History does not include Blacks, and that's why they call it His Story and not Blacks. Other races as well have printed their versions of the Bible.

Chapter 2

The Five-Fold Ministry

The two chapters from Ephesians that you just read were a mouthful. After reading such dynamic scriptures, one would say, "How in the world could anyone ever do all of those things, especially considering the way that we were reared, with both bad and good habits?" We are either on auto-pilot or hypnotized. Whether it's going to church or our everyday routines, we are all hypnotized to do something, but we won't call it hypnosis. Sometimes we need someone to snap their finger and bring us back to the reality of what we are doing and what it costs us.

It is a challenge in all of our lives to continue to do good once we come across the knowledge of what good is. We can point our fingers at others and not at ourselves. "And why behold the mote that is in thy brother's eye, but considers not the beam that is in your eye?" (Matt. 7:3). Regardless of what position you are holding in the church, that passage is for all, from the preacher to the Sunday-school teacher.

We as a people are very slanderous when we think that we don't have a problem in a specific area, yet we still have a problem. Your challenge, which might seem to be so meek and mild, can turn someone off. This is why all of us who live on this earth need help, regardless of our status in society.

Who we are and what we represent will unfold to others around us. Our family name, job title, and the name of the church that we attend all hold a certain amount of clout in the presence of others.

A person who calls himself or herself a Christian will be the center of attraction, regardless of where they go. The job in our lives is to live as per how we speak and preach. Therefore, to become a judge of others, you must put yourself in the seat of Jesus. He is the Perfect One, but he left gifts in others here on earth to help us strive to be perfect.

That's an excellent simple sentence that I've just stated, but it takes an open heart to receive the gifts in which Jesus Christ has left in others. No man has it all, and when he becomes a selfish leader, it will soon lead to a congregation of people thinking just like him or praising him as though he were God.

Instead, we would follow all of man's rituals than do what God has put in our hearts or told us to do. 1 Samuel 15:22- Obedience is better than sacrifice. Some leaders use that passage to get more offerings. God knows the heart of man.

Consider the Jim Jones incident, which happened many years ago in Guyana. People here in the United States made him God, but when he took them to the Promised Land—or so they thought—they realized that the promise was null and void, and many people ended up dying.

If the United States president had all of the answers, there wouldn't be all of the other offices and positions to help run this country, which I might add, still needs help. It doesn't make any difference who will be the next president because we need to make sure that the presidency of Jesus is in us. He already knows the mess that the United States is making and how they will become much colder and more foolish over their decisions and spending.

As you can see, that power is fighting the power in the White House. They'd rather spend thousands on going to court than admit to what is wrong, knowing that there's a fly in the soup and something is not right. You see, when the Devil fights against himself, he has to pull out all of the hidden rules he made, but the Devil never thought he'd have to use them. It's like telling your best friend all of your secrets, but shares your secrets when he or she gets mad or turns against you—it becomes a real war.

It is the same when it comes to the church. Many scriptures have been read in the church, but I haven't seen them being implemented, and when you mention them to others, all they will say is, "Well, you know you're right, but who has the time, or we are still learning?" Take the subject of pure religion as an example: "Pure religion and undefiled before God and the Father is to visit the fatherless and widows in their affliction, and to keep himself unspotted from the world" (Jas.1:26).

How many of us have visited widows, the sick, or even the children who don't have fathers? It didn't say we had to know them. The hospitals are full of them, so there's no excuse for where some might be. The hospital should be turning visitors away. But if we are not raised to do this, then these tasks may seem foreign.

Paul wrote so many epistles to the churches to show us how to act and live. It is just good teaching and sounds excellent to many of us, talking about what **THEY** used to do long ago. And I wonder who changed it or started the fad? God has not changed, neither have the Bible, but I tell you the church has. So why aren't a lot of these great teachings being expedited today?

One of the reasons is that they aren't being taught, nor do they have *power!* Topics may sound good, but you can't do anything without power. You can't drive the most elegant Mercedes-Benz in town unless there's gas in it, and you give it power. The same is true with our Christian path and positions.

God has placed gifts among men to deliver this power to those who believe. Therefore, if churches are not equipped or seeking this power and these gifts, they are like a hollow piece of chocolate, they look good on the outside, but they are empty on the inside and soon will melt when tragic comes.

Thinking about how the church has changed reminds me of a joke. A woman was about to die, and God told her that she had 25 more years to live. As time went by and she thinking about this, she thought she'd get a facelift, new boobs, heavy makeup, extra-long lashes, and all the trimmings to make her extra sexy. Strangely enough, she was in a car accident and died ten years later. When she faced God, she said, "I thought you gave me 25 more years." He said, "I did, but I didn't recognize you."

My point is when Jesus returns, will he recognize the church?" Once I started reading and understanding some scriptures in the Bible, I realized that we live in a messed up and jealous society. If you don't have the five-fold ministry working in your church, you may be going for nothing!

CHURCHES ACT LIKE GANGS, AND GANGS ACT BETTER THAN CHURCHES

Quoted from thebensmartblog.com Some critics of Christianity are keen to point out that, according to best estimates, there are roughly **40,000 Christian denominations worldwide**. This is an astoundingly large figure, and some see it as evidence that Christianity is divided. If Christians can't even agree among themselves, how can they make exclusive claims about absolute truth?

After a quick search online, it's not hard to find a plethora of blog posts commenting on the large number of Christian denominations and concluding all sorts of things: "Christianity has splintered into pieces", or that there are "40,000 groups contradicting each other" and "40,000 different interpretations of the Bible."

Sunday is the most discriminatory day of the week. The Baptist Gang praises God one way, the Catholic Gang praises God another and the same for the Methodist Gang, and it goes on and on. Of course, we call them denominations, in which there are thousands of different denominations. Oh, you didn't know that? Who can deliver our souls from the depths of hell? Nobody but Jesus. That's my own belief, and you have the right to choose yours. As said before, what if you died and found out there was no God, or what if you died and found out there was a God? Uh Oh! It's like insurance; play it safe.

It reminds me of the saying, "Sticks and stones will break my bones, but names will never hurt me." Sounds nice, but I guarantee you that if you don't have the right name branded in your heart when Jesus returns, you will truly be hurt. For those skeptics, if Jesus wasn't real, what have you lost?

Let us look at the main verses in chapter 4 of Ephesians, which are verses 11, 12, and 13: "And he gave some apostles, prophets, evangelists, pastors, and teachers; for perfecting of the saints, for the work of the ministry, for edifying the body of Christ until we all come in the unity of the faith, and the knowledge of the Son of God, unto a perfect man, unto the measure of the stature of the fullness of Christ."

When there is a call of God on your life, some people see it before you can feel it. I can recall that when I would attend services, people would ask me if I were a minister, and I would say no. I thought it was funny whenever they would ask me that, but others would tell me that I would become one. I did not like what the ministry represented, and I still struggle with it today, but I am who God wanted me to be.

As far as I was concerned, my lifestyle was not meant to be a minister. "But many are called, and few are chosen" (Matt. 22:14).

I was merely looking at the word " *gave* " at the beginning of Ephesians 4:11. I interpreted it to mean that when someone gives you something, it is yours. Whether you use it or not, the gift is given to you. He "gave" you something, whether you wanted it or not, and you will not have comfort until you use the gift you're given. Hence, you are to do something with that gift, such as edify the body of Christ by doing the work of the ministry—meaning it is not "yours." You are to give it away, and He will keep restoring the gift that's given.

Another thing that can happen if you are using your gift, especially if you have more than one, people can become jealous. Remember, God gave them to them. Also, although not the main gift, but some gifts are learned or taught in school. Example: If God gave you a gift as a wonderful carpenter, but you had a desire to cook, you end up going to cooking school or as many schools as you would like. God is so creative that most of the things you would like to learn are now on YouTube. There's no excuse. Of course, there's nothing like a hands-on course. You can desire spiritual gifts.

Many have the gifts previously mentioned above in the five-fold ministry, and whether they use them or not, God is holding them responsible for those gifts that He has invested in them. A person may try to do everything except using one of the above gifts if they are called into it, and there will not be any peace until they are working within their calling. We cannot mess up the piece of the puzzle. People are waiting on your part.

We must understand that God has some things that are just divine. A man may dress up and try to act like a woman, but deep down inside, he will always know that he is a man trying to act like a woman. All he did was take part in a play's production, but deep down on the inside, he will never forget that he is, or was once a man—even if he gets to the point of having a sex change. Being who you are is the only freedom you'll have in life, yet it is a task by itself. But what if this is who they feel they are? Although I heard a psychiatrist say that many men who had the sex change regretted it later on. Who are we to judge?

Interestingly, there is a woman in every man, and in every woman, there is a man. What happens on the inside, the psychiatrist can only speculate. A woman may ask another woman why she is gay, and in return, she may ask her why she is straight. You are who you are. The best thing to do is to use the creativity that God gave you regardless, but:

- Why is a person gay?
- Why is a person straight?
- Why is a person bi-sexual?
- Why is a person sexy?
- Why is a person born in death (stillborn)?
- Why is she a whore?
- Why is he a molester?
- Why is a person born cripple?
- Why were they born rich?
- Why were some born poor?
- Why are people jealous of one another?
- Why is there so much jealousy in the ministry?
- Why are some ministers like con-artists?
- Why are there so many denominations and different views of the Bible?

These questions can go on and on. We are so busy with the "why" that we never have time to do what God has called us to do, and that's another reason why television and movies introduce all sorts of ideas.

Psychiatry and Science spend billions of dollars trying to figure out the brain, and they always hit a wall and come up with another study. There is much money made in these areas because they can never get to the truth, and they still keep searching. The heart and brain are very connected.

Above all things, the heart is deceitful and desperately wicked, who can know it (Jeremiah 17:9). We all have a soul controlled by the brain, and no one knows what we are thinking. It is a good thing they don't. Can you imagine if a digital sign went across our foreheads that shows what we were feeling? I know my digital signal would blow a fuse. Whatever turns you on, and a machine is triggered, and it turns you off. We are nothing but a bag of feelings, and we have no idea of what will activate from the time we wake up in the morning. Will we act like we have some common sense throughout the day, or will we become a total fool before the day is over, leaving everyone shocked?

So what if you wear a long cross around your neck? You may murder someone before the day is out. We are all a hair away from being crazy, and I tell people my one strand of hair is split. There's an old saying that tomorrow is not promised to any of us. That sounds nice. However, neither is the rest of the day promised to you. Don't stop reading now; it's just about to get better. Everyone needs some kind of therapist or psychiatrist to talk to once a week. This person shouldn't know much about you because we don't want anyone taking sides. Even the psychiatrist needs a psychiatrist. We were born in a mental world, and we can help each other's minds before it does something drastic. Did you know psychiatrists commit suicide too? They have the highest suicide rate of any profession. May the Lord help us all.

"For the gifts and callings are without repentance" (Rom. 11:29). In other words, your gift is your gift, whether you repent or not. That scripture means that if you don't repent and preach here on earth like you're supposed to, then you might just be preaching where you may not desire—but the bottom line is that you will preach. However, what if we died and found out that there was no heaven or hell. On second thought, what if we died and found out there was. I'm not taking that risk. It's like having life insurance, and Jesus is the beneficiary.

The five-fold ministry's gifts—apostles, prophets, evangelists, pastors, and teachers (A.P.E.P.T.)—holds a specific office in the church. Since you're going to have an organized religion, why not have one wholly for the people. When all the gifts are being used effectively, you will have a well-rounded church to edify Christ and help the saints that attend. When all are not present, you will find a shortage of spiritual growth in the congregation. It's like baking a cake; if one of the ingredients is missing, it's not going to come out right, and more than likely, the cake will not rise or taste good.

Another example is that two people can have the same recipe, but one comes out better, and we can say that person was anointed to cook. People are always talking about lost books, but we can hardly understand the ones we found. Perhaps this is why preachers say, "I believe" when preaching because they don't know but do believe.

Above all, it is the anointing that breaks the yoke. "And it shall come to pass in that day, that his burden shall be taken away from thy shoulder, and his yoke from off thy neck, and the yoke shall be destroyed because of the anointing" (Isa. 10:27). Your yoke could be your burden. Many have heard of the anointing. God's unique gift that the Spirit works through to break every weight or wicked heart amongst a person.

Another way to explain it would be that two people told the same horrific story of a child's death; one person had never experienced such a tragedy, but the other might have been the parent of the child who died.

The latter person will nearly bring tears to your eyes when he or she tells the story; God anointed them to do so through the experience and power of God to lift others who may be going through the same situation. (A sample story in 1 King 3:25- 1 KINGS 3:25 "And the king said, Divide the living child into two, and give half to the one, and a half to the other. Then spake the woman whose the living child was unto the king, for her bowels yearned upon her son, and she said, O my lord, give her the living child, and in no wise slay it).

A person who truly seeks God and spends time with Him will be anointed to preach or teach the Gospel because God recognizes him to do so. However, in some cases, God can just turn you around through an incredible experience.

You are anointed or gifted for something specific. Some people can play the piano and never had a piano lesson because they were anointed to play. It's not that you can't learn, but the outcome may be a little different. There are many ways to explain the anointing, but the bottom line is that God is highly aware of what is going on at present, whether it is a service or one individual. Your Spirit will connect with His, and you will get a feeling of peace, knowing God has sent someone who understands. Whether we want to believe God or not, it would be very enlightening had we tried the things He says, and the outcome is excellent. However, very few churches do it all, and then they wonder!

The five-fold ministry's gifts that God has anointed are vitally needed but are not acknowledged enough. Most pay attention to the pastor or evangelist, not realizing that there are more gifts than that. The question of the calling is, do they have the power to deliver the message? "But ye shall receive power, after that the Holy Ghost comes upon you: and ye shall be witnesses unto me both in Jerusalem, and in all Judaea, and Samaria, and unto the uttermost part of the earth" (Acts 1:8).

Although you have the gift, you still need the power to perform it effectively. Many in these positions will argue with you about what you need and don't need. Some will twist things around because of what they don't have; I just so happen to follow the Bible; even though some things seem a little contradictory, I treat it like a fish dinner, eat the meat, and spit out the bones. Anything that man wrote will have its flaws. However, the WORD was

inspired by God. We all are inspired by God and say things differently. Imagine if you were doing an excellent job of bringing people to Christ, and one day you are filled with the supernatural power of the Holy Ghost. Can you imagine what kind of job you'd do?

The only thing that bothers man is that he can not patent or sell it. If he could, he'd have a Christmas Sale and any other kind of sale promoting it. Acts 8:20- [20] Peter answered: "May your money perish with you because you thought you could buy the gift of God with money!

Let me pause right here for a minute before I continue because I mentioned the word Holy Ghost.

Don't be alarmed or afraid because the Holy Ghost's infilling is in the Bible, and many times if you mention that word, people will tend to draw up or say, here goes another church fanatic. Very sophisticated thinking. I am not trying to make anyone have it, because it's your own choice. It's just like I can mention that a particular store has a 75% sale off on televisions. I just said the whereabouts, but I can't make you go and get one even though you've been sitting home without a TV for a month. However, you can't say that I didn't tell you about it because I had purchased one myself, so it's up to you.

It's just like a Jewish person studying the law, and one day coming to the knowledge of Christ and filled with the Holy Ghost with the evidence of speaking in tongues. There have been groups that started called Jews for Jesus. Can you imagine what type of Jewish person he would become? Sometimes we can't get some things because we don't ask for them. If a son asks for bread from any fathers among you, will he be given a stone? Or if he asks for a fish, will he give him a serpent instead of a fish. Or if he asks for an egg, will he offer him a scorpion? If you then being evil know how to give good gifts to your children, how much more will your heavenly Father give the Holy Spirit to those who ask Him?"Luke 11:11-13

That scripture is in every Bible, but many leaders don't talk about it. However, there's a whole lot that they don't talk about, even though it may be right. That's why non-Christians look at Christians as though they are crazy because they all carry the same Bible but a million different beliefs. But once God opens your eyes and shows you the real church, you will begin to question everything and wonder, how did you get stuck so long?

All I'm saying is that many are in the ministry and don't think they need anything else, as far as the other gifts in the church, yet they are leading a flock of weak Christians who only believe what their leader tells them. In other words, "If my pastor doesn't say it or know it, then it must not be true."

I hate to be the bearer of bad news, but your pastor doesn't know everything, and there are some things that he or she knows but fails to do or tell you about due to conflict. More likely, they will not preach that scripture. The church is supposed to be simple, but man has made a mess out of it. I finally understood why people didn't go.

In addition to the five-fold ministry's gifts, being subject to the higher powers—as they pertain to pastors, teachers, parents, government, and so on—is also essential. This is a lesson by itself, which comes from chapter 13 of Romans, also mentioned later.

I once mentioned to a friend that I was not too fond of airplanes because I didn't understand how all of that weight stayed in the air. He responded that I didn't know much about cars either, but I drive them. So, I hopped on the plane. Lol!

There's a lot that we don't know. On the other hand, we must strive to work on and change a lot of habits. It is a daily walk; you can't get to Friday unless you go through Sunday through Thursday first. We sometimes wake up quickly when a death situation comes to our door, and then we have a quick "Come to Jesus" moment.

To the best of my ability, I will explain the gifts missing in the church, and why many of us are weak. It is only because of our habits, old traditions. The 5-fold ministry is like a business board. Our businesses have meetings constantly and research of how to make it better and more revenue. Sometimes, I feel that the Bible was written by many psychiatrists who forgot to put all the chapters in, but that's another book I may need to write.

Speaking of the books that are said to be lost, such as the letter of Jesus to Abgarus, the Gospel of Nicodemus, the Legends of Paul and Thecla, the Epistles of Clement and Barnabus, the Shepherd of Hermas, the Books of Adam and Eve, the Secrets of Enoch, the Psalms and Odes of Solomon, the many Testaments of the Patriarchs, and many more ancient books which were highly revered, but ultimately left out of the Bible. It's already hard to understand the 66 books that are here, but in the same breath is has to be more because so much is missing from them. Who knows, somebody may be hiding the real truth, hidden, but then what? I still want to know what happened to Eve?

My question is, are you a loving, caring, fair, and honest person. What would those books do, make you more confused? Some people spend their whole life studying and never getting the truth when they should be somewhere lending a helping hand to those in need. I recall watching a movie in which Winnie Mandela said she didn't trust the Bible because a man wrote it. Plus, many people are bound to it, especially the scripture that says: For I testify unto every man who hears the words of this book's prophecy. If any man adds unto these things, God shall add unto him the plagues that are written in this book: And if any man shall take away from the words of the book of this prophecy, God shall take away his part out of the book of life, and out of the holy city, and *from* the things which are written in this book. (Revelation 22:18-19)

With that verse alone, how many things do you think have been added to the Bible? You don't know, do you? How many bibles were before King James? Furthermore, how many books do you believe are not in the Bible? Another question is, how did we get sucked in believing in the pictures of this European Jesus with long hair? Check out this description I read: (Revelation 1:14-15). His head and hair *were* white like wool, as white as snow, and His eyes like a flame of fire; His feet *were* like fine brass as if refined in a furnace, and His voice as the sound of many waters.

That description makes you wonder about the church. They don't know what he looks like if this is the description. This description sounds more like a Black man. No, I'm not saying Jesus was black, but this seems pretty strange to me. Could this be why blacks are mistreated so severely because Satan knows who they are? Could you imagine what would have happened to the world if they had been treated fairly? If all the blacks got together and rebelled against the world, it would be a chaotic mess. However, this is what a particular group of whites did, and not only did they rebel against blacks, but they also rebelled against their own and any other race they feel they could conquer. The Black race has had a hard time, yet they endure and praise God consistently with their many churches, even though many are misinformed on how to run them. Did you know as a painter that you will get black or a very dark color if you mix all shades together? Mmmmmm?

If the Bible is to be simple, how many have read the whole Bible? That's good if you have, now how much did you understand? It's like reading a real estate contract, and they just tell you to sign because more than likely, the agent doesn't understand what it says either until you have a problem, and then he has to seek other sources to possibly explain the details and then point it out in the contract.

Do you ever graduate from church like college and do the work, or do you just study forever? Or maybe there's an Alumni of the church. However, in the Church of Scientology, you just might.

I attended a class at the Church of Scientology, and it was fascinating, and it is not like people always think. Everybody has something to contribute to God's work. They are all about education and becoming free with knowledge. If they were filled with the Holy Spirit, they would go buck wild with what they know. They make their money by mostly trying to get you to purchase courses and read their books. The traditional church makes its money on just taking offerings and listening to a few good sermons.

The following is a comparison of the church to a college degree:

<u>CHURCH</u>

3 times a week, approx. 3 hours = 9 hours
9 hours weekly x 4 weeks = 36 hrs church

36 hours x 12 months = 432 hrs per yr.
432 hours x 4 yrs.= 1,728 hours church
Reward: A tax write off for the year.
Not to mention the many expenses with no benefits.

Whether we want to face it or not, the church is like another bill or expense. Usually, when there is a financial problem at home, and people want to downsize, many times, the first thing they downsize is the money donated to the church. The church has no hold on a person. For instance, if you stop giving to the church, your lights will not necessarily get turned off immediately. But who wants to feel that way? You want to feel good about giving to your church.

COLLEGE (approximately the same amount of hours as the church)

3 days a week class x 3 hours   = 9 hours
9 hours x 4 weeks = 36 hours of school
36 hours x 10 months = 360 per year
360 hours x 4 years= 1,440hrs College B.A Degree
Reward: Certificate to practice their profession for income.

Not to mention the cost of books and materials, and you still can go back to church.
There is less time in college with a degree that you can use for a profession and studied the course and use it.

In the Church, you'll do 288 hours more and no degree. How many have read through the Bible with understanding but made to feel guilty if they don't go? And for some that return home unhappy because of either what was said or done during service. For those who have read it, you would think they would be a little more kind. However, remember it was the Jews (church folk) that persecuted Jesus. I love God, and I love the church, but we have been lied to through the church rituals and habits and not learning to give from our hearts but guilt.

I then read that you have to study the scripture to study to get ourselves approved (2 Timothy 2:15). Study what? Half of the time, the leaders don't understand it, and then they say they have to study in Greek. If that's the case, why don't you just stay in the Greek, and perhaps we all will get a little understanding if things are so.

The best way that I've been able to explain the five-fold ministry is through the following example: If you built a brand-new house and excluded the bathroom and kitchen, it would not be complete. Every day, there would be no place for you to cook or go to the bathroom. Therefore, you would have an empty feeling that something is missing in the house. After a while, you wouldn't be able to take it anymore, so you'd seek a home with more amenities in other neighborhoods.

This is the same thing that sometimes happens in churches. People seek more than what their church has to offer, and deep within, they know that something is missing or not right; therefore, they seek other churches. Be mindful that you can outgrow a church and that God might seek you to move on even though the five-fold ministry is active.

Sometimes, when you start seeking God, one mind tends to visit other churches. Some will refer to this person as a church hopper, but when it comes to your soul, sometimes you just might have to hop around—because we have been misinformed for years. If all the gifts were not working, including the baptism of the Holy Ghost, I would hop away to get just what I needed, and if the Lord directed me back to the church I left, then so be it, but I doubt that He would, in most cases. Let's face it; all these churches are doing is switching members. A visiting church may come with a good choir and speaker, and then some of the members at the host church would like to leave their church to follow the visiting church. They go to one church for a while and then another. Sometimes, they eventually go back to the first one they left. It's the same old sermons and scriptures but different titles. One might preach, "Stay in the Ship," and another might preach, "The Storm is Passing Over." (Acts 27:30). However, many things have been changing regarding church hoppers. It gets to the point that some are tired of hopping, and they refuse to go at all. Same methods, but different faces.

Sometimes it reminds me of going out for a date on a Friday evening. You want to look your very best, but you don't have all you need. So, you might get your shirt from one store, the shoes from another, a tie from another, and the jacket from another. You will seek other stores until you feel complete and ready to give the evening all you have. This is store hopping and just the reverse of church hopping.

Sometimes, the ministry is like that; you may have to visit a few places until you feel complete and come to the full knowledge of who Christ is. After all, you have to admit He's drawing you; otherwise, you wouldn't be reading this book. All sincere people seek more; wherever they can find a little more revelation, it makes things a little better. Even though with much wisdom comes much sorrow. (Ecc:1:18)

You shouldn't stay anywhere that you don't feel comfortable, even if your parents brought you up in a particular church or denomination. You may be used to it, but you're not fully fed, which makes you feel that something is pulling you back without knowing what it is. You either love your church or leave it. Don't be a bad seed in the church gossiping about how you feel and sowing seeds of discord at your church.

Proverbs 6:16-19
[16] These six things doth the LORD hate: yea, seven are an abomination unto him:
[17] A proud look, a lying tongue, and hands that shed innocent blood,

¹⁸ A heart that devises wicked imaginations, feet that be swift in running to mischief,
¹⁹ A false witness that speak lies, and he that sows discord among brethren.

We will always seek God and what He has for us as he continues to give us revelations on things little by little. As the scripture reads: "Whom shall he teach knowledge? And whom shall he make to understand doctrine? Them that are weaned from the milk, and drawn from the breasts. For precept must be upon precept, precept upon precept; line upon line, line upon line; here a little, and they're a little" (Isa. 28:9).

Another thing about the five-fold ministry's gifts is that God can promote you to different ranks, just like in the military. You may start as an evangelist, move on to be a pastor, and later on to an apostle or bishop, helping to create other churches. "For promotion comes neither from the east nor from the west, nor the south. But God is the judge: he puts down one and sets up another" (Ps. 75:6). Some ministers fight over titles, but their work does not follow the title. Some argue that some people don't speak in tongues, but this person is working diligently in the ministry and probably doing more than the person stuck on a person speaking in tongues. Does all speak? (1Cor. 12:30). When it comes to titles, how come they couldn't be just like Jesus and called by the name on their birth certificate. I recall a new minister arguing with the MC at a program because he wanted him to announce him as Minister ___. The MC didn't want to do it. They were arguing in the pulpit before the minister sung. A serious argument too. Can you imagine the disciples arguing because Luke wanted to be called Rev. Dr. Luke? People are getting so dogmatic about titles.

Some women don't like to be referred to as Ma'am because they say it makes them feel old. If you're old, you're just old, and that's how it is, and thank God He has granted you those years. You're not 85 years young, nor is a child a little adult. The child who was taught to address an older person with Ma'am or Sir was being groomed to respect a person older. It was a matter of respect in our days, and now it's cool and ignorant for a child to call an adult by their first name.

I remember when I first got called into the ministry, which was a joyous night. However, everyone has a ministry, but some titles are ignored. I was not a Bible reader—I would read some scriptures here and there—but only when God got on my case. I would buy a book on any topic that impressed me at any chance I could. The next thing I knew, I had a little library, which was very shocking to me. I was a visual person; I liked being shown, and I didn't have to read a lot of anything. Boy, God can make you read!

We all need help, whether or not we feel it at all. Some people act like they were born saved, but we know much better. Saved doesn't mean you're perfect; it just makes you more aware of Christ in your life. It has been said that five is the number of grace. So, as God graced us with these five gifts to help perfect the church, let us govern ourselves.

We all are growing in grace. Same as we grow physically and through education. A child cannot stay in elementary school forever. He has to move on to middle school and then to high school. Sometimes church members tend to move on when they are not growing or inspired.

Remember, it is said to give a person what they want, and they will give you what you want. You get more bees with honey.

Let us begin discussing the five-fold ministry and how it is essential today. Without it, we're like a ship without a sail. Even if our boat has a sail, it will still face storms in the water. The gift of the ministry is like wearing glasses. Some people can only see things far away, while others can see and dissect closely

Gift Number One
Apostle

Paul, a great apostle to the Gentiles, was an excellent example of what an apostle does. The Bible explains how God can change and promote a person, as he did with Paul, also known as Saul, who was a persecutor of the Jews and then converted on the Damascus Road in chapter 9 of the Acts of the Apostles. Sometimes the name *apostle* is transferred by the name *bishop*.

It goes to show you that God can take anyone and turn him or her around. Regardless of your past and what others think of you, when God has a calling on your life, you can rest assured that it will surface.

God can lift anyone up to do what he wants regardless of how someone else may see you. The following was something I came across:

Example here of people God used:

- Abraham was too old
- Isaac was a daydreamer
- Jacob was a liar
- Leah was ugly
- Joseph was abused
- Moses had a stuttering problem
- Gideon was afraid
- Sampson had long hair and was a womanizer
- Rahab was a prostitute
- Jeremiah and Timothy were too young
- David had an affair and was a murderer
- Elijah was suicidal
- Isaiah preached naked
- Jonah ran from God
- Naomi was a widow
- Job went bankrupt
- John the Baptist ate bugs
- Peter denied Christ
- The Disciples fell asleep while praying
- Martha worried about everything

- The Samaritan woman was divorced more than once.
- Zacchaeus was too small
- Paul was too religious
- Timothy had an ulcer
- Lazarus was dead.

Now, what's your excuse whether you're an apostle or not and if he's a good apostle, he recognizes your gift and encourages you to use it. Not as some of the new ones that focus on offerings for a good word or prophecy.

An apostle is a person anointed to raise a church without having a lot of involvement from others. He will help teach and govern the churches that he sets up. The apostle may be blessed with multiple gifts, such as evangelist, prophet, pastor, and teacher, but that doesn't mean he does them all by himself to run a church.

Think of it as a franchise. The originator of Kentucky Fried Chicken will open other stores and have managers or owners to operate them. They will all be taught a particular method and procedure for cooking and selling chicken; therefore, their food will be the same wherever you go.

Another scenario: Take, for instance, a famous restaurant and the head cook leaves, it wouldn't be any problem because the recipes of how the food is prepared at that restaurant are still there. So the new cook fills in where the other one left off. It's like some of these large churches that don't have a good back up pastor. Should the pastor pass away, the members will leave the church because there's no one close to his ministry that can take over because they are not trained due to the pastor not sharing the skills or business part of the church. Therefore the whole church is dissolved.

However, if the church is set up wrong, it teaches others the same thing, and it would be an epidemic around the world, such as today, how a majority of the churches are being run. Remember, Jesus turned over the tables because of the money changers, the same as today, which may be a dignified "prophet or profit or someone preying or praying." Some prophets prey on weak people. I just wonder, do they realize that God knows what they are exactly doing? –**Proverbs 15:3.** One day the member will be like the prodigal son and come to themselves and keep on truckin.'

Matthew 21:12 Then Jesus went into the temple of God and drove out all those who bought and sold in the temple, and overturned the money-changers' tables and the seats of those who sold doves. And He said to them, "It is written, 'My house shall be called a **House of Prayer**,' but you have made it a 'den of thieves.'

Just think if all churches were called a House of Prayer? The only way you would know of which one it was is to give it a location number, such as all the franchises in the world that have a store number. However, if every church were called House of Prayer, someone would creatively come along and say something like House of Prayer of Northside

California instead of leaving it just House of Prayer, trying to make themselves stand out.

Just as the apostle helps set up the church under God's doctrine, all other churches will be set up with the same beliefs, and he also rules his own house well. It's hard to believe people who tell you how dysfunctional your household is, while theirs is giving everyone a problem in the church.

"One that rules well his own house, having his children in subjection with all gravity; (For if a man know not how to rule his own house, how shall he take care of the church of God?)" (1 Tim. 3:4).

In the Bible, apostles set up the churches, not the pastors or evangelists. Today, some pastors are working and doing the work of an apostle, but many are afraid to use that name because it is a term that is seldom heard. Every position has a title, whether we use the title or not. However, some of the modern fancy churches call the pastor by his first name. I guess being like Jesus, it's not Apostle Jesus or Bishop Jesus. It's just Jesus.

Sometimes new pastors set up their own churches because they don't like how their previous church was run. This way, the pastor will not be voted out. They read the Bible themselves and have learned some things and wondered why their ex-leader was not doing or teaching them.

Although you may be doing a pastor's work, your mind is telling you to set up different churches as an apostle. You may find yourself continuing as a pastor and having significant problems because your gift is to set up churches and let a real pastor comfort and take care of the people, as he should. But we all must come under the authority of someone or some organization. There should be some accountability. But everything has become so chaotic and political that no one wants to come under the control of anyone.

Every person has a special gift from God. Many pastors who are apostles have been locked in the position of pastors. Their minds continuously think about starting other churches, but they never get to it out of the fear of what someone may think, including the bunch of unlearned deacons who run the church. Read the book of 1Timothy 3rd Chapter.

These deacons aren't anointed or caring. They are only anointed for what God has called them to do if they'd listen. That is why there are many problems with elders in the church. They are not 'true' deacons. Who would want an un-experienced babysitter watching their newborn?

If it is done correctively, this apostolic anointing that an apostle will have will help perfect many of our nation's saints. The apostle will make sure all the other gifts of the five-fold ministry are present. Unless an apostle sets up the church, today, many pastors do not want to come under any authority, not even the word of God, strangely to say. This process is because there's so much corruption in the church that many don't want to trust anyone. Yet, some leaders will use Psalm 105:15- Touch not mine anointed and do my prophets no harm. We're not trying to make perfect people, but people who have a better life knowing that someone cares even if mistakes are made.

God called twelve apostles to do this work and set up the church, and I'm sure each had a special gift. But because there are so many hirelings in the church, no one trusts anyone.

You will find more apostleship amongst the Methodist/Catholic churches than any of the other faiths among denominations. Once taught, many of their pastors are sent to different churches to the pastor. Many stay several years, and sometimes they are transferred to other places. Although the five-fold ministry is not the main issue in their cases, it would be highly needed for the perfecting of the members.

You will find other denominations that have apostles that raise ministries and do quite well in discipleship. A real apostle operates following the Bible and all of its statures and is chosen by God. "Paul, an apostle, (not of men, neither by man, but by Jesus Christ, and God the Father, who raised him from the dead)" (Gal. 1:1).

If God calls you into a position, he will also equip you with the stamina and resources you need. Can you imagine if all of the Kentucky Fried Chicken restaurants were churches that an apostle set up? My God, the Word would be finger-lickin' good!

At least you would know what you were going to get before you went in there. Nowadays, some ministries might hold the same denominational sign on the outside, but inside you'll get something else. Some are a hair from being a cult.

All I can say is try the Spirit by the Spirit of God that lives within you. If something doesn't agree with you, just shake the dust off your feet and keep moving, and do not try to spend all your time fussing and talking about what someone else did. You don't have that much time and energy. Take heed unless we fall. (1Cor.10:12). Contrary to what we believe, know that we are all in this mess together.

"And this is his commandment, That we should believe on the name of his Son Jesus Christ, and love one another, as he gave us commandment. And he that keeps his commandments dwells in him, and he in him. And hereby we know that he abides in us, by the Spirit which he hath given us" (1 John 3:24).

Usually, a good apostle will govern his bodies of churches well. There are traditionally health benefits and other benefits for its full-time staff, and there are schools for upcoming children who the world system will not teach. The world system teaches us to be ignorant and to be a prime candidate for its prisons. Did you know that nationally, it costs about $33,000 to house an inmate a year? As for California, it cost around

$76,000 per year. Welcome to California, the land of greed.

The Jews will let you know that! Even today, cults are pulling their children out of the world system, although God does not teach them. They know that the government system is corrupt in its thinking and that it is getting worse.

Children are not being educated. They are mentally trained to learn nothing through a slow process.

Gift Number Two
Prophet

God also chooses a prophet or prophetess (woman). This person is used to guide us and sees things in our future and past. Many churches ignore this gift also, which is very prevalent today.

Some of us are prophetic but don't understand it and how we should be used. As a child, sometimes a particular incident will come to mind, and the next thing you know, it does happen. Many times it will go over and over again. When God's anointing comes upon the prophetic word, it usually agrees in the individual's Spirit or helps them take great caution in what is to come. Not all prophesies may be good news all the time, but it can become good news if the proper instructions are followed.

"And Moses said, Thus says the Lord, About midnight will I go out into the midst of Egypt; and all the firstborn in the land of Egypt shall die from the firstborn of Pharaoh that sits upon his throne, even unto the firstborn of the maidservant that is behind the mill; and all the firstborn of beast. And there shall be a great cry throughout all the land of Egypt, such as there was none like it, nor shall be like it anymore" (Ex. 11:4).

That prophecy took a lot of guts. When God says it, rest assured, it will come to pass. It was the same as in the days of Noah, where he prophesied that there would be a flood. It might have taken over a hundred years, but it still came to pass.

Can you imagine all the humiliation he had to go through for all of those years while he was building this great ark? If it were possible, the Devil would have put doubt in Noah, who then would have stopped, then he and all of his family would have drowned.

There's a difference between prophecy and just plain gossip. Some have these prophetic gifts and use them on psychic hotlines. You don't know who's who. Nevertheless, the Devil will financially rip off anyone who is not grounded in the word of God.

Many of these so-called psychics are usually talking straight from their bedrooms, and that's how the lines are set up. The longer they get you to speak, the more money they will make, and the "psychic" will roll over and take a nap until the next call. But the only difference is the church, and it can be just as manipulative in inspiring members to give money. I had a client that was a minister, and she worked on the psychic line, and I would talk to her about certain logical things. She told me that I should work for a Psychic Line because I had a gift. She gave me a phone number and everything for me to call. I called, but I didn't want to do it.

I wouldn't advise this service to anyone because you will get caught up. The following scripture should make you think about it: "And when they had gone through the isle unto Paphos, they found a certain sorcerer, a **false prophet**, a Jew, whose name was Bar-Jesus" (Acts 13:6).

Beware of **false prophets**, who come to you in sheep's clothing but inward are ravening wolves. "Ye shall know them by their fruits. Do men gather grapes of thorns or figs of thistles?" (Matt. 7:15). "Many **false prophets** shall rise, and shall deceive many" (Matt. 24:11). Many prophets know how to raise money, and that's why leaders call them. Unfortunately, it's not necessarily about the soul, but it's about the money.

"For there shall arise **false Christ**, and **false prophets**, and shall show great signs and wonders; insomuch that, if it were possible, they should deceive the very elect. Behold, I have told you before. Wherefore if they shall say unto you, Behold, he is in the desert; go not forth: behold, he is in the secret chambers; believe it not" (Matt. 24:24).

Many things can be said about the **false prophet**, but by studying the word of God and the Spirit of discernment, you will know. You will find many false prophets using God's word and obtaining great wealth by convincing people to give. In other words, many are not prophesying; they are "Prophe**lying**"! $1,000 prayer lines???? Don't try to study people too hard, because you will never know everything about them. Use your mental energy and move on to do what God has urged YOU to do. The heart is deceitful, who can know it. (Jeremiah 17:9).

There's good and evil in all of us. However, many of us can control the bad and not go through with it because the conviction may be firm. I've seen many lines, but where is the line to ask them if they want to be filled with the Holy Ghost? That's a power line that will help. Long ago, many people ran to the church to join or for prayer, but nowadays, it seems like just a thought because now people are running away from the church.

There are so many smooth, easy ways that the churches get money from people using prophets or individuals who know how to get money. I remember a church giving a free dinner to its members at a lavish hotel. Well, that was already strange to me, because there's nothing free. They had hired a speaker, or should I say a consultant, to teach them how to raise money.

So after dinner, he spoke and explained the church building fund. All of a sudden, the conversation switched, and he finished. He convinced many people to pledge for that year for the building fund. So if you promised $1000, well, that's how much your dinner cost as far as I am concerned. Here, you have a large group of people eating a nice free dinner catered at a hotel, and therefore made to feel guilty if they didn't pledge. Yes, they racked in quite a bit of money.

It's so strange to have beautiful places that are only used on Sunday and Wednesday but cost a fortune. Why not rent them out or something. I have no idea in some of these cases of how you may rent.

A prophecy from a true prophet will come to pass. Most of the time, people who tend to depend on psychics don't realize that these people happen to stumble upon specific laws of nature and that they pump you to say just a little, which is the usual conversation of most people who have problems. More than likely, everyone will have a problem in finance, love relationships, health, and spiritual issues, and a prophet can take any subject to what's on your mind and try to give you a common-sense solution. At the same time, it will possibly provide you with hope. If you tell a prophet that someone is beating you, how easy is it for him to say to you that God will soon get you out of that situation? And more than likely, God will. But the scripture tells us all that after we suffer awhile, He will establish us (1 Peter 5:10). We will all go through something.

The law of nature tells you that if your husband is staying out late every night and dressing differently, there must be someone he's interested in besides you. Some things are pretty standard, and so-called psychics benefits because you don't use the gift of discernment that God has given you. Deep down inside, you know the problem. I don't have to go to the doctor for him to tell me that I have a cold if I have been sneezing all day. I go in there telling him I have a cold and hoping he has medicine for me.

A prophet's message is divine, and only through God's eyes can he help—by persuasion, inspiration, and foresight. It is a gift of God and has recently been used widely in the church. Through his spiritual eyes, a prophet can often see things through you, and when they begin to speak, they can bring tears to your eyes—because it confirms in your Spirit. Other times, you will leave curious, wondering when the prophecy will come to pass or how did this prophet know about you?

Prophets and prophetesses were used throughout the Bible. "Be it understood, although you may be prophetic, you may also be without honor. But Jesus said unto them, A prophet is not without honor, but in his own country, and among his own kin, and in his own house" (Matt. 13:57). Sometimes you get respected more by others than those that know you.

Sometimes we may not know when the prophecy will come to pass, but we must go on and live our lives the best we can through Christ Jesus. It's just like a friend telling you that they mailed you a letter; you know they sent it, but you don't remember the exact moment when it will get to you. Anything can happen to the letter at the post office.

I'll never forget prophesying to a lady that didn't care for me. She called me afterward and was upset because she said she didn't feel anything and felt that I was in the flesh." I wanted so strongly to tell her it was a good thing I was in my flesh because I couldn't have told her the full truth at that time. After all, the Spirit had revealed it, and I was trying to be wise in conversing with her. To be truthful, she was one of those church hell-raisers in which we all encounter.

However, I ironed it out by considering a situation as an example where someone told her that a department store was having a big sale. Whether she felt it or not, the sale was still going. Sometimes prophecies will cause people to get angry at you. Some prophets that are not wise spread your business openly. Not everybody is going to like you, and that's regardless of whether you're prophesying or not.

"Despise not prophesying"(1 Thess. 5:20).

Gift Number Three
Evangelist

My, my, my! Who is this firecracker here that has all of this energy and has stirred up the hearts of men? Why he must be an evangelist.

Although some in the five-fold ministry hold different gifts, usually, there is one gift in a person that stands out firmer. This means that we all still need help, but God will allow us to use our gifts until those who have perfected them arrives to help. Trust me; even the evangelist needs to hear from other evangelists and prophets as well.

As you can tell, the evangelist is in the middle of the five-fold ministry. He's the center of attraction—or, we could say, the head of the booster club. He has no problem saying things that other gifts may fear to say. If you don't like the heat, get out of the kitchen.

Sometimes, when we are weak, the evangelist will stir us up and give us a little more hope. Evangelists will stir up other evangelists, too.

The evangelist, most of the time, is full of enthusiasm when he preaches the Gospel. Through the use of God's word, he will compel people to be saved and acknowledge who Jesus is. Sometimes miracles and healings will take place in these services. The evangelist can also preach right to the point of things without sugarcoating the issues.

Sometimes after an evangelist leaves, the pastor has to come in with a fatherly heart to smooth things over. However, he knows what the evangelist said was true. Over time, evangelists have helped build many churches for pastors in their revival meetings and special anniversaries. I won't talk about anniversaries here, because it goes into a different subject. After all, many times, the pressure is put on people, and they give grudgingly rather than willingly with love.

An evangelist does not have a problem telling it as it is, convicting many and leading them to Christ. In Acts 8:5, Phillip went down to Samaria and preached the Gospel of Christ, which brought joy, and an entire city came to Christ. It only takes one to sound the alarm. Such back in our natural history when Paul Revere roamed the streets, saying, "The British are coming."

Many Christians who are filled with the Holy Ghost tend to have a very evangelistic spirit because their conversation is that of Christ, which has given them the power to be a witness for Him. "But ye shall receive power, after that the Holy Ghost has come upon you, and ye shall be witnesses unto me both in Jerusalem, and in all Judaea, and Samaria, and unto the uttermost part of the earth" (Acts 1:8).

There is a special anointing to be an evangelist and preach the Gospel. Evangelists, if not careful, can become very strong-headed due to the excitement. They must humble themselves in the sight of God because it is He that has given them the power to do His will. Evangelists should also be under the authority of a leader.

Loyal evangelists will show the love of God because they will be able to feel the need of the people, letting them know that salvation is more important than anything they can possess.

Evangelists will preach the baptism of the Holy Ghost, which has more emphasis in the Pentecostal Church. Although sad to say—they are usually the only ones that speak about this matter in depth. Other times, they call them the Holiness Church or the Sanctified Church, in which we are all supposed to be holy and live sanctified—set apart. That's why all of the gifts are important; as the old saying goes, everyone needs to bring something to the table, even if it's just the table cloth. Though these scriptures are easy to say, there is still a lot of personal mental work that has to be done for all of us because we fight to undo what was done to us because we didn't get the full revelation of the scriptures. Blessed are those who got the understanding as a very young child.

Many churches argue against this baptism for the mere fact that they have not been introduced to the Holy Ghost. I will explain this to you. Until I had a real revelation of this from God, I too, was a very hardheaded Baptist on the subject.

Jesus told the disciples: "Therefore, Go ye and teach all nations, baptizing them in the name of the Father, and the Son, and the Holy Ghost. Teaching them to observe all things whatsoever I have commanded you; and, lo, I am with you always, even unto the end of the world" (Matt. 18:19).

Many have been baptized in the Father, Son, and the Holy Ghost's name because the scriptures said so. As stated by Paul, "Whatever you do in word or deed, do it all in the name of Jesus." (Col. 3:17). Have you received the Holy Ghost since you believe it? (Acts 19:2)

I never could understand all of these different denominations that carry the same bible. They have their picks and choices about it. And they wonder why people go to church, and those that don't go to church wonder why people do. It has been said that a confused mind does nothing. And the church is good at confusing people. Although baptism may be petty to some, why the churches can't agree with something so little and significant?

Now let's go to the second part. A little more water won't hurt anyone; you can never get washed too much. "And it came to pass, that, while Apollos was at Corinth, Paul having passed through the upper coasts came to Ephesus: and finding certain disciples, He said unto them, Have you received the Holy Ghost since ye believed?

And they said unto him, "We have not so much as heard whether there be any Holy Ghost." And he said unto them, "Unto what then were ye baptized? And they said, "Unto John's baptism." Then said Paul, "John verily baptized with the baptism of repentance, saying unto the people, that they should believe on him which should come after him, that is, on Christ Jesus."

When they heard this, they were baptized in the name of the Lord Jesus. And when Paul had laid his hands upon them, the Holy Ghost came on them; and they spoke with tongues, and prophesied" (Acts 19:3).

All this is to say that they got baptized again, which was in Jesus' name. There is a great argument with the Apostolic churches about this. They definitely believe in being baptized in Jesus' name and filled with the Holy Ghost. Ask, and you shall receive.

(Testimony 1) I recalled going to Mississippi back in the early '90s for just two weeks. As I took this 2 ½ day-long bus ride, I asked God why I was going to Mississippi. He replied that He would show me the root of people's problems, and boy did I get an eye full.

However, I was so busy trying to help that those two weeks turned into 12 years, a story by itself. During that time, my sister Peaches would come into my bedroom, and I would be reading the bible. She was about 26 and got very curious about various things as she was continually seeing me read. One evening she came in asking me about the bible because she felt she didn't know much.

However, I chose the chapters about being filled with the Holy Ghost and speaking in tongues. I knew we had been brought up Baptist, so I asked her whether she did want to be baptized in Jesus' name. She immediately said, "Yes." It was very late that evening and our mother was asleep, so I said, "Peaches, fill the bathtub with water, I will baptize you myself." She smiled and ran the bathwater. So I explained to her that I was going to baptize her again in Jesus' name. I proceeded and praised God. She was filled with the Holy Ghost with the evidence of speaking in tongues, and she has not been the same since, which was over 30 years ago.

I often think about celebrities and wonder how they feel about the Holy Ghost and speaking in tongues. I wonder if they were filled, would they not tell anyone for fear believing they would need to be converted or a shame to let other celebrities know. Maybe it's one reason why the scripture was printed stating if you would be a shame of Jesus that he would be ashamed to tell God about you. What's so strange about many filled with this precious gift that their behavior is worse than someone who isn't, and this should not be so. Some insist on giving another person a piece of their mind if they are crossed. I can't afford to give a person a piece of my mind in that matter, so I pray and keep going.

(Testimony 2) Pastor Beverly asked me to come to speak at her home, where she had services. I told her to have a bathtub full of water before I came because God had put something on my mind. When

I got there, there were about 15 to 20 people there. I began to speak about my concerns about the Holy Ghost. It was quite astonishing after I had spoken, I baptized them all in the tub, and all were filled. There were clothes for them. However, one young lady hopped in the tub with all of her clothes on and left, walking out the front door speaking in tongues while wet. You never know when God is going to fill a person. I was only used as a vessel.

The anointing was so great that the pastor had already been filled before, she decided to hop in for another dip. I am not saying this happens every time, but you never know what God is doing. Several denominations believe in it, but the Apostolic Churches are true to the bone regarding it. You may have to go there if you're highly concerned about it, but it doesn't necessarily mean that you have to stay there and join. You are the church, and you go wherever God leads you, and He may not lead you into organized religion. Getting filled can happen anywhere. Just a reminder, the church is more than just getting filled with the Holy Ghost, but I guarantee you that you will never feel the same should you ask for it, and it happens.

Some churches use the bait and switch method, and you don't know it. They bait you in with kind and loving words, and after a while, they switch their attitude towards you.

(3rd testimony) Why I'm so adamant about God watching over me. Around 1989 after a divorce, I was sleeping in my apartment, and I woke up crying very hard. I had an extraordinary dream that seemed so real. I saw myself on a rollercoaster going up and down the high tracks. As a kid, I never liked roller coasters. In front of the cart was an image of Jesus Christ that was beckoning me to come on. As I was going down the last big hill with great force, I hit two doors at the bottom. After crashing, some fiery flames came up from the ground, writing, "I will never leave you or forsake you." It scared me, and I just cried until I got myself together.

As life would have it, know that God will always send a witness to something in your life. About a few weeks later, I went over to my ex-wife's place to wait for my daughter to come home. I was there alone. I decided to turn on channel 40, TBN, a religious Network. As I sat there watching, a man came on the TV by the name of Ben Kinslow, and he began to speak. "You know life is like a roller coaster, you will go up and down, but Jesus will never leave you or forsake you." I just wanted to holler to the top of my voice. That was many years ago, and that scripture holds close to my heart.

(4th Testimony)- You are who God tells you who you are, whether you want to be or not. I did not wish to be in the ministry. Around the year 1988, as well, one evening after coming home from a high anointed service at church, God took over my mouth and told me about the ministry and what I needed to do. I talked for 3 hours straight while a friend of mine named Ralph witnessed the whole thing. It was amazing! I had no control over what I was saying. I spoke in tongues for an hour and a half, and the interpretation came right behind it for another hour and a half. If anyone knows me, they know that I am a clown 100%, but God did not take my personality away. He told me that I would be different, and some would not accept me, but many would.

(5th Testimony) About 15 years passed after that, and I had another bombshell. I was in Mississippi, and I had converted a Pizza Hut into a hair salon. A beautiful place, but after many trials in the south trying to help, I had had enough negativity. I was running Youth Programs for the Park and Recreation and ran my own programs for children, called The Gulley Institute of Creative Learning as well, and that's another story.

One day I was standing in the salon alone, and I told God I was tired of trying to help these people. I asked Him to please reveal what was in me and what I was supposed to do, and he did. He told me that I was a writer right there on the spot. So I said, "I can't write and do hair too." So I closed the salon within a month, and people thought I was crazy. I hadn't saved any money even though all my bills were paid. I closed the salon and paid my mortgage with a charge card for a year. That first year I wrote five books and moved back to California, and for a while, I stayed with a friend named Michael Henley. I have written about 20 books and six plays. I guess God had always planned to bring me back to writing, which started at age 12. God allowed me to go through many challenges so that I would have something to write about.

I was anointed to write at age 12. During that time, I had written and directed two plays. The church thought I was a genius—these people ranging from about 35 years and over listening to the directions of a 12-year-old kid. After graduating, I went into the hair business for nearly 25 years, beautifying women and men. Does God know what he was talking about when he said I was a writer? I think so. I have so many testimonies, but those were just a few, not to mention all of the schools I had gone to after graduating from high school. I was so glad to get out of high school and said I would never go to school again. My resume today is loaded with schools and classes I've gone to after high school. Just too funny!

Back to the Holy Ghost. This is how I look at it regarding a name. If your name is John and you are a father, and you are a carpenter, that is your skill, but you also are a baker. So if I call you and said John come here, wouldn't the carpenter and the baker come as well? The father, the carpenter, and the baker are all three the same one? The same as the Father, Son, and Holy Ghost are in the name of Jesus.

The following story is an excerpt from my book about the Columbine incident regarding me being filled with the Holy Ghost and the jacked-up educational system.

(**Testimony 6**) We can make lots of money and be extremely busy, but there is always something that tends to catch our attention. I was thirty-two years old at the time, a natural comic full of laughs. During that time, I was a cosmetologist in Inglewood, Calif. I had an excellent clientele, but there was one customer named Jean Allen that stood out. She was a real estate agent that came in weekly, always in a hurry, but always with a joyful personality.

We were both crazy in a way, and we attended different churches. She'd say, "Yeah, but you need to come and visit my church because you need some fire." I would laugh and say, "Yeah, right"— because I thought I was "hot" enough. This went on for months, but the day finally came when I did attend her church, the First Apostolic Church of Inglewood, during that time under the leadership of the late Bishop Wayne Davis. That church does not exist now.

However, I didn't know too much about Apostolic churches. I didn't know much about Baptism either, for that matter, and I'd been attending Baptist churches for years. The service started at 11 a.m., so I got up that morning and put on my duds, thinking I was looking pretty good. I arrived on time, and from the moment the service started, I have to say that the church was really on fire. The whole service was high. The music was great; the testimonies were hot, and there I was, sitting in the middle of all of it, wondering what the heck was going on. Where had I been all the time that I was missing this?

After Bishop Wayne Davis had preached, there was the altar call. Boy, was he punching my card? I was feeling different because I had been in church and had been baptized—my actual problem was that my battery was dead and in need of charging. The altar call continued; people walked down the aisles crying.

Bishop Davis then asked the congregation to turn to one another and ask the person next to them if they were saved. The strangest thing is that when a person asks you if you are saved or not, all of a sudden, you start looking for an answer. Well, a bright-skinned lady was sitting next to me, who had a big mouth, and was on fire. I said to myself, "Lord, have mercy. I hope this woman doesn't say anything to me." She turned to me and said, "Are you saved?" I just looked at her as if one of us was crazy, and then she asked again.

By this time, I guess she knew something was up, so she said, "Hey, I'll walk down there with you." Believe me, I was nervous and partly embarrassed because when I thought about being saved, I had no idea what or whom I was being saved from. Of course, she meant had I accepted Jesus, and did I feel he had saved me from the wrath to come? The next thing I knew, she had my hand, and we went down the aisle. Keep in mind that all of this happened three years before I was called into the ministry. I never could understand how that worked.

There I was, standing in front of the altar, feeling a little paranoid because quite a few members from that church knew me. I was down in front, asking for forgiveness of my sins and confessing that Jesus Christ was the Son of God. The next question was from one of the associate ministers, who asked me if I had been baptized. I told him yes—I had been baptized two times before—but my answer was not good enough for the Apostolic faith. I had been baptized in the name of the Father, Son, and Holy Ghost; in the Apostolic faith, you must be baptized under the name of Jesus.

According to the Bible, as I mentioned earlier, Paul asked a group under what baptism were they baptized; the following took place, as repeated earlier:

He said unto them, Have ye received the Holy Ghost since ye believed? And they said unto him; We have not so much as heard whether there be any Holy Ghost. And he said unto them, unto what then were ye baptized? And they said, Unto John's baptism. Then said Paul, John verily baptized with the baptism of repentance, saying unto the people, that they should believe on him which come after him, that is, on Christ Jesus. When they heard this, they were baptized in the name of the Lord Jesus. And when Paul had laid his hands upon them, the Holy Ghost came on them; and they spoke with tongues, and prophesied. (Acts 19:2)

So, after all of this understanding, I thought one more dip couldn't do any harm. This particular church believed in immediate baptism—they already had a robe and change of clothes ready for me—all I had to do was say yes. There was no such thing as "We'll wait until the first Sunday." The time was now. They escorted me to the back area where I could change my clothes.

Then, there I was, standing in the middle of a pool, being baptized in the name of Jesus by one of the pastors. After coming up out of the water, I thought some kind of miracle was going to happen, but nothing did.

I was asked if I would like to receive the Holy Ghost's power with the evidence of speaking in tongues since it didn't happen immediately. Well, you know I said yes; I wanted to see how this was going to work. I went into what they called the receiving room, which was filled with a group of about fifteen people, all of the different ages. Some were just sitting there saying "Hallelujah"; others were speaking in tongues. "This is going to be interesting!" I said to myself.

The lady in charge of the room told me to have a seat, close my eyes so that I would not be distracted; within my heart, I was to ask God to fill me with the Holy Ghost and keep repeating the word *hallelujah*. So, off I went, "Hallelujah, hallelujah, hallelujah, hallelujah." Nothing seemed to happen miraculously. Maybe God didn't like me.

Unfortunately, because of my creative mind and wild imagination, I had become distracted by visualizing the woman in charge as the Devil. This lady wore a black dress, black stockings, black shoes, a black hat, a black wig, and she was very dark-skinned. I kept saying "hallelujah," but I was also opening and closing one of my eyes just in case I had to body slam her if she were the Devil. Perhaps I was thinking of the scripture that said watch and pray! I didn't want to take any chances. Matthew 26:41

After forty-five minutes of this, I became quite tired and semi-discouraged and told her that I had to go. She said that was all right, that sometimes people don't get filled right away, and could come back anytime that I wanted.

All through that week, I thought about it. Everything started coming to my mind, and I found myself bawling out God. I told him that I had been to church all my life because my mother made sure I went. I felt like He was wasting my time and that this Holy Ghost people were talking about didn't seem to exist.

It seemed that every time I turned around, somebody had something to say about what I should or shouldn't do according to the Bible. I believed that man wrote the Bible and, therefore, he could insert anything in it that he wanted to—even if it frustrated people because man can be crooked like that.

I had accumulated a good amount of anger, and I told God that he had one more time to prove Himself to me; if He didn't fill me with His power,

He wasn't to bother me anymore; I didn't want a bunch of church folks telling me anything because I didn't have the time, I was sick of churches, I was going to mind my own business, and He should do the same. It's a wonder God didn't slap me down because of my attitude. He always shows his mercy. I had been through several different denominations trying to discover who God was until it almost drove me crazy—consider talking to God like that. Well, he cooked my goose, and I mean, well done without a glaze.

The next Sunday, I went back to the same church. I couldn't wait until service was over so I could go back into that receiving room to see what was going down. Before I entered the room, I said, "God, this is your chance to prove yourself." This time there was a brown-skinned younger girl in the room who was neatly dressed. I said, "Thank God."

I took my seat and said, "All right, God." I opened my mouth and began to say the hallelujahs, and within five minutes, the most joyous sound started coming out of my mouth. My tongue turned, and I began to speak this language I had never heard for about forty-five minutes. I was so tickled, and I could not stop speaking in tongues and laughing at the same time. The young lady told me to let it flow: "That's it, that's it," she'd said. She told me that this heavenly language would always be with me and that it took a unique tongue to speak to God. She tried to get my name, but I laughed so hard and spoke in tongues that it made it a little complicated.

She also said that I could speak this language anytime because it was always with me.

I left there with a glow on my face and a new revelation, and I apologized to God. A buddy of mine named Terry Stamps picked me up after church. I had a few things to pick up, so we stopped at a supermarket along the way; he waited in the car. Remembering what the young lady told me about the tongues always being with me, I thought I would test out this marvelous gift. I opened my mouth and down the ketchup aisle, past the mayonnaise and pickles, there I went speaking in tongues.

I said, "Oh, my God, they're still there. I am officially bilingual." I was tickled because the whole event just blew my mind. I realized that my battery had just been charged! If you want some supernatural power, ask God to fill you with His precious Holy Ghost. I guarantee that you may not be perfect, but you'll never be the same. You may not become perfect, but you sure will become instantly wiser.

After coming out of the market, Terry decided we would stop at a restaurant and eat. After telling him what had happened to me, he said, "Stewart, you have this big glow on your face. You make me feel like I'm the Devil." His family was Catholic, but Terry hadn't been to church in a while, so I invited him to go. He said that he wasn't ready yet. Every now and then, I'd ask him again. Sadly, in

1992, he went on to be with the Lord. His sister, Michele, told me that he had found Christ.

Unfortunately, years passed, and Michelle passed away as well.

After being filled, God opened my eyes to things I had never thought or knew. It got to the point where I didn't want to go to church because I kept seeing too much wrong with how the services were being conducted, what was needed or should be eliminated. I told God I just wanted to go to church, sit down, and enjoy the service—unfortunately, that hasn't happened in the thirty-five years since then—so I've just learned to pray. There was a time when I almost got mad at all churches because they were so much against one another, even though they're all using the same Bible, but acting like gangs. Now I know that all they need is to have their batteries charged. Remember, a good looking battery with a dead cell is worthless! *END*

There are over 450 active gangs in Los Angeles. Combined members are over 45,000 individuals. How many church gangs are there?

The third time I was baptized, I did it the apostolic way; I was filled with the Holy Ghost, and I haven't been the same since. I must admit that I had a deep fight about it in my heart, and I had to confront God about it. One day, He revealed to me that it was true. It's like being stunned about some new information that has been here all the time, but no one ever told you.

After this joyous experience, I recall telling a couple of my customers, Jehovah's Witnesses, and they stopped coming to me. As a matter of fact, one of them told me it was Satan. Oh well!

In some stories in the Bible, the Holy Ghost fell, and some hadn't been baptized in Jesus' name at that moment. As I've said, however, a little more water won't hurt.

Many will read this book and think that it won't be necessary to get baptized, but the Devil knows how to work through us all. Some people are so shallow that they believe the only person who can baptize them is the one that did already, and they "don't need anyone else." Try saying that to a doctor who wants to send you to a specialist to save your life. Will you fail to see him because he's not your original doctor?

I admire how God does things; we just have to accept his ways. As the scripture reads, "God's ways are not our ways, neither are His thoughts our thoughts" (Isa. 55:8). *Ye must be born again. (Read the 3rd Chapter of John).*

I feel this way: If a Holy-Ghost-filled evangelist is not coming to you, try to find out where one is, and go to him. We should find out all we can about the power we need to do the work of Jesus, strengthening our faith through trials. Some people may have been raised in a decent Christian family and are doing very well, yet they still need the Holy Ghost's power to do more. People go off to college, trade schools, etc. And they seek more after graduation. Accepting Jesus is like graduation, and when you are filled, you now get a job, which is telling the world about what Jesus is to us.

Some leaders will fight against what I just said, but don't worry. Anything someone doesn't have is always questionable. Some will say that you don't need it, but my response may be, "You don't need three cars, but you have them, nor do you need car insurance, but you have it."

I was almost angry because I had been going to church for years, and most of them didn't talk about it. Life is not easy. You need every tool that you can that will help you have peace.

I thought receiving the evidence was a joke, too, until it happened to me. Even though people have been filled, some still tend to go back to their previous denomination, but you will never forget that experience, and it will always be within you. Your eyes will be open as well, and wisdom will begin to surface. It's like Adam and Eve biting the fruit, and their eyes were opened. Trust me; you will never be the same. When you are somewhere, and the anointing tends to appear in the service, you will try to sustain it to keep people from knowing you have it. Good luck!

Similar to the example mentioned earlier, you can lay your coat on a chair representing a dead spirit. Unless you put the coat on and your spirit in it, the coat will not move. The Holy Ghost is the extra boost you need to do the job you were called to do. However, a person can be rebellious and still not do the job, even though the Holy Ghost is present.

Ask God to fill you with his power. "If a son shall ask bread of any of you that is a father, will he give him a stone: Or if he asks a fish, will he for a fish give him a serpent? Or if he shall ask an egg, will he offer him a scorpion? If ye then, being evil, know how to give good gifts unto your children: how much more shall your heavenly Father give the Holy Spirit to them that ask him?" (Matt. 7:9).

Every church should have an evangelist speak often. They are around, and churches don't have to seek popular ones. A bird in the hand is better than one in the bush.

There are good ministers all day long on different stations for those who have a cable TV or just YouTube. I guarantee you that you will be blessed by the word of God that you will hear through the week. However, there's nothing like being in an actual anointed service. The more you get, the more you can use it. And the more you use, the more the Devil has to flee. That doesn't mean he won't return. It's like killing flies. Yes, you will spray and kill some, but others will eventually return, so don't put your can away. Life is a battle, so keep fighting and don't be ignorant of Satan's devices.

God may talk to your pastor regarding you. All the same, God can speak to you regarding your pastor and what you should do as well. Remember, the pastor answered his call, and you have a telephone in your bosom as well, and you need to answer your own. There is so much we learn day by day. Nevertheless, it has already been given to us. That's why some people seem to be doing God's will, and they don't even go to church. **Hebrews 10:16- This is the covenant I will have with them after those days, says the Lord, I will put my laws in their heart.** Why do you think a two or 3-year-old hides things? Because he knows what is right and wrong and has not been convinced yet of all the other laws man put on a person?

Here's a true story I witnessed. I once was sitting near the back on the city bus. Several adults were talking about God. A young man about 20 years old had the section in a frozen state because he spoke very heavily about God and inserted every scripture he knew relating to their conversation. He was very anointed, I might add. As the bus came to a stop, the young man was at the back door, getting ready to get off, and one of the older adults yelled, "Hey brother, what church do you belong to? He replied, "I don't go to any because all of this is in my heart." He hopped off the bus *END*.

As said, the Devil is not bothering some people because they are walking with him. You'll know the difference when you're trying to do things God's way. Side note: Just because a person is saved and filled with the Holy Ghost, it doesn't mean they are perfect and fully delivered. However, many things will change in their life. Some still make a drink, smoke, have sex, and everything else. This is called being saved and not fully delivered, but things will work out eventually. It's all a process. I can just imagine someone holding up their nose after that statement, but be careful; birds may be flying over and drop you something. Rome wasn't built in a day and in a night either!

Gift Number Four
Pastor

Jeremiah 3:15 - And I will give you pastors according to mine heart, which shall feed you with knowledge and understanding. (Is this happening?)

Ecclesiastes 4:13- Better a poor but wise youth than an old but foolish king who no longer knows how to heed a warning.

Jeremiah 23:2 – Therefore thus says the Lord God of Israel against the pastors that feed my people. Ye have scattered my flock, and driven them away and have not visited them: behold, I will visit you the evil of yours doings, says the Lord

The church is not all about the pastor, as many have made it to be. Before we get started with the pastor, ask yourself this question. What are the benefits of someone coming to your church? Oh, shouldn't there be benefits? Well, let's look at it like this: If a church calls you to be a pastor, wouldn't you want to know the benefits such as salary, benefits, and frills. Now my question again is that what are the benefits of someone coming to your church? Are you just giving a sermon? Or are you saying study to get yourself approved? (2 Tim

2:15). So would that mean they stay home and study by themselves, or are they taught by preacher, teacher, etc.? Better yet; (Rom 10:14) How can they hear without a preacher? But what preacher is telling them right and not for filthy lucre?

As you know very well, some people are so fed up with going to church that they listen to services on the internet or turn on YouTube and thank God for it because he will find a way to pour out His spirit.

Almost like an earthly father, the pastor is like the father of the house. It is almost like when a mother says, "Wait 'til your father gets home." The pastor guards his members and protects them, but these days, it is not always the case; many seek lots of money and don't have a pastor's heart. (**It's not what he can do for his children, but what his children can do for him.**) There are Deadbeat Pastors, the same as dead beat fathers and mothers. We do understand the scripture that says: "Don't muzzle the ox that treads the grain." Those who work deserve pay." But are leaders working or just collecting?

I came across a site that helps churches organize their members and other information. Below was their suggestion of the salary an executive pastor should get a year:

0-500 members = Approx. $69,170 per year
501-1,200 members = Approx. $78,054 per year
1,201 + members= Approx. $103,841 per year

This was just the pastor's salary, not to mention other expenses of the churches. With these numbers in a pastor's mind, he will try to figure out what events and obligations he could put on members that stress them out to give. Of course, we all can't help if a church grows, but instead of seeing souls, we are geared to see the money that is not given willingly, but through many types of events and feelings of guilt through sermons, they will reach these goals. As far as salvation is concerned, it says that by the foolishness of preaching shall save man. Quoted from 1Corinthians 1:21 - For after that in the wisdom of God the world by wisdom knew not God, it pleased God by the foolishness of preaching to save them that believe.

As it has been said, some were called in; some were pushed in, and some just jumped in. "For every tree is known by his fruit. For of thorns, men do not gather figs, nor of a bramble, bush gathers they grapes" (Luke 6:44).

I heard a joke that a man constantly bugged his pastor about how he was called to preach. The pastor just held the man off for a while, but the man insisted on preaching. As time went by, the pastor eventually let the man preach. After preaching, no one saw the man at the church for several months. So the deacons thought they would go to the man's house to see what was wrong. The man opened the door, and one of the deacons said, "Hey brother, I thought you said God called you to preach?" And the man replied, "He did, but after He heard me, He changed his mind." *END*

Unfortunately, the pastor's position has taken precedence over the other four gifts, which should not be so. Many pastors have shipwrecked their congregations from favoritism to manipulation. That is why so many people today refuse to step their foot into a church again. If the pastor supposes to be the father, many are depriving their children of what is needed to sustain and live for the future. If a pastor is wise, he wouldn't have to preach every Sunday, and yet he is still the pastor if he sets the church up, as it should be. It takes hours of preparation to deliver a great message, and contrary to what people may believe, sometimes pastors do not feel like preaching on some Sundays. Everyone gets tired somewhere at something regardless of how good it is.

Hopefully, by the grace of God, people will return to church and find things a little better and in order. As I said earlier, people are becoming wiser and not going for the Okie Doke as they have in the past. They'd rather stay home. If there is no power of authority within the pastor, you will find many problems. The pastor is the shepherd of the flock. A good pastor will see that his children will get all they need.

For instance, they will make sure they will be taught with a teacher's gift; an evangelist will evangelize them, and they will be in the midst of a prophet. All the gifts are essential, and the pastor should make sure they are there unless a true bishop or apostle has set it up.

A pastor will know how to comfort his flock without taking sides with them if they are wrong. One thing about it is that if a pastor is not fair with his members and begins to take sides, he will soon divide the flock. Righteousness is almost common sense. Just be fair.

"Woe be unto the pastors that destroy and scatter the sheep of my pasture! Says the Lord. Therefore thus says the Lord God of Israel against the pastors that feed my people; Ye have scattered my flock, and driven them away, and have not visited them: behold, I will visit upon you the evil of your doings, says the Lord" (Jer. 23:1).

I'll never forget when I started attending a once-popular church, in which I waited to participate until all of its popularity went down. I have always wanted to talk to the leader of a church I am interested in. So, after several Sundays of attending this new church, I spoke with its leader and consulted with him about the gifts God had given me and about how I might help the ministry.

He stated that he had been watching me ever since I began attending the services. I wanted so badly to tell him that I had been watching him too. After our conversation, I understood him. Unfortunately, it wasn't long after that he was up for dismissal, and the church split up.

It is said that many pastors are leading large flocks. But people with no knowledge of the word are being led into the ditch. "Every plant, which my heavenly Father hath not planted, shall be rooted up. Let them alone: they are blind leaders of the blind. And if the blind lead the blind, both shall fall into the ditch" (Matt. 15:13).

Don't worry; in due time, God will uproot many of these ministries that are not doing according to His will. One day, they might have five hundred members, and the next week may only be a husband and the wife. As of this revised writing, the Coronavirus has closed many churches for whatever reason.

If the congregation is taught in earnest, they will understand and learn how also to forgive their pastor if a problem personally occurs with him. The congregation will realize how much good he has done for them. Caution: Just because a church is growing large, it doesn't mean they fully care about the members. Just a new fad in town, and people are flocking until the newness wears off.

Pause for a minute and allow me to interject this story I wrote some time ago regarding getting caught in anything in life.

Don't Get Caught Up In Nothing
By Stewart Marshall Gulley

After a thirteen-hour day of work, a news reporter was headed for home. He was known all over the country, and he became quite wealthy from doing special documentaries on famous people, but he felt something was missing in his life, and he just couldn't put his finger on it. He had a lovely wife, two beautiful children in college, and the finest of everything you could imagine ranging from cars to real estate properties. He lived in an area called Westwood, which was on the other side of Beverly Hills, California.

As he made a right turn onto Wilshire Blvd. heading West towards Beverly Hills, he noticed much traffic and fire engines. Unfortunately, a mansion at 5523 Bedford Drive had caught on fire, which caused this large commotion. The reporter managed to turn off Wilshire and was able to get closer to the fire's location. He parked his car and grabbed his camera, and began to take pictures. Many people recognized him and thought he had been called to do a story, not realizing he was merely on his way home.

After several hours everything died down, and fortunately, the firemen were able to put the fire out quickly. The reporter showed his badge to the firemen, even though they already knew who he was, and he began to ask a few questions. He found out that the mansion was nearly empty, and the cause of the fire was under investigation. As he kept on talking, he also found out that a man was rushed away in the ambulance, and he was described as being elderly with long straggly hair and long fingernails. The neighbors mentioned that they hadn't seen any activity in that house for months, and the man they remembered didn't fit that description.

As the reporter turned to his right, he saw a fireman with a square metal box. He stopped him and asked what was in the box, and the fireman said that he didn't know, but it was probably something that might be helpful. Being a good reporter, he managed to convince the fireman to open the box. Inside, to their surprise, was a small diary. The writing looked as though someone was either nervous or they could barely write. However, the reporter pulled out the diary, not realizing he was getting ready to answer his own emptiness about life. With squinting eyes, the reporter began to read what was in the diary, and it was as though he could hear the writer's voice:

From the diary of Dr. H. D. Lawson, Ph.D.
Dr. of Psychology, Ohio State University
Residence: 5523 Bedford Drive. Beverly Hills Calif. 90210
August 1, 1975, at 4:00 AM, Sunday Morning

Some where in my mansion, in a room I lay alone because I had lost focus and found reality under difficult circumstances, which was not written in a book. It's a cold but strange morning as I sit up in a dying bed. A bed that have no concern, no mind, and the capacity of zero feelings about the fine piece of art it is now holding, which is me. As I lay here in a moment of despair, I realize that my tongue, which is now filled with blistering sores, couldn't lie anymore to anyone about anything or anybody on any given subject. I couldn't even lie on an "I'm gonna' tell it anyhow attitude." Nor lie on income tax, apartment rental, real estate, welfare, or just plain bus fare. My infected palate can not lie anymore.

Right now, I'm feeling my long straggly hair, and my hair haven't been cut in months; strangely enough, my son is a barber, and my daughter is a successful manicurist to the movie stars. My fingernails have grown so very long, and my hands, oh my hands, which are now so crippled, have lost their authority to steal, take or borrow forever. The finest stores in Beverly Hills, such as Neiman Marcus, Bonwit Teller, Saks 5th Avenue, Gucci, Fiorucci, and my old leather buddy Mr. Louie Vuitton are all now at peace because my crafty hands are now at rest. Right now, I am holding my swollen and hurting head, and I realize I can't even fornicate in my mind…I AM SICK.

Yes, it is cold this morning, and the Ortho mattress I'm laying on only has one purpose, which was to hold a dead person, dead in body, dead in mind, and dead in spirit. Yes, a dead person on a dead mattress whose springs had sprung their last spring of sporadic sympathy.

I began to feel the nerves pulsating in this old dying body; as I look up, I can see the cold wind shattering against the crafty French-defined windows. Painfully I'm lifting my body higher, and I look out to the spot where the Rolls Royce had once been parked, driven by the now terminated chauffeur who knew the roads so well. I reluctantly noticed the grass that had grown tall and whose manicure now looked like cuticle fungus on a forbidden island. I am talking about my place. The place where I had labored all the way down to my diseased bones to achieve the luxuries and the beauties of life that the world had given me. A life I am now unable to enjoy because of sickness, pain, lack of money, disappearing children, and unpredictable friends.

As my mind began to wander, I'm turning this feeble body into the best position I can, realizing the utilities have been cut off for some time now, and this room is very cold, and I don't even have a candle to heat a two-by-two square. Slowly turning my head to the right and here facing me is an opened door to a walk-in closet. When opening it, it will surprise you, for it is the size of an average gymnasium. At one time, it had been filled with the finest designer apparel. Unfortunately, my furnishings in my house and the apparel had to be sold to pay the house note for the past eight months. And now, hanging in splendid grandeur on a single department store rack is one Armani shirt that cost me $1,475, one pair of Dolce Gabbana pants that cost me $775, and my eyes are very dim, but I also see one pair of broken-down crutches and a note pinned to the closet door, THREE-DAY EVICTION NOTICE.

And now what do I have to say for myself as I slowly cross my legs, and place my right arm tastefully behind my badly aching neck, my left

arthritic hand pressed against this Ortho-mattress?"
All I can do now is respectfully scold myself and
say, "Self, what have you done? Why did you get
caught up?" The only thing I have to say to anyone
who finds my diary is, "don't get caught up in
nothing."

Don't get caught up on nothing
Nothing here on this dear earth
Don't get caught up in your children
Even though you're the cause of their birth

Don't get caught up on that house
Frustration it will bring
Don't get caught up in that job
Don't know when it's finishing

Don't get caught up on that car
One day it will surely stop
Don't get caught up on parents
One day there's no more mom or pop

Don't get caught up on that business
One day no buyer you will see
For many of them move around
And never will return to thee

Don't get caught up on that person
Because they would not share
Now they realize since you've been gone
That you were the only one who cared

Don't get caught up on that college degree
Even though you studied hard and deep

Someday you'll find that college degree
Won't be enough to buy shoes for your feet

Don't get caught up on that friend
Don't know how long the friendship will last
Don't get caught up on that church
So what if it's growing very fast

Don't get caught up on that sickness
You know it has to leave
Don't get caught up on that long prayer
God already knows just what you need

Do not store up for yourselves treasures on earth where moth and rust destroy and where thieves break in and steal, but store up for yourselves treasures in heaven where moth and rust do not destroy and where thieves do not break in and steal for where your treasure is there your heart will be also. (Matthew 6:19)

Getting caught up will make your way,
Your way so very hard
If you want to really get caught up
MAKE SURE YOU GET CAUGHT UP IN
GOD! *END*

I'm sure that the story made you think. Human beings want everyone except themselves to be perfect. Hopefully, the pastor will lead, but the true scripture is "Let God be true, but every man a liar"

(Rom. 3:4). Members will follow the spirit of the pastor. If he is not a giver, they will not be as well.

Once again, the pastor feeds the flock. He watches them, and he makes sure the five-fold ministry is coming to the church to edify the body of Christ, to strengthen his children because he knows what they need.

Jesus went around teaching in the synagogues, but he was moved with compassion on them when he saw the multitudes because they fainted and were scattered abroad, as sheep having no shepherd do. "Then he says to his disciples, The harvest truly is plenteous, but the laborers are few; **Pray ye, therefore, the Lord of the harvest, that he will send forth laborers into his harvest**" (Matt. 9:36).

When you begin to understand parts of the Bible and all that we as Christians should be doing, we will find out that the "Laborers" are few, including ourselves. Technically a lot has changed, and we can use the bible for our good but continually asking God for wisdom. I heard a question regarding Gay people that was astonishing.

A young girl asked a man why he was gay, and he, in return, asked her why was she straight or what's the recipe? Unfortunately, she couldn't give a direct answer. People worry so much about who's gay or who's democrat or republican they forget about doing good. If God knew you while you were in your mother's womb, then he knew all about you before you got here, listening to the laws and foolishness of men. There is nothing new under the sun. As David wrote in Psalms 199:3- It is He that has made us and not we ourselves.

God already knows our thoughts even before we think about them. It's like reading the manual instructions when there's a problem; it says to call the manufacturer. In other words, the company that made them. God made us, and he is our manufacturer.

Psalm 94:11 -The LORD knows the thoughts of man, that they are vanity.

Psalm 49:10-13 For he sees that wise men die, likewise the fool and the brutish person perish and leave their wealth to others.

2Timothy 2:19- God knows those who belong to him.

Technology just made it easier to get to or hear about things. Many years ago, it was the Pony Express, and you may not get the message until a month after because men on ponies delivered it. Now, if something happens at 8:00, you will hear about it at 8:01.

Same old junk, but the news arrives faster. Within the last 35 years, I may have listened to 2 hours of television news in total. I am too busy trying to go about doing my father's business, and it has not always been easy, I must add. Some people are hooked on the news; thank God I'm not. Still, bad news surfaces on the television.

Some pastors are made to look good as far as the ministry's work is going, and he may not be really called to be a pastor. What has happened is that he may have members who are called to be pastors, have the heart of a pastor, and work well in the church but have not been guided in their ministry. The pastor that is over these more qualified members may be better off as a Sunday-school teacher. Still, his position has been immensely rewarding financially, so he refuses to step down because of the salary, benefits, or power. Uh, oh!

Therefore, the one who is doing all the work is not receiving a salary because no one has considered him. "But let us that are doing good remember that promotion still comes from the Lord." (Psalms. 75:6).

"Jesus said, I am the good shepherd; the good shepherd gives his life for the sheep. But he that is a hireling, and does not own the sheep, sees the wolf coming, and leaves the sheep, and flees, and the wolf catches them and scatters the sheep" (John 10:12).

You will find some pastors who are just hirelings (a person that will follow anyone's order for pay)! In other words, if the deacons are wrong, the pastor needs to tell them; otherwise, he's just a hireling! There's nothing like a weak pastor. It is the same as a woman who wants a man and not a boy and vice versa; a man wants a woman and not a squealing little girl.

The Deacons run some churches. They hire and fire the pastor if he doesn't do what he's told. That's why nowadays, some leaders start their own church without them, and if the members don't like it, they can move on. The church is a strange thing, the pastor better be perfect, but the members feel they don't have to be.

Pastors are getting much older as well as the young pastors are to keep the church exciting. Always invite other good speakers who are either evangelists, teachers, prophets, etc. I never understood why pastors only invite pastors with churches. Do you think they are cunningly trying to get some of their members?

Many speakers will charge high fees, but that's another story of how that works. A pastor is like a producer; he should always search for the right anointed talent to supply his congregation. In the music industry, the producer produces many good talents; he sits back, admires, and checks his bank account. The producer wouldn't call the artist anointed; he would say they are fantastic.

Yes, the harvest is great, and the laborers are few, and now we realize it for ourselves. No pastor can run a church all on his own.

(Exodus 18) As Jethro, who was Moses' father-in-law, said, "And it came to pass tomorrow, that Moses sat to judge the people: and the people stood by Moses from the morning unto the evening.

"And when Moses' father-in-law saw all that he did to the people, he said, "What is this thing that you do to the people?" "Why sit alone, and all the people stand by thee from morning unto evening?"

And Moses said unto his father–in–law, "Because the people come to me to seek God's will. [16] Whenever they have a dispute, it is brought to me, and I decide between the parties and inform them of God's decrees and instructions."

[17] Moses' father-in-law replied, "What you are doing is not good. [18] You and these people who come to you will only wear yourselves out. The work is too heavy for you; you cannot handle it alone.

As I was rewriting this book in 2020, there is a pandemic going on with the Coronavirus, and many are dying and getting sick. If Jethro's method were in action today, many people would get help from the church. I bet the average church doesn't know how many seniors they have as well as young people. How many live alone? Who has a large family that needs help? Who has a disability? Who can't pick up their medications? Who are their next of kin? If it was in order, they could go to the computer and find out the age range, where they live as well what type of income they receive or any social service. The only information many churches have is their address and how much they are giving in the offering, but yet we love one another. Not only does the church panic because of this virus, but many have also temporarily closed. So what about the offering? They will probably receive less because the elderly may not know how to use a computer to donate online. It is said that 20% of the members finance the church as a whole.

Had someone visited them once a week, perhaps they would have given them the offering to support the church still. This virus has made some churches check on the elderly, but something had to occur to make the church get on its job. Thousands have died from this virus and have caused much grief in families. But let's be mindful that plagues have been coming hundreds of years ago. Perhaps this is part of the falling away from the church for other reasons.

"Be mindful: The way of a fool is right in his own eyes: but he that hearkens unto counsel is wise" (Prov. 12:15).

The scripture from Exodus reads on:
[19] Listen now to me, and I will give you some advice, and may God be with you. You must be the people's representative before God and bring their disputes to him. [20] Teach them his decrees and instructions and show them the way they are to live and how they are to behave. [21] But select capable men from all the people—men who fear God, trustworthy men who hate dishonest gain—and appoint them as officials over thousands, hundreds, fifties and tens. [22] Have them serve as judges for the people at all times, but have them bring every difficult case to you; the simple cases they can decide themselves. That will make your load lighter because they will share it with you. [23] If you do this and God so commands, you will be able to stand the strain, and all these people will go home satisfied."

[24] Moses listened to his father-in-law and did everything he said. [25] He chose capable men from all Israel and made them leaders of the people, officials over thousands, hundreds, fifties and tens. [26] They served as judges for the people at all times. The difficult cases they brought to Moses, but the simple ones they decided themselves. *END*

Now that's what I call setting up a camp! Many churches are all looking to one pastor, yet there may be several in the church. By the way, they can be on salary too if they can afford it.

This is why some tend to start their own churches; some leaders have become very selfish, which has had a snowball effect, so now there are many little churches worldwide wondering what's next! Another reason for pastors starting their own churches is that they won't be fired, but they might fire themselves if members don't like what is going on. Today, large ministries are constructing buildings, not churches of God.

Yes, I know many make the statement, "The church is in you." If we took that statement literally, there would be no need for us to go.
. However, I pray that I would be going to the right church where they are putting more church in me with good food and not junk. And stop beating and fussing across the pulpit so much. People work hard, and they are not too interested in paying their money to some church that beats them down all the time, and it's doesn't mean that they just want to

hear some sugar-coated sermon for itching ears. A lot of things that they fuss about everyone isn't doing it. Why don't they go to the person that they know is doing it?

It's like a teacher having a classroom of 30 children, and two of them keep acting unruly. Instead of the teacher taking them out, they remain in class and fuss at those two students during the whole class while the rest of the class miss the lesson. But one of the reasons is that the school will lose funding if the students are not there, so some schools let them do what they want. Same as the church, if you scold a good tithe payer, you just might lose them.

Churches are passing out scraps from the table and not giving the congregation the real food they should receive, such as the five-fold ministry.

Unless God builds the house, the building is in vain (Psalms 127:1). Are we raising buildings for prestige, power, and usury? God searches the hearts, and he knows exactly what is going on. (A con-artist once said: If I know what YOU want, I can take everything you have.)

Jethro was telling Moses to set up what some people today call cell groups. When you have a large congregation and this type of order is not set up, you lead a weak Christian group that don't know it. Some leaders do not like the cell-group style because they think that some will start small churches under them without them knowing it. So what? God calls people to be leaders in different ways. **You do not belong to a church. You**

belong to God. If we were all busy like we should, none of us would have time to go to church at all because church obligations can be very demanding. Some churches have even broken up homes when they should have been binding them together.

This also reminds me why some ministers may leave a church because God may have called them to lead or speak, and the leader may not want to listen or hear what is being said. However, some leaders will not allow them to speak at all, so they decide to leave and do what they feel God has called them to do. Keep in mind; evidently, the pastor is doing what he thought he was to do. How come another member can't feel the same. It reminds me of this song "Listen," sung by Beyonce and written by Beyonce, Henry Krieger, Scott Cutler, and Anne Preven in the musical Dream Girls.

"Listen"

Listen to the song here in my heart
A melody I start but can't complete
Listen to the sound from deep within
It's only beginning to find release

Oh, the time has come for my dreams to be heard
They will not be pushed aside and turned
into your own, all 'cause you won't listen

Listen, I am alone at a crossroads
I'm not at home in my own home

And I've tried and tried
To say what's on my mind
You should have known, oh
Now I'm done believin' you
You don't know what I'm feelin'
I'm more than what
You've made of me
I followed the voice you gave to me
But now I've gotta find my own
You should have listened

There was someone here inside
Someone I thought had died
So long ago

Oh, I'm screamin' out
And my dreams will be heard
They will not be pushed aside or turned
Into your own
All 'cause you won't listen. *END*

We have to trust God. He says, **"All souls are mine."** In other words, they don't belong to anyone but God, who chooses to direct people as he pleases. If you were living in a small town of fifty thousand people and there were two hundred churches, it would mean that each church should have approximately two hundred fifty members each if divided equally.

Sounds nice, but in this day and time, that would be a shock. Many small churches barely have fifty members, and some of these are seeking God without getting impressed by the hype of others. In the same token large churches are losing members. It's always the little things that people fail to do that causes people not to return. It can be a mere "thank you" that someone didn't receive. The courtesy of ushers is significant. .Song of Solomon 2:15: "Take us the foxes, the little foxes that spoil the vines; for our vines have tender grapes."

People must also be mindful that the large churches didn't start as large churches. Someone had to believe in the leader, whether he was right or wrong. It's like the President of the United States. Even though many people dislike Trump, someone still voted for him to win.

Yes, it does look very impressive when you see large ministries on TV, but those that are not as large are also impressive because of the actual work they do to help others.

People are becoming depressed every day, and that's for not receiving the essential things in life. When a person needs clothing or shelter, the church will send them to the Salvation Army or another organization because they do not think in those terms. Does the church have a warehouse to collect good donations? No, but they do have an empty Life Center.

Thank God for the Salvation Army and the Welfare System. There's always a ram in the bush.

How many leaders know everything about their members or their family, such as the next of kin?

Do they all have burial insurance? What's their God-given gift? Do they have a will? Who knows, they may want to donate their belongings to the church if the church acts as if they care because some people who have family members who don't care about them and instead donate to the vet that took care of their dog or to the dog himself.

I heard of a true story that a man placed an ad in the paper to sell a Porsche for $65. Of course, that sounds unheard of considering the actual price of a Porsche. However, a man was selling it because he was preparing for a divorce, and to aggravate his wife, he would rather give the car away than give it to her. Someone got the car for a super deal of $65.When someone dies, love ones scuffle around, wondering what to do? What would have been the person's wish at their funeral? It may sound weird, but some people have their whole life in order before they go.

Every church needs some type of shelter because anything can occur. It's just like having insurance.

These shelters or houses can also be real estate income. People think that McDonald's is into hamburgers, but they don't know the story, but McDonald's is highly interested in real estate of their locations, etc.

Feeding the homeless is excellent because the bible says that the poor will always be with us forever. (Mark 14:7, Matthew 26:11)

The Harvest is great, but the laborers are few (Matthew 9:37). But not only to feed, but it would be nice to find out what their gifts are and what they are qualified to do. Not only that, to help them seek government assistance of some sort. One of the reasons behind having so many homeless on the streets is that some do not know how to fill out all of the red tape information that gets any assistance. So they sleep on the streets. That's a department in itself that the church could have. The government will help you build homes, but we instead build cathedrals. "You have got to be doing something when He comes." What will you be doing?

Ministries today will build million-dollar churches but don't have a shelter or anything similar to one. I know you can't hold everyone in case of a disaster, but at least you have something temporary. Better yet, many years ago, I saw a brand-new church that spent almost $600,000, and they didn't put in a baptismal pool. That was a Pentecostal church, which always speaks of the importance of baptizing. Times are changing. Try building a church today for $600,000. Good luck!

I am not pushing any denomination here, but many Apostolic churches are ready to baptize you right then and there. They will have the clothes and towels prepared for you. I believe that the baptismal pool is more important than the pulpit. However, many try to get the pulpit all lavished and don't think about the baptism. That is the time for salvation. Although water won't save you, it will just get you wet, but it's a start. I've been baptized three times, and it's a wonder I haven't drowned. Some of us take a little more water.

First two times under the Baptist doctrine and the third under the Apostolic Doctrine. Wow! What a difference. Of course, someone might say, I wasn't ready to receive Jesus yet during the other baptisms, and I was just getting wet.

As I previously said that I don't like bringing up denominations, but I guess you have to call it something. I just can't figure why all these bibles can't get on one accord. Why do you think the world look at people who go to church as crazy or hypnotized? I call it a bunch of Water Sports, and may the best baptismal swimmer win.

Now back to speaking about Jethro's pattern of concern. **Pastors should know what is in their church, regardless of the number of members. Know them that labor among you. (1Thessolonians 5:12).**

Promotions come from the Lord. Some pastors want a large congregation, but they don't want the real responsibility of being one. So many young ministers are coming along; they see the ministry as being very lucrative and easy. They feel all they have to do is get a group of people to follow them and drop off a sermon for Sunday morning and get paid, but it doesn't work like that.

If the leaders and members were paid a commission, they would have no problem going into the highways and byways to compel people to Christ (Luke 14:23). I would be trying to bring them by truckloads, and so would you. Like a person who works in a department store, the behavior is different from a person on salary, and one is on commission. The salaried person doesn't care if you purchase or not because they already know how much they will get an hour, but the commission person would try to sell you back your own underwear if they could.

Speaking is the most lucrative business there is in the country. One message to many (thousands), but you had better have something to say. Even though some have made it a con game, people will pay you to listen to what you have to say, especially if they feel they are getting help. Proverbs 25:11 A word fitly spoken is like apples of gold in a setting of silver.

The only time it gets tough in the church business is when you start constructing buildings, and someone has to pay for it. Luke 14:28- For which of you, desiring to build a tower, does not first sit down and count the cost, whether he has enough to complete it? Otherwise, when he has laid a foundation and is not able to finish, all who see it begin to mock him, saying, This man began to build and was not able to finish.

So you have conventions, revivals, sell books, tapes, pledges, and any other thing you can think of to help pay for the building, and when you pay it off, there's still always something new to be added, but what about people's hearts and what they need. I guarantee that if you had gotten into people's hearts, in what they needed, the building would have been paid off faster and willingly. There's an old saying: "Give them what they need, and they will give you what you need."

Back to knowing about your member, there should be a meeting involving every department head stating the new change. They should know the necessary information about each person in their department of what other skills they may have to help or ideas they may have to make things better not only for the church but for themselves. This information needs to be written down and not just kept verbal. We can fix our mouths to say anything. However, understand that there are church meetings often, and they don't go too well because there is always someone who will try to go against the pricks, and you will see their real personalities.

There should be an advertisement in the back of the Sunday program with a picture of the member and information accessible for members of those that own a business so that other members may support them and refer consumers to them. You can charge a minimal fee for this, and this is for members only. If outsiders use it, would they give the church a percentage? Or would they increase their offering? How would you monitor that when people use your members for their gain and not supporting your church?

Face it. We come across many advertisements all day long. An average consumer sees about 3,000 ads a day. Check out on YouTube: 15 Things you didn't know about the advertising industry. Advertising dictates what we eat, wear, our careers, and so on. Of course, now, the church is doing it too. However, most of the church advertisements are to support something that benefits the church and not necessarily the members' needs.

Church members are continually going out in the world, supporting non-Christian businesses, and why? Because they own the companies.

If we supported our own somehow, it would bring more tithes to the church for those who believe in tithes or more offerings. Also, understand that all offerings are not planted in good seed, and for those that are produced in good seed, it will show. In the same breath, all great ministries are not always doing the will of God, and it just looks that way. Understand that the devil has many followers as well. Just a thought!

Your offerings can be more than your tithe as well as someone else's tithe so that God's work will continue; even if they didn't pay tithes, they would give something. If you can convince a million people to offer you one dollar, how much would you have? That's right, one million dollars. Why do we work for the wicked? "The wealth of the wicked shall be laid up for the just" (Prov. 13:22).

They should be bringing the saints' money too. It seems like the wicked are the ones that own the businesses, and the saints don't. We must remember that a church is God's house, not a marketplace like some have made. Very few members have businesses, and I could never understand why church people are the most broke people I know. Yes, the church is a business, but a particular type of business.

Church announcements: If you want to mention all of the events and burdens you wish to put on people, why not send them a letter? Might end in the junk pile? Why get them all depressed and make them feel obligated? They do not hear you; all they are thinking about is the burden you're trying to put on them. Eventually, they will get sick of you and all of your obligations. Some can barely feed themselves for being pressured to give to the building funds, and no one ever sees the building they are talking about, building what? Are there any benefits for the members in the announcement section? Some people would love to go to your $75 banquet, but they can't afford it. Do you ask whether any members would like to sponsor someone to go?

Furthermore, churches strive to pay off the mortgage, but who does it benefit even if they do? They will continue to come up with something else to pay for, which has only things to do with beautifying the church and not personally beautifying the members. Are there teachers showing members how to pay off their mortgage quicker? I am definitely for a beautiful church; however, the members should be just as beautiful financially and spiritually. Who's teaching finance? A small piece of the lesson wouldn't hurt on Sunday morning service.

I know we like to share our experiences and some of God's things to help the ministry and encourage others. A funny expression that many people use is, "My life is an open book." Some people talk too much and need to close their books.

Even God didn't allow everything in His book. It would have been too much to handle with all the other numerous books to be read and studied. That sounds good, but what if the wicked men took some of the books out. People are arguing over His sixty-six books. Do they need more? So why is your book so open? Many religions are coming up, but people want people who care about them. You may know your Jesus, but people like you to show your Jesus!

In reality, you're not telling it all. I'm sure if it were an open book, there would be a lot of things you wouldn't want a person to know. We need to forget some things. God does. "We overcome by the words of our testimonies, true enough, but you had better be wise in your testimony, which will go better to a person who can appreciate it who may be going through the same thing that you overcame" (Rev. 12:11).

Many Christians talk on the surface, in which the pastor has to seek the heart of God to know who is sincere. A woman may stand up and testify to a congregation that she is an ex-prostitute; thus, the other women in the congregation will start holding on to their husbands and will not want to see that woman near him. Before long, the ex-prostitute will feel it and will not go to that church because she feels too significantly judged because of what she used to be. But as far as that is concerned, no woman can take another woman's husband; he wanted to go, and vice-versa, a man cannot take another man's wife; she wanted to go as well. Some churches cut out testimonials.

Yet, the person that stands up and says that he or she is an ex-drug addict doesn't bother anyone, and they will applaud, making them feel they've done something great, but the prostitute will be judged harshly from the point she has opened her mouth. The congregation fails to realize that the ex-drug addict was probably also a prostitute to get money for the drugs. Who knows who might be in the congregation that's not delivered and looking for drugs or to purchase sex?

A friend of mine says that his cousin goes undercover to the rehab programs to sell drugs because everyone is there for that reason trying to break from the habit, but he knows their weakness and financially benefits from it.

That's why a good pastor is exceptional and seeks God's wisdom. A person has to be loving yet strong enough to be a pastor. The pastor is the head of the house.

For example, a couple would not let just anyone come into their home and teach their children or stir up strife, so why should a pastor let just anyone come into the house of God? Now the television has moved into the house and teaching God's word. Many people are tired of going to the fanfare. Large conventions, why? People now have D.I.Y.C (Do it, Yourself Church). Once again, why are they coming to yours? Are they staying? Yes, there's a large congregation on Easter Sunday, but what about the Sunday following? That's the Sunday everything should be in order hoping they would like to come back. Yes, all across the nation, on Easter Sunday, they tell the story about how Jesus rose, but just remember he got off the cross and got busy.

Many go to these large conventions to take vast offerings and come back to their church and run it the same way, but not the proper way because most keep repeating the same methods. I look at these large conventions and wonder who do they help? What's their conversion? I'm not knocking them, but I just wonder what the success results are. Or was it just a good gospel hangout? I'm sure if they did the things in this book, they would come back mentally exhausted, which is not what I'm trying to create. I'm just trying to show how far we are behind in our religions, across the board. How many times can they nail Jesus to the cross? I thought he got down. These conventions and Camp Meetings make a lot of money, not to mention the enormous amount specific guest speakers get. It's all about money, which there is nothing wrong with it because it takes money to do things. However, look at the same methods they've been using for years. They charge for each church representation as well as a fee for each delegate. Some churches, such as the Methodist, are required to bring in so much money every year to the Methodist Organization. They raise the money in whatever way they can, and it's way up in the thousands of dollars, so the pressure is not on pastoring but to raise the money to represent. It may be 50 or $60,000 or more a year, almost like a Franchise.

And if some of these leaders were busy, they wouldn't have time to go to a convention anyway because they would have too much to do at their home church. Mostly when they return, they tell you that they had a good time and the classes were terrific, but continue doing the things as before. All the rules of how to run a church are already in the bible. So, what are they doing to convince you to come to the convention? They say the church is like the hospital, but what do you do when the doctors are sick too?

Some pastors are fearful of their members. I'll never forget many years ago when I was directing a choir at a church in the rough parts of Los Angeles. During choir rehearsal, a young lady insisted on talking. To my understanding, she was one of the hell-raisers and relative to an official in the church, but I didn't care even if she had been the pastor's daughter. Enough was enough, and right is right. Perhaps some may think I should have handled it another way. I knew the only other way was to grab her by the collar and drag her out of the church. Oh no! She would not have acted that way on her job, especially if she worked for a TV studio that was recording, and the director said, "Quiet on the set." Church people need influential leaders and yet with a heart. Her behavior could be the very reason people would fail to join the choir. I need to inject the following real quick. The reason I know this is because I joined a choir that sung beautifully on Sunday morning. I went to my first rehearsal, and I left the same night. I have never seen so much foolishness in a choir rehearsal. In other words, the night I joined was the night I quit.

Once again, speaking of the young lady in rehearsal. After the third disruption, I told her that one of us would have to leave the choir stand tonight. Being the "tough girl" she was, she stated that she wasn't going anywhere. So I kindly picked up my briefcase and left the rehearsal. One bad apple can spoil the whole bunch. Same as: /Galatians-5-9
Other Translations. A little leaven leavens the whole lump. A little yeast corrupts the whole lump of dough.
The president of the choir didn't have anything to say to her, either. Of course, the pastor heard of the problem, but he never said anything about it, nor did I ever return after that day. I'm still waiting on his call; it's been over several decades ago. I hope they haven't killed him.

Another incident occurred when I was directing a different choir. We had always had a good time, and we enjoyed each other. During that time, I was making good money through being the owner of a hair salon, and my tithes were $100 per week;

however, my salary for directing the choir was also $100 per week, so I was directing the choir for free. I was not a member there, but since I was there, I paid my tithes.

I discovered that our pianist played in nightclubs besides in our choir, which was her own business. However, every time that she would come to rehearsal, she would never have a new song or go over a song that I would ask her to—more so, she was always late.

I went to the pastor about three times regarding her conduct, asking if he would talk to her. The next thing I knew, I received a letter in the mail stating that my services were no longer needed, and I couldn't understand why. I'm sure the pastor's wife was puzzled because she and I had a great time in service.

A few months later, the pastor's daughter came into my salon for service, and she happened to get on the subject of my dismissal. The only time in my life, I had been dismissed from a job, and now you will learn the crazy reason why. With a smile on her face, she told me why it happened because I kept going to the office complaining about the pastor's girlfriend. Uh, oh! Not pointing a finger because we all have issues to deal with, but look at the cost.

All I can say is, I don't care. However, my problem was that the pastor would instead have sacrificed the uplifting of a whole congregation for his girlfriend—while his wife was in the choir stand. "A little leaven and leaven the whole lump" (Gal. 5:9).

When it comes to pastoring, you can't let anyone hinder the work of God. One bad apple can spoil the whole bunch. You have to be strong and get them out; if not, they will eventually get you out.

I know that full-time pastoring takes a lot of work. Taking care of yourself is a lot of work and now trying to take care of others is a bigger job. How some are pastoring two churches, I do not know. Are they just dropping off a sermon, collecting a paycheck, and going on about their business, or are they taking the time to feed the people, taking care of their needs, and seeking the other gifts the church needs? Or maybe they have the gift of an apostle and don't know it but need to focus on it and do it right. **Who knows besides God?**

You have to look at your church like an artist that is too close to his painting. He only sees what's close on the canvas, but he can see the flaws that may need correcting when he walks back and looks at the picture. Sometimes a person has to bring things to the leader's attention.

An old saying: "What you see is what you get."

12 Leading Causes of Deaths in America

Are churches prepared for any of this? While writing this included section, as mentioned in 2020, is the pandemic Coronavirus. However, many other diseases and deaths are still occurring, and leaders should be aware and not just focus on the

Coronavirus. The same happened when AIDS started back in the '80s, and many were dying. Many people concentrate on AIDS that they forgot that other deaths and venereal diseases such as gonorrhea, syphilis, and chlamydia were still rising. Healthline.com reported the 12 Leading deaths in America as of 2017. Of course, many of the numbers have increased, and who knows how many are caused by doctors' misdiagnoses due to medications and wrongful operations? I use to think when I heard that whatever field the doctor studied was his practice; I would say it was. He was practicing on you to see what may work and what didn't work. Yet, we must understand in this process that many people die from certain diseases until they come up with a cure, while the pharmaceuticals make billions of dollars on medications they still send out. We never know how much is covered up by the medical field, so there wouldn't be another suit. The average annual number of lawsuits filed each year is about 85,000, with the actual number of medical injuries estimated to be about one million per year. The medical numbers have increased highly, and approximately 440,000 people die a year just from doctor's mistakes. It used to be said that there were 100,000 a year, and now the numbers have jumped tremendously due to many more people living on earth for them to test on.

Quora.com: There are approximately 100,000 diseases known to man at the moment, and there are most likely more to occur in the future. Viruses can potentially mutate and affect humans.

Overview - The following information by Trusted Source: For more than a decade, heart disease and cancer have claimed the first and second spots, respectively, as the leading causes of death in America. Together, the two diseases are responsible for 46 percent of deaths in the United States.

Combined with the third most common cause of death — chronic lower respiratory diseases — the three diseases account for all deaths in the United States.

For more than 30 years, the Centers for Disease Control and Prevention (CDC) has been collecting and examining the causes of death. This information helps researchers and doctors understand if they need to address growing epidemics in healthcare.

The numbers also help them understand how preventive measures may help people live longer and healthier lives.

The top 12 causes of death in the United States account for more than 75 percent of all deaths. Learn about each of the leading causes and what can be done to prevent them.

The following data was taken from the CDC's 2017 report Trusted Source.

1. HEART DISEASE

Number of deaths per year: 635,260

Percent of total deaths: 23.1 percent

More common among:

- men
- people who smoke
- people who are overweight or obese
- people with a family history of heart disease or heart attack
- people over age 55

What causes heart disease?

Heart disease is a term used to describe a range of conditions that affect your heart and blood vessels. These conditions include:

- heart arrhythmias (irregular heartbeats)
- coronary artery disease (blocked arteries)
- heart defects

Tips for prevention

Lifestyle changes can prevent many cases of heart disease, such as the following:

- Quit smoking.

- Eat a healthier diet.
- Exercise at least 30 minutes per day, five days a week.
- Maintain a healthy weight.

2. CANCER

Number of deaths per year: 598,038

Percent of total deaths: 21.7 percent

More common among: Each type of cancer has a specific set of risk factors, but several risk factors are common among multiple types. These risk factors include:

- people of a certain age
- people who use tobacco and alcohol
- people exposed to radiation and a lot of sunlight
- people with chronic inflammation
- people who are obese
- people with a family history of the disease

What causes cancer?

Cancer is the result of rapid and uncontrolled cell growth in your body. A normal cell multiplies and divides in a controlled manner. Sometimes, those instructions become scrambled. When this happens, the cells begin to divide at an uncontrolled rate. This can develop into cancer.

Tips for prevention

There's no clear way to avoid cancer. But certain behaviors have been linked to increased cancer risk, like smoking. Avoiding those behaviors may help you cut your risk. Good changes to your behaviors include things like:

- Maintain a healthy weight. Eat a balanced diet and exercise regularly.
- Quit smoking and drink in moderation.
- Avoid direct exposure to the sun for extended periods. Don't use <u>tanning beds</u>.
- Have regular cancer screenings, including skin checks, mammograms, prostate exams, and more.

3. ACCIDENTS (unintentional injuries)

Number of deaths per year: 161,374

Percent of total deaths: 5.9 percent

More common among:

- men
- people ages 1 to 44
- people with risky jobs

What causes accidents?

Accidents lead to more than <u>28 million</u> emergency room visits each year. The three leading causes of accident-related death are:

- unintentional falls
- motor vehicle traffic deaths
- unintentional poisoning deaths

Tips for prevention

Unintentional injuries may be the result of carelessness or a lack of careful action. Be aware of your surroundings. Take all proper precautions to prevent accidents or injuries.

If you hurt yourself, seek emergency medical treatment to prevent serious complications.

4. CHRONIC LOWER RESPIRATORY-

Number of deaths per year: 154,596

Percent of total deaths: 5.6 percent

More common among:

- women
- people over age 65
- people with a history of smoking or exposure to secondhand smoke

- people with a history of asthma
- individuals in lower-income households

What causes respiratory diseases?

This group of diseases includes:

- chronic obstructive pulmonary disease (COPD)
- emphysema
- asthma
- pulmonary hypertension

Each of these conditions or diseases prevents your lungs from working properly. They can also cause scarring and damage to the lung's tissues.

Tips for prevention

Tobacco use and secondhand smoke exposure are the primary factors in the development of these diseases. Quit smoking. Limit your exposure to other people's smoke to reduce your risk.

5. STROKE

Number of deaths per year: 142,142

Percent of total deaths: 5.18 percent

More common among:

- men
- women using birth control
- people with diabetes
- people with high blood pressure
- people with heart disease
- people who smoke

What causes a stroke?

A stroke occurs when the blood flow to your brain is cut off. Without oxygen-rich blood flowing to your brain, your brain cells begin to die in a matter of minutes.

The blood flow can be stopped because of a blocked artery or bleeding in the brain. This bleeding may be from an aneurysm or a broken blood vessel.

Tips for prevention

Many of the same lifestyle changes that can reduce your risk for heart disease can also reduce your risk for stroke:

- Maintain a healthy weight. Exercise more and eat healthier.
- Manage your blood pressure.
- Stop smoking. Drink only in moderation.
- Manage your blood sugar level and diabetes.

- Treat any underlying heart defects or diseases.

6. ALZHEIMER'S disease

Number of deaths per year: 116,103

Percent of total deaths: 4.23 percent

More common among:

- women
- people over age 65 (the risk for Alzheimer's <u>doubles</u> every five years after age 65)
- people with a family history of the disease

What causes Alzheimer's disease?

The cause of <u>Alzheimer's disease</u> is unclear, but researchers and doctors believe a combination of a person's genes, lifestyle, and environment impacts the brain over time. Some of these changes occur years, even decades before the first symptoms appear.

Tips for prevention

While you can't control your age or genetics, which are two of the most common risk factors for this disease, you can control certain lifestyle factors that may increase your risk for it by doing the following:

- Exercise more often than not. Remain physically active throughout your life.
- Eat a diet filled with fruits, vegetables, healthy fats, and reduced sugar.
- Treat and monitor any other chronic diseases you have.
- Keep your brain active with stimulating tasks like conversation, puzzles, and reading.

7. DIABETES

Number of deaths per year: 80,058

Percent of total deaths: 2.9 percent

More common among:

Type 1 diabetes is more commonly diagnosed in:

- people with a family history of the disease, or a specific gene that increases the risk
- children between the ages of 4 and 7
- people living in climates farther away from the equator

Type 2 diabetes is more common among:

- people who are overweight or obese
- adults over age 45
- people who have a family history of diabetes

What causes diabetes?

Type 1 diabetes occurs when your pancreas can't produce enough insulin. Type 2 diabetes occurs when your body becomes resistant to insulin or doesn't make enough of it to control your blood sugar levels.

Tips for prevention

You can't prevent type 1 diabetes. However, you may prevent type 2 diabetes with several lifestyle changes, like the following:

- Reach and maintain a healthy weight.
- Exercise for at least 30 minutes, five days a week.
- Eat a healthy diet with plenty of fruits, vegetables, whole grains, and lean proteins.
- Have regular blood sugar checks if you have a family history of the disease.

8. INFLUENZA AND PNEULMONIA

Number of deaths per year: 51,537

Percent of total deaths: 1.88 percent

More common among:

- children
- the elderly
- people with chronic health conditions
- pregnant women

What causes influenza and pneumonia?

Influenza (the flu) is a highly contagious viral infection. It's very common during the winter months. Pneumonia is an infection or inflammation of the lungs.

The flu is one of the leading causes of pneumonia. Find out how to determine if you have the flu or a cold.

Tips for prevention

Before the flu season, people in the high-risk category can and should get a flu vaccine. Anyone else concerned about the virus should get one, too.

To prevent the spread of the flu, be sure to wash your hands well and avoid people who are sick.

Likewise, a pneumonia vaccine is available for people with a high risk of developing the infection.

9. KIDNEY DISEASE

Number of deaths per year: 50,046

Percent of total deaths: 1.8 percent

More common among:

- people with other chronic conditions, including diabetes, high blood pressure, and recurrent kidney infections
- people who smoke
- people who are overweight or obese
- people with a family history of kidney disease

What causes kidney diseases?

The term kidney disease refers to three main conditions:

- nephritis
- nephrotic syndrome
- nephrosis

Each of these conditions is the result of unique conditions or diseases.

Nephritis (kidney inflammation) can result from an infection, a medication you're taking, or an autoimmune disorder.

Nephrotic syndrome is a condition that causes your kidneys to produce high levels of protein in your urine. It's often the result of kidney damage.

Nephrosis is a type of kidney disease that ultimately can lead to kidney failure. It's also often the result of damage to the kidneys from either physical or chemical changes.

Tips for prevention

Like with many of the other leading causes of death, taking better care of your health can help you prevent kidney disease. Consider the following:

- Eat a lower-sodium diet.
- Stop smoking and drinking.
- Lose weight if you're overweight or obese, and maintain it.
- Exercise for 30 minutes, five days a week.
- Have regular blood and urine tests if you have a family history of the disease.

10. SUICIDE

Number of deaths per year: 44,965

Percent of total deaths: 1.64 percent

More common among:

- men
- people with brain injuries
- people who have attempted suicide in the past

- people with a history of <u>depression</u> and other mental health conditions
- people who misuse alcohol or drugs

What causes suicide?

<u>Suicide,</u> or intentional self-harm, is death caused by a person's actions. People who die by direct suicide harm themselves and die due to that harm. Almost <u>500,000</u> people are treated in emergency rooms each year for self-inflicted injuries.

Tips for prevention

Suicide prevention aims to help people find the treatment that encourages them to end suicidal thoughts and start finding healthier ways to cope.

For many people, suicide prevention includes finding a support system of friends, family, and other people who've contemplated suicide. In some cases, medication and in-hospital treatment may be necessary.

If you're thinking about harming yourself, consider contacting a suicide prevention hotline. You can call the National Suicide Prevention Lifeline at 800-273-8255. It offers 24/7 support. <u>You can also review our mental health resources list for more information about ways to find help.</u>

11. SEPTICEMIA

Number of deaths per year: 38,940

Percent of total deaths: 1.42 percent

More common among:

- adults over age 75
- young children
- people with a chronic illness
- people with an impaired immune system

What causes septicemia?

Septicemia is the result of a bacterial infection in the bloodstream. It's sometimes called **blood poisoning**. Most cases of septicemia develop after an infection somewhere else in the body becomes severe.

Tips for prevention

The best way to prevent septicemia is to have any bacterial infections treated quickly and thoroughly. If you think you may have an infection, make an appointment with your doctor. Complete the full treatment regimen prescribed by your doctor.

Early and thorough treatment can help prevent the spread of any bacterial infection to the blood.

12. CHRONIC LIVER DISEASE AND CIRRHOSIS

Number of deaths per year: 38,170

Percent of total deaths: 1.39 percent

More common among:

- people with a history of excessive alcohol use
- a viral <u>hepatitis</u> infection
- an accumulation of fat in the liver (<u>fatty liver disease</u>)

What causes liver disease?

Both liver disease and <u>cirrhosis</u> are the results of liver damage.

Tips for prevention

If you feel you're <u>misusing alcohol</u>, see a healthcare provider. They can help you <u>get treatment</u>. This may include a combination of:

- detox
- therapy

- support groups
- rehab

The longer and more you drink, the greater your risk for developing liver disease or cirrhosis.

Likewise, if you receive a diagnosis of hepatitis, follow your doctor's instructions in treating the condition to prevent unnecessary liver damage.

Death rates that have decreased

Though it's the most common cause, heart disease deaths have been falling over the last 50 years. However, in 2011, the number of deaths from heart disease began to rise slowly. Between 2011 and 2014, heart disease deaths rose 3 percent.

Deaths from influenza and pneumonia are also falling. According to the American Lung Association, deaths from the two diseases dropped an average of 3.8 percent per year since 1999.

Between 2010 and 2014, deaths from stroke dropped 11 percent.

This falling number of preventable deaths suggests that health awareness campaigns are hopefully increasing awareness of preventive measures people can take to live a longer, healthier life.

Rising death rates

The gap between heart disease and cancer was once much wider. Heart disease's hold on the number one spot was wide and demanding.

Then, American health experts and doctors began encouraging Americans to curb smoking, and they started treating heart disease. Because of these efforts, the number of heart disease-related deaths has been falling over the last five decades. Meanwhile, the number of cancer-related deaths has been rising.

Just over 22,000 deaths separate the two causes today. Many researchers suspect cancer may overtake heart disease as the leading cause of death in the coming years.

Accidental deaths are also on the rise. From 2010 to 2014, the number of accident-related deaths increased by 23 percent. This number is primarily fueled by substance overdose deaths.

Leading causes of death worldwide

The list of leading causes of death worldwide shares many of the same causes with the U.S. list. These causes of death include:

- heart disease
- stroke

- lower respiratory infections
- COPD
- lung cancer
- diabetes
- Alzheimer's disease and dementia
- diarrhea
- tuberculosis
- road injury

Takeaway

While you can't prevent every cause of death, you can do a lot to lower your risks. Many of the leading causes of death, both in the United States and worldwide, are preventable with lifestyle changes.

Same statistics of deaths WORLDWIDE from www.worldometer.info

2020

4,892,605 Communicable disease deaths
183,482 Seasonal flu deaths
2,864,717 Deaths of children under 5
16,024,185 Abortions
116,491 Deaths of mothers during birth
41,796,759 HIV/AIDS infected people

633,567 Deaths caused by HIV/AIDS
3,095,321 Deaths caused by cancer
369,679 Deaths caused by malaria
9,406,556,640 Cigarettes smoked
1,884,057 Deaths caused by smoking
400,000 Deaths caused by Corona Virus

Psalm 103:3 He who forgives all my sins and heals all my diseases

.

Hebrews 9:27 And as it is appointed unto men once to die, but after this the judgment.

Although this list shows the many deaths, that we shall not live forever in our fleshly bodies. We are like ants, for they do not know when someone will come along and step on them and destroy them, but yet they stay busy. Same as we that are human, we will never know when or the cause of death that we shall leave here or perhaps raptured, but we continue being busy as in the days of Noah. It is also written that God will send many plagues amongst the earth.

Romans 8:36- As it is written, For thy sake, we are killed all the day long; we are accounted as sheep for the slaughter.

Matthew 24:36-47

36 No one knows about that day or hour, not even the angels in heaven, nor the Son, but only the

Father. As it was in the days of Noah, so will it be at the coming of the Son of Man. For in the days before the flood, people were eating and drinking, marrying and giving in marriage, up to the day Noah entered the ark. And they were oblivious until the flood came and swept them all away. So will it be at the coming of the Son of Man. Two men will be in the field: one will be taken, and the other left. Two women will be grinding at the mill: one will be taken, and the other left.

Therefore keep watch, because you do not know the day on which your Lord will come. But understand this: If the homeowner had known in which watch of the night the thief was coming, he would have kept watch and would not have let his house be broken into. For this reason, you also must be ready, because the Son of Man will come at an hour you do not expect.

Who then is the faithful and wise servant, whom the master has put in charge of his household, to give the others their food at the proper time? Blessed is that servant whose master finds him doing so when he returns. **47** Truly I tell you, he will put him in charge of all his possessions.

We started dying from the day we are born. We go through a period of ups and downs, or we can say many happy days and trials and some tragedies that are called part of life, and then we die, but you don't know when. As said by Job 1:21, "The Lord gives, and the Lord takes away; blessed be the name of the Lord."

Jesus affirms this in Matthew 24:14, which states that 'this gospel of the kingdom will be preached in the whole world as a testimony to all nations, and then the end will come.'

I hear many say that their loved ones are in heaven, but I'm not sure from the following scripture.

1 Thessalonians 4:16 For the Lord himself shall descend from heaven with a shout, with the voice of the archangel, and with the trump of God: and the dead in Christ shall rise first:
But before our loved ones can be in heaven, according to the scripture, the dead in Christ has to rise first, don't you think? As far as the dead are concerned:
"For the living know that they will die, but the dead know nothing, and they have no more reward, for the memory of them is forgotten. Ecclesiastes 9:5.

*
We never know when we will leave this earth.

Psalm 49:10-Those who are wise must finally die, just like the foolish and senseless, leaving all their wealth behind.
Many quote the scripture Psalm 90:10 below referring to 3 score and 10 equaling 70 years. People misunderstanding the scripture. If they come they will have trouble and sorrow. For in much

wisdom is much grief: and he that increases knowledge increases sorrow. Ecclesiastes 1:18

Our days may come to seventy years, or eighty, if our strength endures; The best of those years are but trouble and sorrow, for they quickly pass, and we fly away.

Many babies, teenagers, and young adults would not have died so early if this were true. It's a beautiful thing if you make it that far, however as Genesis 2:17 says, referring to Adam and Eve., but the tree of the knowledge of good and evil you shall not eat, for the day that you eat of it you shall surely die. The man was initially designed to live a very long time, but it was cut short starting in the Garden.

Briefly take a look at this graft on the next page. Following the steps will make you think about your life and the many years that have gone by swiftly. Whether you have wasted them or made good use of them, but you will never be able to get them back. What will you do if you live out your life with the rest of the years? Make an X in every box until you get to your age. The X represents the years you have already lived. If you're given 70 to a hundred years, look at how many years you'll have left if you make it that far.

1	2	3	4	5	6	7	8	9	10
11	12	13	14	15	16	17	18	19	20
21	22	23	24	25	26	27	28	29	30
31	32	33	34	35	36	37	38	39	40
41	42	43	44	45	46	47	48	49	50
51	52	53	54	55	56	57	58	59	60
61	62	63	64	65	66	67	68	69	70
71	72	73	74	75	76	77	78	79	80
81	82	83	84	85	86	87	88	89	90
91	92	93	94	95	96	97	98	99	100

Don't you wish all of the scriptures were in chronological order that you didn't have to skip around? Perhaps this is why it says to search the scriptures. John 5:39 Search the scriptures; for in them ye think ye have eternal life: and they are they which testify of me. I guess those who have not read the bible do not know this but just believe they will leave the earth because they have accepted Jesus and moved on with their lives.

Whether we are absent from the body, judged, appointed to die or healed, and any other scripture that concerns our lives, from statistics, none of us will live here on earth forever. Maybe they base it on people misquoting the scripture saying being absent from the body is to be present with the Lord. This is what it says:

2 Corinthians 5:8- "We are confident, I say, and willing rather to be absent from the body, and to be present with the Lord."

Paul is saying in our time here; he'd **rather** be absent from the body and be present with the Lord. Although many say to be absent from the body is to be present with the Lord, and he only says he'd **rather** be present with the Lord than here on earth. However, everyone will not be present with the Lord, according to the scriptures. I'm sure some would be hoping for immunity.

Job 14:5 A man's days are numbered. You know the number of his months. He cannot live longer than the time You have set. So now look away from him that he may rest, until he has lived the time set for him like a man paid to work.

Job 14 "Mortals, born of woman, are of few days and full of trouble.

I say: "Your days are numbered, and your nights are registered."

And after you have suffered a little while, the God of all grace, who has called you to his eternal glory in Christ, will himself restore, confirm, strengthen, and establish you. 1Peter 5:10

Matthew 5:11 - Blessed are you when they revile and persecute you, and say all kinds of evil against you falsely for My sake. Rejoice and be exceedingly glad, for great *is* your reward in heaven, for so they persecuted the prophets who were before you.

"You are the salt of the earth; but if the salt loses its flavor, how shall it be seasoned? It is then good for nothing but to be thrown out and trampled underfoot by men.

"You are the light of the world. A city that is set on a hill cannot be hidden. [15] Nor do they light a lamp and put it under a basket, but on a lampstand, and it gives light to all *who are* in the house. [16] Let your light so shine before men that they may see your good works and glorify your Father in heaven.

There is no greater love than to lay down one's life for one's friends. John 15:13

Even though we are the light of the world and in God's hands, we are still challenged. Some of us are told no in situations, knowing we should have been allowed to do a certain thing because we were well qualified for the position. If something is yours God will see to it that you will eventually get it.

Ezekiel 21:27 I will overturn, overturn, overturn, it, and it shall be no more until he comes whose right it is; and I will give it unto him.

What if God hardened someone's heart to say no so that we may do something else, or had we taken the position, it could have been the worse choice of our life.

Remember, He hardened Pharoah's heart. (Exodus 9:12) But the LORD hardened Pharaoh's heart, and he would not listen to Moses and Aaron, just as the LORD had said to Moses.

Not only that, but God has allowed many to be destroyed, whether young or old.

The LORD Rejects Saul

(Exodus 9:15) And Samuel said to Saul, "The LORD sent me to anoint you king over his people Israel; now, therefore, listen to the words of the LORD. ² Thus says the LORD of hosts, 'I have noted what Amalek did to Israel in opposing them on the way when they came up out of Egypt. ³ Now go and strike Amalek and devote to destruction[a] all that they have. Do not spare them, but kill both man and woman, child and infant, ox and sheep, camel and donkey.'"

I'm sure all of the about information, including the diseases, would make a good Sunday morning sermon. They've heard the sermon a thousand times that Jesus died on the cross, but how much of ALL the above information have they heard?

Gift Number Five: Teacher

The gift of a teacher is one that opens a person's understanding. Many of our large megachurches have massive teaching ministries, but I must admit that I would have enjoyed their services better with a little fiery dessert with the message and some good, uplifting songs. Today, people are told that it doesn't take all of that, but that's because they ran into a sophisticated God that's very bougie. However, if they went to the night club, it had better be rockin'. We have to be taught how to live here on earth, learn God's will, and still have a good time. Eat, drink and be merry with wisdom.

We have never been here before. It's just like traveling to England. If you have never been there, you need to study their rules regarding how to address the queen and other rituals. Remember, you've never been there before. Same as learning God's ways. You've never met him before, so you have to learn, and there will be some rough days as well as good.

The pastors in some of these large churches also have the gift of teaching. Many times, when a person is being taught and begins to get a revelation on life, he or she tends to want to come back and get a little more. Some large churches are known for their great choirs, but they are not knowledgeable in understanding the Word. There is power in knowledge.

As stated before, a pastor, and an evangelist, can also obtain this gift—as well as a person with knowledge in the word of God and can teach it well. Some people are naturally gifted when it comes to studying, and they have no problem taking up to ten or twelve hours just to deliver a one-hour message. Searching the scriptures is a joy, and the revelation and understanding of specific passages make the hours worthwhile.

Even so, the teacher will get a kick out of people when they ask him questions; he should be able to deliver the answers. Sometimes a teacher is so thorough in his teaching that there are no questions asked after the lesson. It is just a pleasant evening of divine revelation and wisdom.

There is a saying that goes, "What you don't know can't hurt you." I beg to differ. What we don't know from our Bibles causes us to live a life of misery right here on earth. The only part that we often wonder is what part is genuine if there is so much missing. The teacher will bring things to a great understanding. "The way of a fool is right in his own eyes, but he that listens to counsel is wise." (Prov. 12:15).

A real teacher that is filled with the Holy Ghost, the anointed power of God, realizes that "God also hath made us able ministers of the New Testament; not of the letter, but the spirit; for the letter kills, but the spirit gives life" (2 Cor. 3:6). Here it is explained through Apostle Paul that the Old Testament was of the letter meaning the law; however, the apostles were not just ministers of the letter but also of the Spirit, which is mentioned in the New Testament. Where the Old Testament was the ministration of death, the New Testament is the ministration of life.

The teacher will help you understand that "if any man among you seem to be religious and bridles not his tongue, but deceives his own heart, this man's religion is vain. Pure religion and undefiled before

God and the Father is this, to visit the fatherless and widows in their affliction, and to keep himself unspotted from the world" (James 1:27). Have you ever been told that?

This may be a good time to talk about tithes as well. The teacher will also let you know the real truth about tithes and what they were originally for in the bible. (Malachi 3:9) This subject has been a big controversy in the church, which is 10 percent of your earnings. More than likely, people wouldn't mind paying tithes, but they are so beat down by so many other obligations, and I will not go down the list. Being part of a church can be a tremendous responsibility if wisdom does not take place. Burdened down and pressured doesn't seem like the love of God. Life doesn't have to be so hard, but the churches have made it that way, especially putting burdens on people. Of course, going to church is not supposed to be a free ride. However, you wouldn't mind tipping if they were a little more caring. How many times have you stayed away from the church for months, and no one knew you were missing? And soon as someone sees you, "I was just thinking about you."

Let's talk about Malachi 3:9 for a brief moment. **Ye _are_ cursed with a curse: for ye have robbed me, _even_ this whole nation. [10]**Bring ye all the tithes into the storehouse, that there may be meat in mine house, and prove me now herewith, says the LORD of hosts, if I will not open you the windows of heaven, and pour you out a blessing, that _there_ shall _not_ be room _enough_ to receive it.

My understanding of tithes was that if the priest brought in their 10% of crops, herds, and flock, and food was brought into the storehouse for the Levites on Temple duty. So since we have navigated to a better life, have the tithe been considered in monetary terms? Because we don't have crops, herds, and flocks. Why doesn't the church have a real storehouse? Just because your member is wearing a fur coat doesn't mean they have money to buy food now because of losing a job. They purchased the coat when they had the money, and now they are just keeping warm. I just heard your thoughts! Perhaps they should sell the coat, you would say, but that's for how many meals and people are not going to pay you what you paid for the coat. Don't beat me up; I'm just asking a question about the real church storehouse. You read it yourself. The church can have its own personal Goodwill store or warehouse.

People want to trust God second; they want all of God's benefits but do not want to obey Him in any way. In the same token, very few people are real representatives of Christ, making it hard for the outsiders to believe, but yet He lives. However, some people tithe their time. If they were getting paid for the service, it would be more than their tithes anyway. I know what you're saying, "It's for the Lord." Well, He must need a lot according to all of the things people are obligated to donate to, which is all financial. Some people are made to be embarrassed because they are not a tither. Come offering time, they ask all of the tithers to stand up or who will stand that will give $100 in this line.

Sometimes, the leader will mention how much they are starting the offering, putting guilt on deacons and other department heads to follow. Indeed after the offering, the pastor can re-coop his $100 back. I thought what you gave in secret he'd reward you openly. (Matthew 6:4). You can still give the amount, but who has to know it?

As a kid, I remember that whatever amount of money you put in the envelope on Sunday, it would appear in the church bulletin beside your name on the following Sunday. Because I was a kid, many times, there would be $1.00 by my name, but I was proud to see that $1.00. Everyone knew how much money you gave. If you wanted to look like a game player when it came to church, you had better put a decent amount of money in your envelope. And if you were a tither, you were at the top of the list, and people could estimate how much money you make from your job.

Some people are puffed up in what they are giving by standing in lines that ask for high amounts of money. They are already given their reward because they want to be praised because of what they offered. (Matthew 6:2)- "So when you give to the needy, do not announce it with trumpets, as the hypocrites do in the synagogues and on the streets, to be honored by others. Truly I tell you, they have received their reward in full.

Try giving $500 in the line when they ask for those to give what they can. That should be a humbling experience. In many things, let every man be persuaded in his own mind. (Rom. 14.5).

Although many ministers use certain scriptures to persuade people to give and to make them feel guilty. Such scriptures as (a) Mark 12:41, Luke 21:1 – The woman and her pennies and she gave all she had. (b) Acts 4:35—Where those who sold land and gave things and brought the money and laid at the feet of the prophet. **34**There were no needy ones among them because those who owned lands or houses would sell their property, bring the proceeds from the sales, and lay them at the apostles' feet for distribution to anyone as he had need. That passage has been another fad. More than likely, the prophet put the money in his pocket and buy something he wants. Sorry, but it is what it is.! Another one they use is 1Tim. 5:18 –Don't muzzle the ox that treads the grain, referring to giving to the pastor or the laborer is worthy of his hire. Meaning if someone works for you, they should get paid.

Let me pause here for a second and back up to where they laid proceeds to the apostle's feet. The people sold things and made sure that everyone had what was needed to live decently. What kind of inventory are churches taking to see who needs what? However, people will do just about anything free for the church. Yet, you should know that Jesus knew about money or some type of exchange. He was a carpenter, so do you think he picked up wood for free and built things for free?

There are many scriptures used that can be twisted to make people feel guilty. Still, if you read the whole story, you will see why some gave the way they did, but since many don't understand things of the bible, they just take for granted what is said, and the anointing is high, and they give out of their pockets and go home wondering what did they just do.

I heard of one true story where an evangelist/soloist raised a $10,000 offering in the church, and when the service was over, he said that was his money and cursed the pastor out because he didn't want to give it all to him. Unfortunately, I later heard that this particular soloist passed away. We never know what goes on after the offering. However, just give from the heart, but with wisdom. Give the church your light bill money, and you will be sitting in darkness because no one came to check on you while you thought you were doing something great. What do some of these people in the ministry do to help and inspire others? I can inspire you, but that doesn't mean I'm physically helping you. By praying for me because I'm hungry, do not solve my problem. Can I at least have a peanut butter and jelly sandwich so I can think?

Plus, we must be aware of moochers that can come to the church. It's like graduating from college without ever having taken a single course. Believe me: God will not let you pimp him; you will pay. Now say "Amen" to that!

I will say further that the teacher will let you know that "when the Son of man shall come in his glory, and all the holy angels with him. Then shall he sit upon the throne of his glory; And before Him shall be gathered all nations; and he shall separate them one from another, as a shepherd divides his sheep from the goats; And he shall set the sheep on his right hand, but the goats on the left. (It's incredible how we can believe this, not knowing if it's true, but yet we believe and how it is given some are frightened to death, but rejoice, Jesus has your back for those that believe.

The following passages should make us learn about visiting the sick and giving according to a person's needs, especially when we have plenty. If we are taught from youth and not conned as adults, we would trust more and would have done more. However, as many revelations come to us, we are inspired to do better within our power.

Matthew 25:34-[34] "Then the King will say to those on his right, 'Come, you who are blessed by my Father; take your inheritance, the kingdom prepared for you since the creation of the world. [35] For I was hungry and you gave me something to eat, I was thirsty and you gave me something to drink, I was a stranger and you invited me in, [36] I needed clothes and you clothed me, I was sick and you looked after me, I was in prison and you came to visit me.'

[37] "Then the righteous will answer him, 'Lord, when did we see you hungry and feed you, or thirsty and give you something to drink? [38] When

did we see you a stranger and invite you in, or needing clothes and clothe you? [39] When did we see you sick or in prison and go to visit you?'

[40] "The King will reply, 'Truly I tell you, whatever you did for one of the least of these brothers and sisters of mine, you did for me.'

(When was the last time we have done something unto the Lord and didn't look for a lot of praise because it was something we were all called to do?)

[41] "Then he will say to those on his left, 'Depart from me, you who are cursed, into eternal fire prepared for the devil and his angels. [42] For I was hungry, and you gave me nothing to eat, I was thirsty and you gave me nothing to drink, [43] I was a stranger and you did not invite me in, I needed clothes and you did not clothe me, I was sick and in prison and you did not look after me.'

[44] "They also will answer, 'Lord, when did we see you hungry or thirsty or a stranger or needing clothes or sick or in prison, and did not help you?'

[45] "He will reply, 'Truly I tell you, whatever you did not do for one of the least of these, you did not do for me.'

[46] "Then they will go away to eternal punishment, but the righteous to eternal life."

With all that you just read, many would think, how could a loving God allow this, especially for those who tried, and He is their father. Would a father do this to his children? Just another thought, I'm sure.

(Matt. 25:31–46). I'm sure that was a questionable chapter for you. Not only that, but you also don't hear such chapters being read much in the church.

"Let brotherly love continue. Be not forgetful to entertain strangers: for thereby some have entertained angels unawares" (Heb. 13.1).

1John 3:17- But if anyone has this world's good, and sees his brother have need, and shuts up his bowels of compassion from him, how dwells the love of God in him?"

I do have a suggestion, regardless of what bible the pastors use, all members should have the same one. That way, when the pastor mentions a particular scripture, he can tell the congregation the page number that the scripture is on. People are more familiar with the numbers than they are with the scriptures. Of course, today, many people now use their cell phones because the bible is online. It's a new day. People are not trying to remember how many books are there, but how to remember to be righteous and bridle their tongue in certain instances. It used to be a bragging right if you could quote all of the scriptures in the bible, but the bragging right should have been how many people we have helped in our ability that we've come across.

The people who brag about how they know all the Bible books and find them might easily be the biggest Devil of all in the church. Don't you think the Devil know scriptures? Who knows, he could have created a few. It's not about who can find the word; it's about who will do it. The Parallel Bible—where King James is on one side and the New International Version, which explains the Bible in laymen's terms, is on the other—is even better. Every little bit helps. Stop being so puffed up because you know where they are! Who knows if the bible is real or not, but we still believe. However, remember that during translation, words get lost. Some relate to what's written in Hebrew, and that's the problem. If it was said in Hebrew, let's just stay in Hebrew, but we have to go back and forth, making ourselves look intelligent because we went to the Hebrew. Regardless of where we seemed to take a look at the world, know it's in a mess, Hebrew or not.

For the teacher, the previously mentioned scriptures in this chapter are entirely meaningful to the Christians. Many of us have gotten so caught up with the matters of the world that we don't have time to visit anyone. Yet, if each of us would take one or two hours a month just to show some kindness, I'm sure the receiver would be happy.

Many people in the hospital today whose own families do not visit them yet attend the family member attends church weekly as though they are doing God's will. The issues of the world have confused and frustrated most of us. If we were to count all of the holidays in the year—let alone all of the birthdays, anniversaries, weddings, and funerals in between—that the world tries to force us to celebrate, many would not be able to come up for air. Being caught up in Christmas alone can almost send you to the mental hospital.

I'm no Scrooge, but I'm sorry to say that Christmas is the biggest joke in the world and how it's been turned around with parties, gifts, shopping, programs, and manipulative giving. Believe it or not, it is considered the most depressing time of the year for many people. But that's another subject as well. The Coronavirus turned around everything this year, and it made people think about the real meaning of Christmas and not all of the fanfare. Things you thought you needed, you didn't get.

Someone is trying to do the will of God regardless of the Christmas story or what the world is trying to dictate, says the teacher. If you are not happy seeing other people happy, then there might be a little problem in your heart. By the way, during Christmas, did you take someone a gift to the hospital that you didn't know? I didn't, which means I fell short of giving too.

When it comes to holidays, you are better off celebrating the Jewish holidays, regardless if they are under the law; at least there is a true biblical meaning behind their celebrations. We preach about their experiences in our churches.

"Study to show thyself approved unto God, a workman that needs not to be ashamed, rightly dividing the word of truth" (2 Tim. 2:3). The teacher has no problem in this area because he wants to break the Word down in every phase as possible so that his listeners almost can't wait to return to hear the next message. Everyone can't read, so they will have to hear divine wisdom.

The teacher realizes that the letters of Paul— Thessalonians, Galatians, Acts, Romans, Colossians, Ephesians, Philippians, Philemon, Timothy, and Titus—are significant in our Christian walk and way of living. Not to sleight or forget any book in the Bible, but all scripture is given by inspiration of God and "is profitable for doctrine, for reproof, for correction, for instruction in righteousness; that the man of God may be perfect, thoroughly furnished unto all good works" (2 Tim. 3:16). My favorite books are Proverbs and Ecclesiastes because they are about wisdom.

People in the bible have had experiences as we all have had. As far as I'm concerned, we too can add a book to the Bible; If your name is Larry, it could be Larry's book with 23 chapters because God also inspired Larry. Thousand of books today have been inspired by God, but we don't call them bibles. But when it comes to the bible, it says the following:

For I testify unto every man that hears the words of the prophecy of this book, if any man shall add unto these things, God shall add unto

him the plagues that are written in this book. And if any man shall take away from the words of the book of this prophecy, God shall take away his part out of the book of life and out of the holy city, and from the things which are written in this book. Rev. 22:18-10)

This can be frightening to hear, and I'm sure scholars will go back to the Greek and find an answer. My question would be that I can't add to this book, but someone skips years of incidences and revelations in the book, and I'm wondering what happened in that space. And if I find the answer, I'm not to write it in a book? It makes you think, huh? Sounds almost like politics. The mistake of one word or a comma can change a whole meaning. Example: Let's eat Grandma or Let's eat, Grandma.

Welcome to the English language, wherein the Oxford Dictionary states that there are over 171,476 words in current use and 47,156 obsolete words. Who can keep up with them, and many of the words have the same meaning, but they want to see how astute you are. To me, they are so creative in coming up with words but have no love in their hearts. I heard a story of a famous newspaper that used about 650 words to print the whole paper. I get so tickled when you have some pastors speak and use such grand words, and the congregation is hollering "Amen" and don't understand what the word meant. Lol

When it comes to being astute, if a person wants to learn something, I'd say study the book of proverbs, and it may teach some of us how to live without knowing some fancy word. It's like going to the doctor, and he gives you some fancy name, whereas you just have a cold, which will, in turn, cost you $400 to hear that fancy word.

It is the same in voting. If people understood in plain English what the ballot is saying, many people would not vote. I have always believed that if an eleven-year-old child can't understand a contract, there is something crooked in it, ranging from real estate to insurance and expensive purchases. The United States is so greedy, unorganized, and uncaring in certain areas. However, they are also pushing toward one-world money. You may not believe the information about "the chip" under your skin to purchase goods, but keep living, and you will see it flourish. They've already been testing it for years on animals and some humans to enter individual buildings.

Why should you have to vote for better schools or march to raise money for breast cancer, march for a cure for diseases, or better medical help? We should have it anyway; other countries do. The pharmaceutical companies are racking up as they give you diseases and make you pay for it. It almost reminds me of slavery where they had many black slaves, and now they've made movies to show what whites did to the blacks, and they turn around and make you pay at the movies to see what they did. Who do you think is making significant money from it again? Have you heard of these great producers giving money to educate your children in fields that would benefit the family? If they do, it will only be their own. I don't wear designer clothes, and if I did, the name would be hidden. Why give them free advertisement and they only help their own.

Furthermore, they stretch out the education to the 12th grade to get your child addicted to foolishness. It is said that six families run the entire country. I don't know, but it is quite disturbing, but in the end, whether we see it or not, they will reap what they have sowed. Those they have mislead "They are coming home to roost!"

Trying to understand a voting ballot is ridiculous, so some people choose not to vote at all, and it's not always about the candidate. Yes, there's the freedom to vote, but the smooth thing is that you won't understand the language. Go ahead and decide to go to meetings and talk with your councilman or whoever. Those who say that's what your congressman or congresswoman is for, you'd be surprised that they are trying to figure it out themselves. The government usually have it fixed just like they want it. Although they mention the electoral vote and the popular vote, it is just a procedure. People feel if it depends on the electoral vote, why should the rest of the country vote? I say they want you to vote just to know where you are planted and grouped. I wouldn't be surprised if the Publisher's Clearing House was connected in helping to find out where people are. The prize money may just be a bait to get your information and whereabouts. You rarely hear about it, and after it's over, who is the winner? People love free money, and what good bait would that be to find out where you are. The government is not giving you a free phone for nothing, but they want to know where you are. You will learn that there is nothing free, and there's always something attached to the word free. Whether they get what they want now or later, there will definitely be a cost for more.

I heard a story one time that the police were looking for a particular man. They mailed him a professional-looking letter stating that he had won a large sum of money, but he needed to come in person. When he arrived at this particular location, they arrested him.

The government knows where you are because anything free always collects your email information. The only thing they cannot pinpoint is the cash that you may receive. However, they are still checking your bank account if you put money in there, and if it is a large sum of money, they want to know where you got it. I believe it's $10,000 or more. Many businesses take cash only and not putting it in the bank or reporting it. Uncle Sam wears the low and middle class out as far as taxes.

What do you think about the following Willie Lynch Story written in 1712 regarding teaching Blacks and restructuring their minds? Blacks seem to have been the backbone of this world until tortured. Many ideas are stolen from Blacks, and they were not given financial compensation. **1 Corinthians 1:27** but God chose the foolish things of the world that he might put to shame them that are wise; and God chose the weak things of the world, that he might put to shame the things that are strong.

As you know, when you are in a bad situation, you began to create and come up with ideas of how to make things easier for you. Others gleam on your idea or concept and manufacture it. However, even though some have become wealthy, they are miserable. This story is repeated twice in this book for emphasis.

Chapter 3:
The Making of a Slave

This speech was said to have been delivered by Willie Lynch on the banks of the James River in the colony of Virginia in 1712. Lynch was a British slave owner in the West Indies. He was invited to the colony of Virginia in 1712 to teach his methods to slave owners there.

Greetings,

Gentlemen. I greet you here on the bank of the James River in the year of our Lord one thousand seven hundred and twelve. First, I shall thank you, the gentlemen of the Colony of Virginia, for bringing me here. I am here to help you solve some of your problems with slaves. Your invitation reached me on my modest plantation in the West Indies, where I have experimented with some of the newest and still the oldest methods for the control of slaves.

Ancient Rome would envy us if my program is implemented. As our boat sailed south on the James River, named for our illustrious King, whose version of the Bible we cherish, I saw enough to know that your problem is not unique. While Rome used cords of wood as crosses for standing human bodies along its highways in great numbers, you are here using the tree and the rope on occasions.

I caught the whiff of a dead slave hanging from a tree, a couple of miles back. You are not only losing valuable stock by hangings, but you are also having uprisings, slaves are running away. Your crops are sometimes left in the fields too long for maximum profit; you suffer occasional fires, your animals are killed. Gentlemen, you know what your problems are; I do not need to elaborate.

I am not here to enumerate your problems. I am here to introduce you to a method of solving them. In my bag here, **I HAVE A FULL PROOF METHOD FOR CONTROLLING YOUR BLACK SLAVES**. I guarantee every one of you that, if installed correctly, **IT WILL CONTROL THE SLAVES FOR AT LEAST 300 HUNDRED YEARS**. My method is simple. Any member of your family or your overseer can use it. **I HAVE OUTLINED A NUMBER OF DIFFERENCES AMONG THE SLAVES, AND I TAKE THESE DIFFERENCES AND MAKE THEM BIGGER. I USE FEAR, DISTRUST, AND ENVY FOR CONTROL PURPOSES**.

These methods have worked on my modest plantation in the West Indies, and it will work throughout the South. Take this simple little list of differences and think about them. On top of my list is "AGE," but it's there only because it starts with an "a." The second is "COLOR" or shade. There is **INTELLIGENCE, SIZE, SEX, SIZES OF PLANTATIONS, STATUS** on plantations, **ATTITUDE** of owners, whether the slaves live in the valley, on a hill, East, West, North, South, have fine hair, coarse hair, or is tall or short.

Now that you have a list of differences, I shall give you an outline of action, but before that, I shall assure you that **DISTRUST IS STRONGER THAN TRUST AND ENVY STRONGER THAN ADULATION, RESPECT OR ADMIRATION**. The Black slaves, after receiving this indoctrination shall carry on and will become self-refueling and self-generating for **HUNDREDS** of years, maybe **THOUSANDS**. Don't forget; you must pitch the **OLD** black male vs. the **YOUNG** black male and the **YOUNG** black male against the **OLD** black male. You must use the **DARK** skin slaves vs. the **LIGHT** skin slaves, and the **LIGHT** skin slaves vs. the **DARK** skin slaves.

You must use the **FEMALE** vs. the **MALE**, and the **MALE** vs. the **FEMALE**. You must also have white servants and overseers [who] distrust all Blacks. But it is **NECESSARY THAT YOUR SLAVES TRUST AND DEPEND ON US. THEY MUST LOVE, RESPECT AND TRUST ONLY US**. Gentlemen, these kits are your keys to control. Use them. Have your wives and children use them, never miss an opportunity. **IF USED INTENSELY**

FOR ONE YEAR, THE SLAVES THEMSELVES WILL REMAIN PERPETUALLY DISTRUSTFUL. Thank you, gentlemen." *END*

P.S. And may I add that these methods are still valid today, including in our churches. Some blacks that attend white churches feel they have mentally arrived!

However, all churches should be mixed, but that is just good sounding talk. I recall attending a mixed church, and approximately 95 percent of the people were Black, but those that held official positions were all white, including the pastor.

Should the above letter by Willie Lynch be true, perhaps the following scripture is true as well. Keeping mercy for thousands, forgiving iniquity and transgression and sin, and that will by no means clear *the guilty*, visiting the iniquity of the fathers upon the children, and upon the children's children, unto the third and to the fourth *generation. Exodus 34:7*

Do not be deceived. God cannot be mocked. A man reaps what he sows. Galatians 6:7

It's not a matter of how, but when!

Off the Record

Traditions have torn our churches apart, and some call it organized religion. Many are scratching their heads and wondering why. Jesus i's not looking for a flea market. All of the bad habits in the ministry that have been passed down have made many weak Christians continuously pass it on to others without knowing why. After a while, you began to wonder who this Jesus is that allow all of these things to happen. Of course, someone will say we have free will. Is it a free-will, or was it designed to happen?

The following is an old story that has been passed around for years. Once a young girl was watching her mother prepare a ham. Before the mother put the ham in the pan, she would cut both ends off. The young girl asked her mother why she did that. The mother replied, "Well, my mother used to do it always, so I do it too."

The little girl became very curious, and so she went to her grandmother and said, "Grandma, Mama cut the ends off of the ham before she put it in the pan, and I want to know why you do it too." The grandmother replied, "Yes, I do, and I do it because my mother taught me to do it that way too."

The little girl had one more place to visit. Through the grace of God, her great-grandmother was still living, so she went to her and asked, "Why do Grandma and Mama cut the ends off of the ham before they cook it?" The great-grandmother sat and laughed and said, "I don't know why they cut it off, but I used to cut it off because the ham was too big to fit in the pan, so I cut off the ends."

All of that is to say that no one knows why he or she does some things. It is all because of traditions. No one knows why it is that in some churches, all the deacons have to pray or why they have so many anniversaries. Some practices may be useful; others need to go. But you very seldom see them doing the cultures in the bible. You may not hear a sermon on it. We love to listen to sermons that say what we should be doing, but we have mentioned the word "we" so much that we think we are doing something but are not doing anything. It just sounds good, and we say Amen! It's almost telling a child I'm going to spank you, but you never do it.

I must admit that I don't know whether to dance or have a candlelit dinner for someone I'm trying to entice when it comes to many of the songs in the ministry today. Songs long ago had meaning and feeling, but now we just listen and say, "That was a cute song."

The church is like a hospital; the doctor is to meet all of our needs. Many churches have become hospitals where the entire staff is sick, including the leader, and God's anointing needs to meet them there. That's why the five-fold ministry is so important.

Some of these church hospitals send for specialists. Some ministers, being scared of their congregation, need a real good shot of boldness.

God will back them up. The church is supposed to be exciting, yet it has become one of the most depressing places to talk about—and that is not supposed to be so. Jesus is alive! All of this is why there is a falling away from the church. There's nothing to hold them. How many times are they going to nail Jesus to the cross? When you get down from something, you can work and get busy, and that's what he did, but we are to be followers. When we learn what Jesus did and what the people did long ago, most of us find ourselves too old and tired to move and realize it was in the bible. Go ahead and say we need to read it for ourselves. If that's the case, why do we go? What's the purpose of the pastor, etc.

I have been wondering for years why the leaders tax the church members. There's money for Women's Day, Men's Day, the church's anniversary, the pastor's anniversary, the choir's anniversary, and any other anniversary they can think that would be profitable.

Many will hold a revival all week just to raise money for a pastor's anniversary. I thought revivals were to get people saved and lift them. Maybe I'm confused!

Someone may hate me for this next statement, but so be it. The church is the most stingy and cheapest place I know. They never want to pay anybody for anything, but they are always begging. Sure they like to say, "It is better to give than to receive," but I guess it doesn't work like that for them in reverse.

They come up with all of these events because people don't believe in tithes. As far as giving is concerned, we have learned to give in the little areas of life. We are challenged in our lives to pass people who have a small cup or ask for a quarter.

I guarantee you that if we were to take out $10 a month, which is forty quarters, we would not give them all out to those on the streets who asked for one. You will hear my story about that later.

I learned a lesson from my mom discussing why she gave a drunk a dollar. Even if he didn't get anything to eat and bought a beer, perhaps he was going through something in life, and that beer could have calmed him down instead of him being frustrated and going to jump off a bridge or hurting himself. We thought about it and felt her answer was wise and sympathetic, but you still need wisdom.

In some churches, you almost have to have a second job to keep up with the obligations. No one is getting saved or renewed at all of these anniversaries and musicals. Be assured that if you invite fifteen churches to come to your program, sit back and wait because you will be getting fifteen invitations in the mail to return the favor.

It's enough dealing with the hell-raisers; they go to church to create problems, let alone having to take your time and spend your money going to an **un-anointed service**. (J o b 1 : 6) "Now, there was a day when the sons of God came to present themselves before the LORD, and Satan also came among them."

Church has almost turned into a circus, and the ringmaster is counting dollars instead of souls. I understand why Jesus came in and turned the tables over, saying, "You have made my house a den of thieves (Matt.21:13)."

I shall never forget when I went to visit a church for the first time, and I was on my knees for the devotional prayer. Just as I was trying to get up off my knees, the lady leading the prayer had ended the devotion and came straight over to ask if I wanted to donate money for the pastor's birthday. Look! I didn't know the pastor, and I was thinking about God at the moment and meditated on him, and all of a sudden, here comes one of the trained church hustlers I felt. Sorry for the expression, but that's how I felt.

But who cares these days? I may have mentioned this already, but some pastors request members to bring $100-$500 for their anniversary. I know a person that took out a loan to give the pastor $800 for his anniversary because that's what he was asking from each member. Absolutely sickening! Of course, if you're a board member, you definitely have to lead by example and give it. All you have to do is manipulate and control a person's mind, and they will provide you with anything you want. All they have to say is "God told me," and the rest is history.

Church has almost become a hustle, but you have to stand firm and know your rights and go to hear the word of God. The Devil attends services, too; he ushers, preaches, speaks in tongues, wears long dresses and no makeup, and builds large buildings. "The heart is deceitful above all things, and desperately wicked; who can know it" (Jeremiah 17:9).

He comes in so many disguises, so we have to stay on guard. "You shall know them by their fruits" (Matt. 7:16). And some fruit is rotten. One bad apple spoils the whole bunch, and sometimes that apple is the leader.

Many churches have gotten themselves into debt, and the sales go on. There is faith, and there is foolish faith. All of a sudden, everything is a blessing if you donate. What happened with the tithes and offerings? Have our leaders outstretched their faith and now have to beg their way through? Once again, have they counted up the cost? I heard one pastor say if they didn't do the things they did, they would not get any money. It was just not enough coming in the regular offering. Why? Because the people couldn't understand where it was going, nor did the church care or address their personal needs. No one educated them on life and how to save or invest. So basically, they just give the church a tip. I recall a church having a Zodiac Club, and each month their sign had to represent financially. I came across a site on the internet: "How to find the 12 Zodiac Signs & Meaning in the bible." Interesting! After that knowledge, then what???

The church has to go to the so-called heathens for loans and everything else. What is wrong with this picture? In a book, I read that the Jews will give their people a loan, but there were no interest charges (usury), depending on the situation. Somebody is not doing it God's way. There is so much good sitting in the congregation, but people don't give because of greed and selfishness. Even the sinner can see if people are being manipulated.

You may get over, but you won't get by.

If people see through you the first time, rest assured there will not be any repeated business, and you will not grow. Sometimes listening to announcements, you'd think you were watching QVC, the home-shopping channel on TV.

Churches need to open car washes, hair salons, markets, mechanic shops, restaurants, and the names go on. All the Christians are working for the heathens and can't mention God on the jobs, or else they'll be looked at like they're crazy or possibly fired. As said, "I hired you to work, not talk about Jesus."

Some people do not worship God or witness to others that Jesus is soon to come. However, we have been saying that Jesus is soon to come for hundreds of years but has not arrived. Or we also may say that he is coming any day now. Or what if he's here and his spirit will be leaving soon? Or perhaps he's coming soon for anyone of us individually.

2 Peter 3:8
But, beloved, be not ignorant of this one thing, that one day is with the Lord as a thousand years and a thousand years as one day.
Regardless of how we calculate, "Be ye also ready for we know not the day the Lord shall arrive.

Mark 24:44
For this reason, you also must be ready, because the Son of Man will come at an hour you do not expect.

Mark 13:32
But as for that day or hour, no one knows, not even the angels in heaven, nor the Son, but only the Father.

We should work on getting ourselves cleaned up regardless of who we are, but do it in love and not fear. You will feel better about yourself. Just as we do not take clean clothes to the cleaners, we do not go to church already having come to Christ. Usually, we are at our worse and keep going until we get cleaner and cleaner. When others see the change and begin to hear the sincerity and difference in our speech, they may desire to do the same. You never know who's watching you. For example, in doing "theatre." You're backstage peeking through the curtain, not realizing the audience sees you as well as you are seeing them.

Many have taken it for granted that people are saved and know about God. I had a new revelation about worshiping God; we can worship Him by doing God's will and giving Him the praise for enabling us to do it. People will realize that you are heaven-sent even though you may not talk a lot of scriptures. (Matthew 15:8- People honor Me with their lips, but their hearts are far from Me). People will know you by the fruit you bear.

The fashion show for the church has become greater and greater. Everyone has to have designer clothes. These designers probably have no idea who God is, but they will live lavishly because it is another form of the lust of the eye, and the church people flock to buy their expensive clothing. Proverbs 27:20 –The eyes are never satisfied. (Also Ecclesiastes 1:8). Even if I had said it earlier, I have to put this in, but people saved a lot of money during COVID and not going to church.

The trend today, people are saying the bible says, **"Come as you are."** However, "Come as you are" is not in the bible, but some people have taken it to dress any kind of way when coming to church, but when we go out to clubs, etc., we dress our best instead. More so, it reads, "Man looks at the outward appearance, and God looks at the heart.1Samuel 16:7. And no one knows the heart but God. The heart is deceitful. Jeremiah 17:9 "The heart *is* deceitful above all *things,* And desperately wicked; Who can know it?

Yes, it is come as you are in your heart and has nothing to do with clothing. All dressed up and feeling sad and lost is not impressive. Because the new thing is to wear jeans to church, the designer creates jeans that cost as much as suits. No one knows that you were that foolish to pay that much for them, but you and those that recognize the label. I don't like labels on my clothes, and people have given me things with small labels on them, of which I try to cut them off or color them.

Sometimes your friends may not come to your church because your church seems like a very dressy place, and they are embarrassed by what they have. Trust me; a robe will cure it all. Having a wealthy look but no money in their pockets or bank accounts because they are not taught. This will probably be mentioned several times in this book. I know this may sound funny, but can you imagine the magical feeling of everyone being on one accord with the same color and design by wearing a robe for all. That's for the choir and members too.

I've seen robes from $9.98 to hundreds of dollars. I'm not sure what the robe looks like and being that cheap, but I've seen them posted on the internet. It doesn't have to be anything fancy, almost like a plain college robe. You can have members purchase their own robe or have a cloakroom for visitors to put one on; if there are not enough robes for some reason, those that don't have one need to sit in the back or not enter at all. It is what it is. People make all kinds of excuses, especially when it comes to church, but if your job requires you to wear a uniform for you to work, then that's what you'll do if you want a paycheck, and it won't make any difference what color it is, whether it makes you look larger or smaller. I'm only suggesting the feeling of unity. The K.K.K. knows what unity is, so how come the church doesn't get it. Look how wise they are about unity. It's a unique energy when you all look alike. They felt they had power when they all wear white sheets.

And the lord commended the unjust steward because he had done wisely, for the children of this world are in their generation wiser than the children of light (Luke 16:8).

Some believe that if they do not fall out when hands are laid on them, the prayer is not working. My, my, some don't have faith unless they can see something. I've been healed many times, and no one has touched me. But all of the laying of hands and blowing in the faces excite people. Even if it's a simple headache and you don't have it anymore, you've been healed. Some people had headaches that turned into aneurisms and have passed away.

Nothing is wrong with the anointing and the falling out. I've fallen out and have prayed for some, and they did the same, but the Christian life is more than that. People just love a show, so they flock to it.

I would get excited if all of the TV ministries took the millions they are making and built Christian schools so that the world would stop teaching Christian children. Then I'd think they were doing something. Television is costly.

The original design was not that the world would teach our children, but the Devil was so smooth that he made schools cheaper, and now he dictates with a white glove about how children should be taught and disciplined. Furthermore, the parents were supposed to raise the children, but nowadays it's the parents out on the streets—with their children out looking for them.

Something else has crossed my mind: Why is it that when visiting preachers are late for church, they come to the front of the church and shake everyone's hand along the way across the pulpit, thereby disturbing the congregation? Indeed everyone is looking at them, and whoever is speaking may have had a good point or blessing for someone, but he or she becomes distracted. It's enough that the ushers are bringing people in and seating them everywhere. Unless they are speaking, they should sit with everyone else, and if need be, the pastor will call them up later. It's like a medical doctor doing open-heart surgery on a patient, and his phone rings that he forgot to leave in his office. What a disturbance at the wrong time!

I've gone to churches where the ushers guide people to the front until all seats are full. That way, if anyone comes in late, they will have to sit in the back because there will be no spaces upfront. I think this is very effective, but there is always the one who will try to squeeze his or her two-hundred-and-fifty-pound body into a space left to hold a one-hundred-pound person comfortably.

Here's another thing that has puzzled me. I realize that God's word is God's word and that His anointing is His anointing. However, some churches act like there is something wrong with how they praise the Lord, so they adopt another church's pattern. I hate to say this, but some churches are so dead it's like watering dead plants. What are you learning or getting out of it?

I've gone to black churches looking for some good, soulful music and thought that I was in a traditional white church because of how they were acting and the songs they were singing. Don't get me wrong; there is nothing wrong with it, but it's not the norm. (It's not stereotypical, but as a rule, white folk eats cauliflower, and black folk eats collard greens). And we won't base that on a few people that may eat the opposite.

The Black culture has the African Drum rhythm from their ancestors, and that's who they are. African clothing is some of the most beautiful clothing that there is, but the Americans have influenced the black, and Gucci is happy because they know that the eyes are never satisfied (Ecc.:1:8), so they are continually putting out new clothing, the same as car dealers design new car models every year. Can you imagine how much they'd lose if the church congregation and choir all wore robes?

When there has been good rhythmic sound, possibly by a visiting choir, it was as though they knew good and well they wanted to break loose with a good patting-the-feet song but that it wasn't permitted because their new leader had slowly taught them that blacks get too excited. I want you to know that God is exciting, but there are times when we need to worship and slowly meditate on slower-paced songs. I've also gone to white churches where all they played was soulful black music. Say what you want, but you know I'm telling the truth. The mixture is good.

You'll have a person say that the black church is trying to be white, and the white church is trying to be black. It's like an interracial couple. They know people are looking at them. However, we all understand that it's all God's music, and it doesn't differ in our skin color. Some believe that what made them feel so good long ago is now suddenly totally wrong because of trends.

I read a medical report that said 99% of our bodies are the same. That's why we can use each other's blood or body parts, and 1 % has to do with the features and skin color. That 1% has caused a whole lot of chaos in the world.

I'm sure that if a Mexican were invited to dinner by some Italians, he or she wouldn't expect Mexican food. But then again, if you're hungry, food is food regardless of the type. As said, breakfast is the most important meal of the day, but I say that if you're hungry, food is important at any time of the day.

If God didn't want things mixed, he would have had one type of Christian music for us all, and who's to say He didn't, and someone changed it. I don't know. Like I said earlier that churches should mix their music. There are good praise songs, as well as good hand-clapping songs. Have you noticed that when white people praise God, it is different from when black people do the same? White people pat every beat, and blacks pat every other beat. It's still all praising God. There is no white God, nor is there a black God. I have finally realized that God and the Devil have something in common: Neither of them are prejudice, and they use the same people. It's a good thing that we don't teach our animals to be prejudice because the dog's color would reflect the race of the house. I'm sure some people train their dogs to be prejudice. Prejudice is still here today. There are people mad because Disney is remaking The Little Mermaid, and she's black. I recalled seeing the white version of the movie Pollyanna, produced by David Smith, Disney, which was initially released in 1960, based on a book by Eleanor H. Porter, and it was great, and I loved it and heard much about it. Then came along the black version of the movie just called Polly 1989, produced by Frank Fisher, James Pullium, and choreographed by Debbie Allen, with Keshia Knight Pullium and Phylicia Rashad. The same version and it was super fantastic. And I'm not saying it because they were black. It's just that it was done over very well, but did you hear a lot about it? It's on YouTube and will blow your mind. Other famous shows, The Wiz, with Michael

Jackson and Annie with Jamie Fox. These classic shows should be seen once a year expressing the creative Black Culture. From history in school until today, much of the black talent is suppressed because it is energetic and can show things better. It is ok when whites steal black ideas, but when blacks re-do what whites have done, it is suppressed and made not famous. Many White TV shows produce violence, and when Black copy it in the streets they are labeled because their gangs do it, but who did they get the idea from? Blacks are extremist when it comes to ideas, while Whites are extremist when it comes to word usage. Look at the many contracts they create that most people don't understand, not even their own. Blacks appreciate much of what the whites have done, but Blacks only want the acknowledgment returned. When white shows were produced, no one hired black writers or directors to ask them their opinion. When Blacks were able to create a duplicate of the show and made them more vibrant, the black version was played down. We all have talents regardless of race.

When I see prejudice at work, all I can say is the mind is a terrible thing to waste, and there is nothing that God doesn't know about, and it's all about a matter of time.

Believe it or not, all races have the same problem within their race, but you know thoroughly about your own because that's who surrounds you. However, when you hear of other race problems, you know some of the same issues are in your own family. It's like Kool-Aid, it's all the same water, but the only change is the flavor you put in. There is nothing new under the sun. I had a strange thought; what if people went to heaven, and all of the angels were cursing? You'd be in shock. But to hear God say that the problem wasn't the cursing on earth, but them doing the work I called them to do. Could you imagine if God said, "Adam, I told your a_ _ is not to eat that d--n fruit." Who created cursing? I tried to look up various curse words to see their origin, and it was quite interesting. I saw on Netflix "The History of Swear Words." Cursing? What about it? There's nothing new under the sun. We just don't like to hear it. We were taught that certain words were bad words to use, even though they were used only to emphasize a phrase or sentence. Did they smoke marijuana in the bible before we knew about it? Of course, once again, there's nothing new under the sun. So many chapters are missing in the bible. Who decided to omit them?

What if there was no such thing as the church, and God wanted to guide each of us individually and not come together as a gang, making people feel guilty for not coming to a church. Organized religion? Food for a crazy thought: Did the Devil create a church, and all of the sincere people are out doing the real work and don't have time to sit in church? Even though they don't go to a church because they were not hypnotized? All that sounds crazy, but life is full of surprises. What if you died and a second after you see God, and he says, "None of the things you saw in the church were me because I have real integrity. I kept telling you over and over. "I talked to your pastor the same as I talked to you."

Some people are so far behind that they think they are first. There is nothing new under the sun, and we should stop making church so dull. The main problem, may I say, is that they need the Holy Ghost. Some think they have the Holy Ghost, but they have the powerless Casper the Friendly Ghost. Don't be so small-minded because God could have told you something that he hasn't shown the pastor yet. You are God's child too. Understand that God showed him something as well before he became a pastor. The pastor was not designed to run the church all by himself.

Every Sunday should be like a production seeing God's gifts at work. A man's gift makes room for him and brings him before great men. Proverbs 18:16. Your gift also helps with your vision.

Proverbs 8:12 I wisdom dwell with prudence and find out knowledge of witty inventions.

The church is filled with people that have different talents. Secular artists do it every week, and many church members go to see the secular artists and clubs, but the church represents God with all the gifts sitting in front of them, but boring. The church should have an orchestra. Evidently, they told God to go to sleep, and they will do it their way. Does your church do any of the following?

Psalm 150
Praise ye the LORD. Praise God in his sanctuary: praise him in the firmament of his power.

² Praise him for his mighty acts: praise him according to his excellent greatness.
³ Praise him with the sound of the trumpet: praise him with the psaltery and harp.
⁴ Praise him with the tambourine and dance: praise him with stringed instruments and organs.
⁵ Praise him upon the loud cymbals: praise him upon the high sounding cymbals.
⁶ Let everything that hath breath praise the LORD. Praise ye the LORD.
And you wonder why one of the reasons attendance is low?

Pertaining to Gifts

Philippians 1:6- Being confident of this very thing, that he which has begun a good work in you will perform it until the day of Jesus Christ:
Hebrews 13:21- God will equip you with everything good that you may do his will, working in us that which is pleasing in his sight, through Jesus Christ, to whom be glory forever and ever.
Romans 8:30 - And those he predestined, he also called; those he called, he also justified; those he justified, he also glorified.

"He who wants friends must show himself friendly" (Prov. 18:24). Some churches build their ministries solely on being friendly, but they lack the five-fold ministry's gifts. Regardless of how cults are started, they have found it's better to get bees with honey. And if the honey supply keeps coming, it would be hard to leave where it was found. Just being helpful and friendly to people pulls a lot of weight because most people haven't seen it in the church.

Once again, "The children of this world (unsaved) are in their generation wiser than the children of light" (saved) (Luke 16:8). Think back to the sixties: Love and Peace! The church should have tried it and kept it. Saying "Peace" is a better greeting than just saying, "How are you." Everyone automatically says, "Fine," knowing that a lot is going on, and you don't have time to hear it. But the word "Peace" is praying for hope in their hearts. When Jesus entered a room, he said, "Peace be with you." He didn't say, "How are you?"

One day, I heard a joke that a homeless man was sitting on the doorstep of a church just crying away. Jesus came along and asked the man what was wrong. The young man replied, "Jesus, they won't let me in the church." Jesus replied, "Don't worry, son, they won't let me in either."

Pray that when Jesus does return that he will find us at least trying to do his will and not sitting around figuring ways to use his people. God may allow things to go on for a while, but he truly knows how to stop them. (Hebrews 10:31 - It is a fearful thing to fall into the hands of the living God). Millions of dollars are spent on the beauty of buildings; very little is spent on the torn-up heart.

The church has become a market place, but if it is done correctly, it wouldn't be as bad as it is. But they are selling and conning folks in all kinds of ways. I recall taking notes at a particular church, and for each transaction or anything they did, I gave it a number. For instance, if they sang three songs, that was 3. If there were five announcements, that was three plus five equal to 8. This church had 63 actions in one service. I was waiting for Jesus to come along in one of the preliminaries. And Jesus said unto them, It is written, My house shall be called the house of prayer, but you have made it a den of thieves (Matthew 21:13).

The best altar call song I've ever heard in a church was "Give Yourself to Jesus." I was first introduced to it in 1970 by James Cleveland's Southern California Choir and then later was a song by Aretha Franklin on her Amazing Grace album. You can listen to it on YouTube as well.

GIVE YOURSELF TO JESUS

Give yourself to Jesus
You don't have much time
Give yourself to the MASTER
He'll make your life sublime
Give yourself to Jesus
He's waiting just for you
Just put all your trust in Him
God will take care of you.

Chapter 4
Music/Dress

I know this book's main subject is the five-fold ministry, but I just could not help myself by mentioning music and how people dress in the church. If you want to call it judging, all I can say is, " Help yourself." It is almost ridiculous how music has changed our churches, and people look like they are going to the Blues Festival. Absolutely unrespectable, and yes, I said it. They have become the center of attention.

Of course, we judge each other all day, and it's like a monkey behind bars, but the look of bars are on both sides. We see one monkey in a cage, and he sees a lot of monkeys (people) looking at him, and the monkey may be saying, "Look at all of those monkeys in that huge cage, and I'm free and not bothering anyone."

Some people are so far behind thinking they are first, as I just mentioned a few paragraphs ago. Meaning they believe they have discovered something new and judge others who don't know it yet, but later found out they were behind because of their thinking.

I touched on this subject earlier and thought it would be of excellent value if repeated.

Go ahead and say, "You are supposed to come as you are."—Yes, come as you are in your mental condition about life and what you're going through because none of us are perfect. And it also says that man looks at the outward appearance, but God looks at the heart. So when you are coming to God, he knows your heart's sincerity, but a person knows what type of look they are trying to portray. A skirt that stops just below your private area, isn't that a joke? That's why they tell speakers when they speak not to wear something very gaudy because we are all humans, and it's a distraction because people will be looking at all of that flashy stuff and not listening to you.

God forbid what these people are wearing in these praise groups *with all of these open blouses, tight pants, and skirts.* Yes, I *repeated it*! If you want to call me old fashion in that respect, I will accept it. People are upstaging the anointing of God. Yes, and I *have repeated it*! I think the choirs should go back to robes and the praise groups as well. And if you want to know the truth about it, as I said earlier, the whole congregation should wear a robe, and that way, when you enter the church, you will look like everyone else and not give a fashion show.

Therefore, if you have to be seated in the front, you won't look any different than anyone else; you will *also* save a lot of money for clothing. Gucci and all of the other designers will *probably lose a lot* of money. A lot of the superstars would hate this.

By the way, What church do these designers belong to, or who do they support? How much do you get for advertising their names across your chest? What is so ironic about clothing is that long ago in the bible days, everyone wore some type of garment that looks like a robe, and that was both men and women. Who invented pants?

The earliest existing pair of pants was found in China and dates to around 1000 BCE - within 1000 years of the time when horses were initially domesticated. Pants were made of wool multiple panels.

I feel that the gospel music change happened around 1968 when Edwin Hawkins Singers released "Oh Happy Day." That song swept the nation. I was a kid, and it was my favorite song. It was like it drove me crazy. If someone heard it on the radio, they hollered for me and said it was on. You would walk down the street and past churches, and they would be singing Oh Happy Day.

It was a new style and sound of music until the flame caught on, and the contemporary world got stronger. And to this day, people still love Oh Happy Day, it's like an old Beatle song that comes on, and your mind goes back and smiles, saying, "That's my song."

We have so many gospel celebrities that we don't know whether to ask for their autograph before prayer or after. Suppose we ask for before, they may not have time because they need to concentrate on their delivery, and if we ask after, they won't have time because they have to rush somewhere and leaving you a little saddened. Of course, now and then, you will hear of them being involved in a worthy cause, but everyone wants to feed the homeless, give them a blanket and throw them a sandwich or two and give backpacks to the children to take to school to learn nothing because the school system is corrupt.

Why not help build Christian schools or donate money to help pay for a child's music lessons or classes that structure their gifts. Many teachers today have to buy some of their supplies for schools to show how corrupt and uncaring the school system is. There are homeless that have talents too. Half the kids get out of school and don't know how to balance a checking account. They can't count because they use calculators and don't have to write cursive. If the schools didn't teach the whole bible, they should teach Proverbs, Ecclesiastes, and the Beatitudes. Churches receive, but do they give, especially those that are able? The church is the root of our souls, and it has become corrupt and flashy.

Some celebrities are more like most of us. Having gone through the church seeking help but unable to find any support or encouragement to push them in their craft or skill, so they went out on their own, fought it out, and made something of themselves. Now they are afraid to give back to the church because of what they have seen in them— mainly how it is supported by all the anniversaries, etc. Church people should be the wealthiest people there are, but they seem like the most broke. People would instead take their chances of going to the Casino than to the church, hoping they will receive, even though the risk is high. Why do you think the casinos are rich? Surely the church people don't go and take the Sunday School money there. Lol.

Music in the church, by all means, sounds good, but there is no anointing on a lot of it. I never thought I would be the one to make a statement like that, but the truth is just the truth. I'm not old-fashioned by any means. It's like having a good steak, and you know when it's good and when it's not.

When I would dance in the clubs and much younger, I must admit that I was one of the best dancers on the floor. I could work a beat on the floor; my partner and I would always draw a crowd at the club or house party. So, I know secular music well and quite familiar with the beat. God gives us the talent. I had such a strong urge to dance that I would go to Sunday morning service, then to happy hour at a club, and then back to evening service and maybe the club again afterward.

Unfortunately, secular music is quite prevalent in our churches today. Don't get me wrong; the music sounds good, but where's the anointing? For those churches with quite a few young people, you will notice them jumping up and having a good time getting their groove on because they recognize the beat from the night before.

It's not the words they are familiar with; it is the music. You will notice the elderly are just sitting back and watching. And it is not always because they are unable to keep up but because they have learned, through the spirit of God, what it is all about. Remember, the elderly were young first.

The Jim Bakker Story

I enjoy dancing, but I think that they should have a special night for the people who like this music to come and dance in a safe environment. Let them create some dances such as "The Moses Shuffle and an amusement park. I use to think about things like this when I was much younger, and people would tell me that I was before my time.." And behold, someone else was dreaming the same thing I was. A brief dream and idea of this were in 1987 by the Evangelist Jim and Tammy Faye Bakker.

Heritage USA was a Christian-themed amusement park opened in 1978 by televangelists Jim and Tammy Faye Bakker. At its peak, it was the third-largest park in the **USA** behind Disney World and Disney Land, with almost 6 million visitors annually. Only a few remnants of the park are **still** visible today.

FORT MILL, S.C./

CHARLOTTE OBSERVER.COM

It was a chilly January night in 1987, and then-PTL president Jim Bakker had invited top leaders from York County to Heritage USA, his Christian theme park in Fort Mill. He wanted to share his dreams for expanding the 2,300-acre complex, which had attracted nearly six million visitors the year before with, among other things, its 52-foot water slide, Bible-based shops along a pretend Main Street, and a TV studio spotlighting the talk show that starred Bakker and then-wife Tammy.

Bakker's vision, he told the leaders, included a roller coaster ride through "heaven and hell," a 30,000-seat replica of London's Crystal Palace, even a five-story, Greek-style mausoleum.

Construction had already begun by then on two other mega-projects: A sandcastle with a 10-story turret that would house the world's largest Wendy's restaurant and a high-rise hotel called Heritage Grand Towers. When finished, reported the Heritage Herald, a weekly newspaper for tourists and those living on the PTL property, the tower's "elegantly furnished" 500 rooms would include 100 honeymoon suites "for couples who come to Heritage USA to renew their marriages."

Two months later, Bakker suddenly resigned amid financial and sexual scandal. His plans were scrapped, the ongoing construction halted. Today, three decades after Bakker's dreams gave way to a nightmarish spell of bankruptcy, lawsuits, and prison, many of the magnets that once drew people to Heritage USA are long gone.

Most of the land that **Heritage USA** once sat on is now housing developments and commercial buildings. Only the abandoned 21-story hotel, Upper Room Chapel, and **Heritage** Grand Hotel (now **Heritage** International Ministries Conference Center) remain.

That's an amazing story, and if the ministry was targeted like Jim Bakker, there would be a lot of leaders going to jail along with all of the scandals. Blessed be the name of the Lord! But to my surprise, with all of the millions of the "perfect" Christians in the world, no one could step in and take the project over. The fight would be what denomination it would represent. We are now addicted to Disneyland, which today costs at least $104 per person to enter, and the price goes up depending on additions. Do you want to stay in the hotel? You don't want to hear the price.

Usually, most church people sit around and gain weight talking about everyone else and have no choice to lay before the Lord because they are too heavy and don't have the strength anymore. Weight has slowed down most of us. But when they were younger, they partied and danced and did the same thing, but not as wild as those today. It seems after a person gets around 25 and in the church, they stop everything.

The school system has already taken P.E. out of school, meaning you don't have to take it if you don't want to. Why don't you have aerobics on bible study night? For bodily exercise profits a little, but godliness is profitable for all things, having the promise of the life that now is and that which is to come. (1Timothy 4:8) It may profit little, but it does profit.

I remember, after being "saved," that I still wanted to dance. Dancing is just all in my bones. I found a Jewish synagogue that danced every

Wednesday night, and boy, did we have a good time! There were no alcoholic beverages there, just soda and chips, but I learned the different religious dances, and it was terrific. They said there were over 100 Jewish Dances.

Some of those dances made you sweat and get your groove on. Even though there were no alcoholic beverages there, the Jews are known to drink plenty of it. I recalled going to a Bar Mitzvah when the Jewish boy turns 13 years old; the celebration was at a synagogue. There was a petition dividing the sanctuary from the reception hall. After all of it was over, I never saw so much alcohol and good food in my life that was behind the petition, and I was only about 14 years old myself. It made me want to be Jewish. lol

David danced before the Lord, so why can't we? But it is how you dance and what you're dancing about that makes a difference. As repeatedly said, there is nothing new under the sun. Who knows, David could have been doing the Electric Slide, smoking a joint and cursing while he was doing it. How do we know? None of us were there. Music can be for created dance, as well as for praise. Nowadays, you turn on the gospel station on the radio, and you think you have it on the wrong station. So you wait to see if someone is going to mention Jesus or God, and then you say, "Oh, that's it."

It's incredible how brilliant the Devil is. He has people saying that you have to change the music and beat for the young folk to get them to Christ. I guess this would be a good time to use Malcolm X's phrase, "By any means necessary."

What was calling us to Christ before long ago? As they get older and wiser, they begin to see things that don't make any sense. Years ago, they were coming to Christ without the beat, so who changed the rule? The Devil got smarter, and the church got dumber. John 15:16-You did not choose me. I chose you and gave you this work; to go and produce fruit, fruit that will last. Then the Father will give you anything you ask for in my name.

You were running so well, who hindered you from obeying the truth. (Gal.5:7) A little leaven levels the whole lump. (Gal 5:9)
You always see gospel artists changing their beats to secular music. It is a real rarity to see a secular artist trying to change his album to a gospel beat.

Some of this music reminds me of a scripture that reads: "This person draws near unto me with their mouth and honors me with their lips, but their heart is far from me" (Matt. 15:8). I know some people believe that this music draws the young folks, but drawing them to do what? If they do attend church and don't receive the five-fold ministry or the baptism of the Holy Ghost, what have you done? Or is it the offering, in which some would say, "Every penny helps"? By the way, a lot of young folks are not going to church. Look at your congregation. If you have a large young congregation, consider yourself blessed. However, you better educate them or become the elderly and wonder why they were not taught when they were young while their mind was new and fresh. This pattern is repeated continuously until you end up with a nation that doesn't care, because many say they are young and they need to spread their wings a while. Later, to find out that their wings won't help them fly anywhere because they don't know anything and don't have a direction.

If this music is a must, the pastor should insist on mixing it with some authentic gospel songs. More than likely, if you have a young musician, you will have to take them the song and insist on the choir learning it. Many musicians are gifted. However, I'm sure that if the right music gets in their hands, they will become anointed!

Remember that the elderly were the prayer warriors before we got here, so why move them out? A little good music is like chicken soup for the soul. The only good thing to me is when they have monitors with the words of the songs and in the bulletin. However, I've seen songs on the monitor with the songs the choir will sing for the day. At least you will know what some of them are saying. So many times, I would just make up a word to fit.

When attending a concert or service with a lot of contemporary music, I'm sure you have noticed that all of a sudden, an artist or choir began to sing a good old song with a lot of feeling, and the anointing came, and everyone was rejoicing.

There was a time that when you heard church music, you knew that's what it was, but now you have to ask, "Was that a church song?" I do believe in the anointing and the understanding of the church. It is said, by the foolishness of preaching, man shall be saved. (1Cor.1:21). Yes, there is some foolishness in the pulpit, whether it is preaching or in song.

However, some people still come to Christ with it, but then revelation comes. No church is perfect, but many are not trying and only existing. They throw a sermon at you, tell you to pay your tithes, and repeat it the next Sunday. Phooey! With all of the talents in the church, each Sunday should be like a major production. The congregation has actors, singers, writers, and people in movie production, cooks, and so on. It all boils down to the sermon to introduce the acceptance of Christ and asking for His will to be done in our lives. He has already written most of his will: Feed the hungry, visit the sick, and help the elderly.

Going to some of these services or concerts is like going to a big sale at a department store; everything is so lovely, but you leave empty-handed because there was nothing there that suited your fancy. Churches now entertain; they don't enlighten and reveal. That might sound contradictory to what I said above regarding the talents in the church, but the entertainment is definitely for the show, but how it's done and how the gifts are being used may become anointed. A little leaven leavens the whole lump. (Galatians 5:9)

Some people try to offend the audience by saying, "If you didn't get anything, it is because you didn't bring anything." I would love to respond by saying, "The reason I didn't get anything is that I couldn't find anything I could connect with."

God will always reign, regardless of the habits the church adopts. When they come to their senses, they will fall on their knees and realize that God reigns forever.

Although some music is not scriptural and a few words might need to be changed, it can still hold the rhythm. It's just like the song "Walking around Heaven All Day"; I doubt very much that when we make it to heaven, we will be walking around heaven all day. God will give you something to do. What about "Rejoicing around Heaven All Day" instead?

We have to understand what happens with the words we are always singing. If words are appropriately written, there can be a whole sermon in a song. Thou art snared with the words of thy mouth; thou art taken with the words of thy mouth. (Proverbs 6:2) And this can be anything.

Choirs are one of the church's significant entities, but when you have a choir whose members party all night and do everything all week, don't expect a great anointing from them because they are too tired to give it all. They should have gone out Friday night instead.

Just listen to music and pray for them. Trust me; I've been in the car with people who smoked a joint before they went to sing, so I know what I'm talking about! Not realizing how strong the odor was, I did not judge them; I was just worried about the smell being on my clothes.

In the Acts of the Apostles, they were seeking God; in the new millennium, they are seeking fame and fortune. Deliverance is the key to any ministry. If the members are not changing for the better, realize there is something wrong, and why are they going to your church?

Repeating the same pattern as others, you will be getting the same results.

Titus 2
Doing Good for the Sake of the Gospel

You, however, must teach what is appropriate to sound doctrine.[2] Teach the older men to be temperate, worthy of respect, self-controlled, and sound in faith, love and endurance.

[3] Likewise, teach the older women to be reverent in the way they live, not to be slanderers or addicted to much wine, but to teach what is good. [4] Then they can urge the younger women to love their husbands and children, [5] to be self-controlled and pure, to be busy at home, to be kind, and to be subject to their

husbands, so that no one will malign the word of God.

[6] Similarly, encourage the young men to be self-controlled. [7] In everything, set them an example by doing what is good. In your teaching, show integrity, seriousness [8.] and soundness of speech that cannot be condemned, so that those who oppose you may be ashamed because they have nothing bad to say about us.

[9] Teach slaves to be subject to their masters in everything, to try to please them, not to talk back to them, [10] and not to steal from them, but to show that they can be fully trusted so that in every way they will make the teaching about God our Savior attractive.

Let me pause here for a minute. There has been a lot of controversy about the above passage regarding slavery. Because man has written the bible supposing God's inspired word, do you think this passage was added to condition slaves to be slaves and not wanting anything but to serve the white masters? Would God encourage this, or did God say this? If you understand life today, you would know that this is not a discriminatory statement and that whites are against blacks. There is a group of whites that run our country, and they wouldn't care if you were black, white, yellow or brown, because this group manipulates their own as well. Some people in this group will kill their own parents for the insurance money. There are many manipulative and deceiving laws that no one understands but lawyers. The reason it seems like blacks have it so hard because they were taught to be against each other, as in the Willie Lynch story. However, in their training to destroy themselves, there are prejudiced whites that do their damage on all people, and now the blacks have a double scoop of negativity. Whites have learned that if you can keep blacks separate from their own wisdom, they will not conquer anything. Such as the example of the bumblebee. According to the theory of aerodynamics, the bumblebee is not supposed to fly because the size, weight, and shape of his body in relation to his wingspan make flying impossible. But you see, here's the problem: somebody forgot to tell the bumblebee about this theory, and he goes ahead and flies and makes a little honey every day! No one could manipulate his mind and say to him that he couldn't fly.

Blacks have come up with thousands of ideas and did not receive credit or compensation. I often think Blacks were the real chosen people because you have never seen a group of people who have gone through so much hardship put on them by whites, and they still bounce back one way or the other and are happy and always praise God. There is something in them that can't be destroyed; even now, they are trying to destroy the Black race through poisoning, the internet, medications, abortions, and anything they can. Reaping and sowing will become a sad day for some who have treated them wrongly. Black people were not taught prejudice like others; they were taught to obey, love, and survive at their expense. The only discrimination they were taught was to be against themselves, in which later they found out it was a ploy to destroy them and keep them from being conquerors. If the tables were turned and what I understand about the Black race and how we trust in God, there would be no way we would have treated whites the way they have treated us. Did God know this?

I know other races have gone through some of the trauma, but the black and white fight has always been in the limelight for some reason. One of the reasons why it's like a magician, he keeps your eyes focused on one hand, and the magic is on the other hand. While whites have taught the world to focus on blacks and whites to be against one another, they manipulate all the other races that are not paying attention to what is going on. Therefore, Hispanics and any other race will be empowered by them if they are not paying attention. However, people are beginning to wake up, and I think of that scripture that says that the first shall be last. Matthew 19:30

But we must also understand that there were white slaves too. The Forgotten History of Britain's White Slaves in America. Slavery in America, typically associated with blacks from Africa, was an enterprise that began with the shipping of more than 300,000 white Britons to the colonies. This little known history is fascinatingly recounted in White Cargo (New York University Press, 2007).

My mind keeps going back to Harriet Tubman, which proves come hell or high water, if you stick together for what is right, they would have to change. This was not about running to voting polls; this was strict action. Can you imagine if everyone stuck together and said they wouldn't catch an airplane for a month because the prices are too high, no bereavement flights, and carry-on costs too much? What a change, What a transformation! Whether it's in my lifetime or not, I feel that one day the world will rebel, and it's not going to be a pretty sight, and we all will be saying, "Come Lord Jesus."

Teaching a person from youth to adult age can be very dangerous. If they are taught wrong, they will teach their children the same thing, and it will go on and on. Although many slave owners thought they would get away by their wrongdoings. It reminds me of the old saying, "The chickens are coming home to roost. Meaning your actions will be returned to you. Galatians 6:7- You reap what you have sown. Everything is a matter of God's timing, whether you receive the consequences personally or someone in your family.

The Willie Lynch Speech, which was repeated earlier in this book about how to control slaves.
Reread the following article because it needs to stick to show how cruel people can be when they want to train someone to be ignorant, such as the children in our school system. The problem is people forget that these ignorant people are going to grow up and give them hell. Don't be offended by it being repeated because many things are repeated in the bible as well.

The Making of a Slave
(Repeated)

This speech was said to have been delivered by Willie Lynch on the bank of the James River in the colony of Virginia in 1712. Lynch was a British slave owner in the West Indies. He was invited to the colony of Virginia in 1712 to teach his methods to slave owners there.

[beginning of the Willie Lynch Letter]

Greetings,

Gentlemen, I greet you here on the bank of the James River in the year of our Lord one thousand seven hundred and twelve. First, I shall thank you, the gentlemen of the Colony of Virginia, for bringing me here. I am here to help you solve some of your problems with slaves.

Your invitation reached me on my modest plantation in the West Indies, where I have experimented with some of the newest and still the oldest methods for the control of slaves. Ancient Rome would envy us if my program is implemented. As our boat sailed south on the James River, named for our illustrious King, whose version of the Bible we cherish, I saw enough to know that your problem is not unique.

While Rome used cords of wood as crosses for standing human bodies along its highways in great numbers, you are here using the tree and the rope on occasions. I caught the whiff of a dead slave hanging from a tree, a couple of miles back. You are not only losing valuable stock by hangings, but you are also having uprisings, slaves are running away, your crops are sometimes left in the fields too long for maximum profit, you suffer occasional fires, your animals are killed.

Gentlemen, you know what your problems are; I do not need to elaborate. I am not here to enumerate your problems; I am here to introduce you to a method of solving them. In my bag here, **I HAVE A FULL PROOF METHOD FOR CONTROLLING YOUR BLACK SLAVES**. I guarantee every one of you that, if installed correctly, **IT WILL CONTROL THE SLAVES FOR AT LEAST 300 HUNDRED YEARS**.

My method is simple. Any member of your family or your overseer can use it. **I HAVE OUTLINED A NUMBER OF DIFFERENCES AMONG THE SLAVES, AND I TAKE THESE DIFFERENCES AND MAKE THEM BIGGER. I USE FEAR, DISTRUST, AND ENVY FOR CONTROL PURPOSES**. These methods have worked on my modest plantation in the West Indies, and it will work throughout the South. Take this simple little list of differences and think about them. On top of my list is "AGE," but it's there only because it starts with an "a." The second is "COLOR" or shade.

There is **INTELLIGENCE, SIZE, SEX, SIZES OF PLANTATIONS, STATUS** on plantations, **ATTITUDE** of owners, whether the slaves live in the valley, on a hill, East, West, North, South, have fine hair, coarse hair, or is tall or short. Now that you have a list of differences, I shall give you an outline of action, but before that, I shall assure you that **DISTRUST IS STRONGER THAN TRUST AND ENVY STRONGER THAN ADULATION, RESPECT OR ADMIRATION**. The Black slaves, after receiving this indoctrination shall carry on and will become self-refueling and self-generating for **HUNDREDS** of years, maybe **THOUSANDS**. Don't forget; you must pitch the **OLD** black male vs. the **YOUNG** black male and the **YOUNG** black male against the **OLD** black male. You must use the **DARK** skin slaves vs. the **LIGHT** skin slaves, and the **LIGHT** skin slaves vs. the **DARK** skin slaves. You must use the **FEMALE** vs. the **MALE**, and the **MALE** vs. the **FEMALE**.

You must also have white servants and overseers [who] distrust all Blacks. But it is **NECESSARY THAT YOUR SLAVES TRUST AND DEPEND ON US. THEY MUST LOVE, RESPECT AND TRUST ONLY US**.

Gentlemen, these kits are your keys to control. Use them. Have your wives and children use them, never miss an opportunity. **IF USED INTENSELY FOR ONE YEAR, THE SLAVES THEMSELVES WILL REMAIN PERPETUALLY DISTRUSTFUL**. Thank you, gentlemen." *END*

After reading this, I thought about reparation when it was said that black former slaves had become free.

During the end of the civil war, freed slaves were given 40 acres of confiscated land and a mule.

However, once Andrew Jackson became the president, the land was given back to the ex confederates.

The following from Africanamerica.org

However, the unfulfilled promise of 40 acres per family also provides a means to gauge the magnitude of reparations owed to the descendants of those enslaved. A conservative estimate of the price of land in the USA in 1865 would be $10 per acre (Mital and Powell). An allocation of 40 acres to a family of four would imply 10 acres per person, hence a value of $100 per ex-slave in 1865. If we also take as a conservative estimate of the total number of ex-slaves who had attained emancipation at the close of the Civil War of as 4 million persons, 40 million acres of land valued at $400 million should have been distributed to the ex-slaves in 1865. The present value of that sum of money compounded from 1865 at 6 percent (5 percent for interest earned and one percent as an inflation adjustment) would amount to more than $1.3 trillion. If there are approximately 30 million descendants of enslaved Africans in the USA today, the estimate based upon forty acres yields an allocation of slightly more than $400,000 per recipient.

My thought: This would probably never happen because of the way that blacks had been trained; all of the money would be spent and given back to white businesses for lavish purchases. And

Also, understand that all whites are not interested in all other whites to become rich; they still have their prejudices within their own race to make them superior overall. The White House is not named the White House for nothing. That not a prejudiced statement for those who like to make something out of nothing. Just look and understand what race is in there. If a person is doing right, it doesn't make any difference in your race, but if some are doing wrong, know that the whole race suffers.

We all have been trained to think a certain way. Do you think the media will always tell you the truth? That's why I don't watch the news. In our thinking, we've been trained so long that it's tough to believe when the truth appears. The following is another creative story that I heard as a kid that may help you with the concept of being free.

There was a little boy that kept a jar of fleas. He punched tiny holes at the top of the jar so that the fleas could breathe. The fleas always jumped around and went to the top but could not get out. After keeping them in the jar for some time, the little boy decided he would take the lid off and let them go free. To his amazement, they would not jump out because they were trained only to jump so high. They were now free, but would not learn and explore the world. Might I add; this is the type of training that was done to our children in the school system. Had they been given the correct information, they could have been doctors by 12th grade—controlled thinking in America.

Even though we are to forgive a lot of wrongdoings, many people quote the scripture referring to forgiveness 70 X 7.- Matthew 8:21 -21 Then Peter came up and said to him, "Lord, how often will my brother sin against me, and I forgive him? As many as seven times?" Jesus said to him, "I do not say to you seven times, but seventy-seven times.

Christ was just giving an example and not necessarily 490 times. Who forgives someone that many times? Usually, we forgive them once, if even then, and it's a blessing we don't hold a grudge afterward. Christ was alluding to the 490 years the Jews were in captivity and slavery and taken from their homeland. Christ knew forgiveness was hard. Harboring un-forgiveness in your heart is not suitable for anyone.

The Lost Seniors and Youth
(Don't forget those in between need help as well)

I spoke on this a little bit earlier, but here is the whole enchilada.

James 1:27 - Pure and undefiled religion before our God and Father is this: to care for orphans and widows in their distress and to keep oneself from being polluted by the world.

Just think if this is what we were really taught with action, but instead, we were taught a lot of bible stories. When we did learn this, we were too tired to be concerned about anyone but ourselves or told to study to show ourselves approved. Well, what was the purpose of the teacher? I shouldn't have to go to Sunday School after sitting in a morning service for 3 hours. You would have thought they would have educated me during that time. Not only about life goals and entrepreneurship, but the bible as well. It's incredible how many people have been in church for 20 and 30 years and haven't read the whole bible. They only know the scripture given to them in the Sunday morning text, not knowing that the previous verse that was not read would have made things clearer. If people read the bible, they would question themselves say, "Who is doing this stuff?"

Deuteronomy 4:9

Only be on your guard and diligently watch yourselves so that you do not forget the things your eyes have seen and so that they do not slip from your heart as long as you live. Teach them to your children and grandchildren.

Many children are being taught the latest hip hop artist music or designer clothing. So sad!

Deuteronomy 11:19

Teach them to your children, speaking about them when you sit at home and when you walk along the road, when you lie down and when you get up.

Today, parents smoke marijuana with their children, and the children tell their friends that they have hip parents, but parents forget to teach them manners. Still, they will teach them how to roll a joint, not realizing these children will grow up and disrespect them and any other adult and guide their children the same. Willie Lynch's story makes you think, huh?

Deuteronomy 4:9

Only be on your guard and diligently watch yourselves so that you do not forget the things your eyes have seen and so that they do not slip from your heart as long as you live. Teach them to your children and grandchildren.

How are grandchildren helping seniors? It's incredible how time has changed, and the seniors are slowly booted out of the church, and yet they were the ones that helped build the church. And now the word is that they need to attract the young folk. Attract them to do what?

The young folk today have lost all of their manners and respect. You always hear about the children of the future. Oh my God, it will almost make you afraid of the future. A sophisticated group changed the education and discipline laws strictly for their children. However, they did not realize that their children have to walk through some of the same streets as the uneducated, and they will be in fear. The sophisticated drive in their limousines, but they ride the same freeways as the drive-by shooters that are not educated. The school system is ridiculous. How they got their foot in the door, I have no idea. Some said it was because prayers were taken out of the school system with the encouragement of Madalyn O'Hara, a white woman, but life is more than prayer; there is action needed. Did it affect whites as well as blacks and other races? I have a book that is not yet published, *"If You Thought Columbine Was Something, You Haven't Seen Anything Yet."* A person can be praying, and it not evident whether prayer was taken out of school. A man should always pray (Luke 18:1). I heard that if you want your grandchildren to visit you, make sure you have plenty of money to give them.

Many people will say regarding the seniors, "Don't they have children that look out for them?" That's like asking a dog if he knows how to fry chicken just because he was lying around the kitchen and watching the owner cook. A person can have eight children, and there will only be one that may be concerned, and this one sibling may also have their hands tied with their own family and can't get sisters or brothers to help do anything. The family structure was not taught, or as the bible says, men will become lovers of themselves (2Timothy 3:2). Many families' curiosity; is there anything left in the "WILL" for them, and that's it.

However, this older adult has gone to your church for years and has been ignored, yet their monies add up. Even if you had a large congregation and there were only 100 older people giving $20 a month, that's $2000 more than you had. I'm sure they gave much more back in their younger days to help build the church. People used to love the church until it got dignified and cunning. That can be turned around if we see what worked before. Because of technology, we can do more if we use technology right. Whether the church uses it correctly or not, the government will use it consistently to control it.

I heard a heartbreaking story. I attended a friend's mother's funeral, who was about 80 years old. She was a Catholic and had raised her children in this particular church for 40 years or more. She had gotten ill and didn't attend the church for a little while, and when she passed, the church did not allow them to have a funeral there. Furthermore, how many of them cared that she was ill, but everything was fine as long as the money was coming. This kind of stuff discourages people from churches and everything else.

Churches love the fad in building life centers. How come they won't build a convalescent home that is decent? The government would help them, whether it's through grants or philanthropists. Philanthropist doesn't mind, but they will not throw their money away to any church mess. Half of these convalescent homes are nasty and don't care. In the same token, if someone from the outside were assigned to a person once a week to come there, perhaps they would do a little better for the person fearing that someone would report them.

My sister Peaches have worked in-home care for over 30 years, and thank God they love her. I recall going to see one of her clients in a private home. He and his wife were in the same room. Both of his legs were amputated, and his wife was a vegetable, not being able to move at all while she was frail and curled up. Their insurance was paying the home over $5,000 a month. I got a chance to talk to the older man, and he said he had been to some of the finest rehabilitation centers and homes that were gorgeous, and that didn't mean anything to him because of the terrible care he had gotten. The bottom line was that it wasn't important how the place looks, but the respect and care he had obtained from the right nurse. Unfortunately, since this writing, both had passed away.

So many people just drop their loved ones off, and once again, what responsibility does the church have in visiting them, regardless if they know them or not. What if we were taught on our birthday that we are to stop by a hospital and give someone a gift and tell them to share your day with you instead of us waiting for a person to bring us a gift. If we had been taught this as children, this would have been a natural thing to do, but we were taught to go to church on Sunday, dress up and pay tithes, offerings and prepare for the next anniversary or revival. I've gone to visit the elderly myself but had slowed down, and as I'm writing this, I need to start back again.

The time it would take a person to make someone feel good is when it would take to watch one of their favorite TV shows as they watch people on television create a story and get paid for it, while the viewer doesn't get a dime. If anything, he has to pay to watch cable, which costs over a thousand dollars a year, and there's nothing on it. That's a mini-vacation and a pot of flowers to someone in the hospital.

What service do you have to help seniors who use the internet and get ripped off in their bank accounts? I know this may sound redundant, but it stays on my mind. Seniors that try to take care of business on the phone with these half hours to hour wait and then they give up, possibly forget, and then charged again for something because they failed to try to cancel again.

There are discount services they can use and don't know anything about it. What gets next to me is when someone says, "Someone in the family should help them." What family? There is no such thing as the American family anymore. Many are for themselves in this high tech world. (The love of many will grow wax cold (Matt. 24:12). The only thing they care about for a senior did they leave them as a beneficiary. As mentioned earlier, back in 2018, U.S. Citizens paid over 30 billion dollars in bouncing check fees and overdrafts, and late fees. These figures rise up and down, so they will never know the exact amount. I wonder how many of them were seniors that didn't know what they were doing? Companies charge a small fee for electrical and gas bills that are late. Pennies make dollars.

AARP states that older Americans lose roughly $3 billion to fraud each year.

Ushers

So you feel the pastor is essential, and I do agree? However, one of the other most critical positions in the church is the usher **because you will meet the usher before you ever reach the pastor, and that's if you reach him at all.** And if there are thousands of members, you may never meet the pastor one to one. And sometimes, you have no idea why your membership is declining. Who do you have at the front door? If they don't go through an extreme etiquette program to meet and greet a person, you will run into a problem and more than likely will not get any return visitors. There was a survey by barna.com that stated 2 out of 5 people go to church. **Proverbs-18:19 -A brother offended is [harder to be won] than a strong city, and contentions are as the bars of a palace.**

Some feel they don't need a class for that and want to do it the way they've been doing it for the past 30 years, and unfortunately, they will get 30-year-old results. I have met some nasty and mean ushers and couldn't wait to get out of that particular church. My spirit was killed before the service started. Of course, I can hear someone say, "Well, you shouldn't worry about that; you are coming to hear from the Lord." That might be true, but I don't think the Lord wouldn't want the devil to greet me at the door. Who knows, had I listened to the Lord first, I would have never stepped a foot in that church. The first person you meet holds a lot of weight in any business. Whether you're a secretary, bartender, manager, cashier, salesperson, usher, waiter or any other service business, these people can either make or break your business.

Church Ideas

Ecclesiastes 9:10
Whatever your hand finds to do, do *it* with your might; for *there is* no work or device or knowledge or wisdom in the grave where you are going.

There are ideas I'm sure that you may have never thought of, but remember, the church must be in order as much as possible. God gave man the wisdom to create the internet and technology, and if it is appropriately used, the church will benefit from keeping track of the needs of the people. Whether the church wants to use it or not, it is here to stay. I bet a person can pull up your church on the internet, can't they? People are looking for excuses not to go to church. Let's give them love and reasons they'd want to come. Many homes are spiritually divided, meaning there can be 5 or 6 adults in the same house, and 3 of them may go to different churches or not at all. Why? There used to be a time when the whole family attended the same church. What makes your church better than another person's church?

1. Someone should make a call a week to the seniors just to see how they are doing? Not just seniors only, but anyone who is a member. For example, if you have 500 hundred members,

there should be 50 people who make ten calls each to them. Of course, the member has to agree to opt-in to this service. Anything can happen to a person in a day.

2. Get one of their children as a witness to the senior's bank account to understand what they are paying monthly. Companies are ripping them off every day. I recall a story about a lady spending about an extra $15 a month to the telephone company for about 15 years that she didn't know about. When it was found out, they only returned her money for half of the time for about seven years. Why not all of it? Some foolishness about the statute of limitations. Had someone known and checking her account, they would have caught it. This type of service should be for everyone.

I received a call from a rip-off telephone company, and as I was talking to the salesperson, they stopped and asked me could they put me on HOLD. I said yes. Later, they asked a few more questions like a survey, thanked you, and hung up. For a couple of months, I kept seeing the word HOLD on my phone bill, and when I questioned it, the operator said that HOLD was the name of the company and charging me $4.95 a month. How slick was that, and of course, I said take it off? I wasn't a senior during that time, but con-artists will get anyone they can.

3. Helping seniors know what benefits they can get and find out what kind of insurances they have would be very helpful if they become deceased.

Of course, a family member needs to be a witness because they will say you are taking advantage of them. However, if the senior is sitting there with a sound mind, this will not be so. Some elderly don't want to leave their families anything because they were not there to help when needed, so they may want to leave it to the church. Ironically some leave some large funds of money to their pets, forget about the family. Leaving wealth to a pet or leaving them $1.00 is a slap in the face.

4. **Special Note**: Children's Insurance may only cost $15 to $20 a month. Children do pass away, as well.

5. Some seniors need rides. Who helps them? I recall a particular church that had a carpool after service that was willing to take a person home, and you didn't have to be a senior. They would hold up a sign in the lobby of the cross streets they were near, and if you were going that way, you would get a ride.

6. What about the Medical-Alert chains that seniors or disable wear in case of an emergency at home? Who knows, there may a discount if you get a large amount of them to join. What if the church paid for it out of a particular fund.

7. If a senior lives alone, you could have a person stop by once a week for a minute to see if their house is intact. In the bible, they had all things in common. There is so much for individuals to do in the church when set up correctly. Most of the time, you either sings in the choir, usher, or just a bench member. Be more than a bench

member; use your gift, be part of something, even if you have to ask the pastor if you can start it yourself. Your gift is worth more than a dollar. They always want to put the help they need on the senior's children's family. However, their children may not attend your church or care for your type of service.

8. The following from Redteam.com - Despite good health, good finances, so many people die a few years into retirement. Many retirees suddenly find themselves with no friends, no money, and no purpose. You'll have a tough time getting up in the morning if those three things are absent. And again, no matter how old you are, be planning the next 25 years.

There are approximately 10,000 people who turn 65 every day, and amazingly about 4,900 die every day. Who's counting?

What about "Sen/Yo Day?" Where a senior and a young person go to lunch once a month. Or bring lunch to them and sit for a little while.

Also, I don't think that God didn't mean that some can retire to sit around and do nothing. Some are still energetic and will get more out of life if they volunteer or help a cause. I heard that many that retire die soon because they have nothing to do.

It's hard to do nothing and too tired to do something! SMG

It's like a car; if it was not getting used, it will sit, rust, and not be suitable for anyone. I have so many stories I can tell, but I will share this one. Many leaders sometimes have speakers come in regarding special occasions that may be regarding something financial. This leader may also get a monetary percentage of the member's donation. However, in this situation, I will never forget. I attended a trendy church and a visiting minister who was also a businessman who spoke regarding foreclosures and how he could help people. I thought it was quite admirable and interesting, although many times, the help was to get a person out of debt or satisfy their credit. I decided I wanted to go work with the company, even though I had a real estate license. I went to the first meeting in his small office. There were probably about seven people there interested in working. However, when you got there, the minister's whole personality changed, and this is what he said. "If yall here and trying to have compassion on people, this is not the place. I'm trying to make some damn money."

Of course, my eyes flew open. After his little shocking speech, he went down the hallway to get some papers out of another room for everyone to sign up. By the time he returned, I had tipped out of the office and never returned. That is the kind of crap people deal with within the church and sometimes don't know it. I wanted to go back and tell the pastor, but I didn't know him very well, and he could have been working with him; I have no idea. Perhaps I could have mailed an anonymous letter telling him that a wolf came in sheep clothing.
9. Theatre night- Get a giant movie screen and turn your sanctuary into a theatre.

10. .Junior Duty- An adult counsels a child or teenager about their future, encouraging in what they would like to be and see what steps they are taking once a week.

11. Take 20 to 30 minutes during morning service to educate people on insurance, wills, finance, health, diabetes, etc. Employment, unemployment benefits, special sales, government grants, brief information about how stocks work, and what happens with foreclosures? These are things that have to do with everyday life that the congregation has to face. Now is the time to attract them to the stuff of life. Letting them know that you are not just interested in their offering but there well being. The Educational Hour. Making the best of people's time. When leaders learn about the stock, why don't they t teach their congregation? It's like an inside luxury, and next, you hear about donations for the pastor's anniversary. If members are trained to earn as well, they would probably be more eager to give. You would think that if the pastor is making money, he would want his members to make some money as well. Wouldn't it cause them to give more to the church? Pastors always want you to come to another meeting when some of this. You already have a captive audience. **(Ecclesiastes 2:26 To the man who is pleasing in His sight, He gives wisdom and knowledge and joy, but to the sinner, He assigns the task of gathering and**

accumulating that which he will hand over to one who pleases God).

3 John 2 - Beloved, I pray that you may prosper in all things and be in health, just as your soul prospers.

12. Prepare an anonymous survey, ask members about particular views and what they want or how they feel regarding a specific plan or situation. After all, they have so many other church choices. The list ranges from the selection of music, which has changed because of the director. If you have many members saying the same thing in any area, know that you have a problem which is like a seed and can grow into a tree, which will cause the loss of members.

13. Why not start at the beginning of the bible and give 15 minutes of the bible study during Sunday morning service and give them a chapter or two to read for the next Sunday. This part has nothing to do with the morning message. What is the purpose of Sunday School when some of the education could be taught during morning service? After two hours of service, what did you learn? Nothing strenuous. For those who want to come to bible study during the week to skip around to other chapters, let them do so. Members have been in your church for 20 and 30 years and have never gone through the whole bible. However, if they did, they just might be shocked at how you're handling things and stop giving.

14. Church Suggestion - BOX…(Companies have these all the time, or they will send you a survey after you have talked to one of their representatives). Although this is repeated, this is very, very important. As leaders, we set up our groups or congregations on how we feel or what we saw other churches do. However, you would not believe what type of people are sitting in your congregation. You will know what they think or what their profession is. You may have some millionaires there; however, if you do, perhaps, you should think about it twice before trying to suck up to them. Trust me; they know who is sincere. First, take time on a Sunday morning and pass out a suggestion sheet, asking them what do they feel would make their church better (That's all).

Put card suggestions in a group and make sure you go through every one of them and see what they are thinking. You can go as far as giving visitors a call and asking them what they enjoyed about the service or what they least enjoyed. Anything you can correct quickly, and it is possible to do, perhaps you can do that first and then work on the other suggestions if desirable to do so. After the first launch, you can just leave the box at the front entrance.

Or you can give a gift to new visitors that fill out the cards. They can fill out their personal information, and another is an anonymous card on how they felt about the service. Sometimes beware of those who give large sums of money and their sincerity if they are on one accord to help the ministry properly and not run the church. Who knows they may pay for the church because they feel the love?

I recall reading about a large company that hired a consulting firm and paid them $25,000. The company that hired them still wasn't satisfied with the results. However, a suggestion came that they should have asked the workers; after all, they are the ones doing the work.

The director thought about it and questioned each employee, and also had a suggestion box. Sometimes people have ideas and thoughts and won't tell them in person, so the suggestion box is excellent. After reading the cards, the owner found things or understood things that the consulting firm didn't. He used the suggestions, and his business doubled.

What personally happened to me about 25 years ago was I had gone to Capstone Mortgage School in Marietta, Georgia. One day I was trying to make my classwork easier regarding mortgages. Kathy, the owner, looked over my shoulder and asked me what I was doing because I had all of the extra lines on my paper, and I showed her how I was making my work easier. She thought it was fascinating during that time, and she recreated the form. After I finished school, I came back and worked just for a little while, and Kathy had a class in session while I was working in the office. She came to my desk and told me to go with her and that she wanted the class to meet me to let them know that I was the one that created the additional information on the worksheets that made the work easier. I'm saying that you never know who is sitting in front of you to make your job easier. Suggestion boxes make people feel comfortable in their comments.

I recall a story where there was an office full of employees. One particular employee sat in his chair and stared out of the window most of the time while all the other employees were at work. The employees began to complain about him doing nothing but staring. The boss stopped them all and said, "The last time he opened his mouth, he had an idea that made us over a million dollars, so leave him alone. *END*.

My point is that you never know who can give you a better way of looking at something.

A wise man seeks wise counsel. (Proverbs 12:15) There is nothing new under the sun, but you won't know what's under the sun if you don't ask.

I know that churches take up time to acknowledge visitors. Years ago, I often wonder, when thousands of people gathered together, did they acknowledge the visitors or had testimony service? Can you imagine how much time that would have taken? Also, the sky's acoustics must have been phenomenal because there weren't any sound systems when people spoke, only the use of some horns made from a ram or kudu. These horns were called Shofars.

15. Business Sunday - How many members own a business that belongs to your church? A church may have 500 to 15,000 members or more, and I know that many own a business in that crowd, but our congregation doesn't know it, nor does the pastor. How much more would it increase the finances of your church if they supported each other? Create your church business discount card if necessary.

The plan would be that all those who own a business of any sort meet after service. In this meeting, you would have forms stating the member's name and their type of business. Plan on them submitting a picture of themselves with the company. An up to date photo of them is crucial.

Tell them on a particular <u>Sunday; you will put an advertisement for their business in the back of the program along with their picture.</u> You will also announce their name and the type of business that you will pray for them as a whole to bless their business. Better yet, they can come upfront and allow them to do 60 seconds about their business.

If it's a lot of owners, you can do so many per Sunday until you've reached them all at least one time, but still, print all of the businesses. This introduction can be once a year, starting the first Sunday of the New Year or every six months. You will put this ad in the bulletin free for the first time. Each Sunday after that, you can charge a small fee ranging from $5 to $25, depending on what you decide. The decision could be to charge one price for all adds to keep the size equal or charge more for larger adds. Your bulletin is like a magazine, so treat it like one. Why not feature members on the front cover? They already know who the pastor is. If the pastor owned a business, I'm sure the whole congregation would know what it is because he would ask them to support it.

I think all the ads to be the same size to make everyone feel equal, but the choice is yours. For example, you have 25 business owners paying $10 per Sunday, which's $250 per week, and that's $1000 per month or $12,000 a year to help print and inform the church's ministry.

Owe no man anything, but to love one another: for he that loves another has fulfilled the law. **Roman 13.8**

The rich rules over the poor and the borrower is a servant to the lender (Prov. 22:7). Also, talk about usury as the bible does, referring to all of these loan sharks, etc. After that message, someone teaches about credit and how much you're paying, and how much they make if you're late. There are approximately 15 billion dollars made a year on overdraft fees, late fees from credit cards, mortgages, and more. Teach them that they can pay off their mortgage in half the time. However, many churches want you to come out on a Wednesday meeting and talk about this, but why? They are sitting in front of you now. They spent time and money to come and learn, and now you want them to come out again? It's unnecessary. Make your members wise, and they will appreciate you.

16. Have a nutritionist talk on Sunday morning. Diabetes, heart attacks are running rapidly all over the world due to non-education about them. Healthy members make active members.

17. Who helps the people with voting ballots or any kind of contract? The language on them is ridiculous and usually does not benefit the consumer if they sign. You need lawyers to look over contracts or a suggested company that helps with everyday problems. Any legal aid?

18. Are there lawyers that volunteer their services, and of course, they will eventually get paid in some cases? Should a person plead guilty for a lesser charge even if they didn't commit the crime?

19. What about having a church fast, but this one you eat, oppose the other ones when you don't eat. Eat plant-based foods for 21 days and watch the energy of your congregation by not eating meat. Watch on Netflix- What the Health and Forks Over Knives to give you a kick start. That video could be your morning service. I was a Vegan for only eight months, but I did feel a difference.

20. Have each member write their vision for what they desire in life and to make it plain and post it somewhere in their home that they may be

reminded. What about praying and anointing picture frames that they will put their vision in and post it on the wall?

Habakkuk 2:2 "Write the vision and make it plain upon tablets that he may run that reads it. For the vision is yet for an appointed time, but at the end it shall speak and not lie. Though it tarry, wait for it, because it will surely come; it will not tarry.

We must realize that all of our ideas and great visions come from God, and he began the work in us and will finish it. Philippians 1:6

Jeremiah 29:11 For I know the thoughts that I think toward you says the LORD, thoughts of peace, and not of evil, to give you an expected end.

Where there is no vision, the people perish: but he that keeps the law, happy is he. Proverbs 29:18

"Don't create a perishable congregation."

Helen Keller, who was blind, became a great American author, and one of her famous sayings was: "The only thing worse than being blind is to have sight and no vision."

Chapter 5:
Why Your Members Are Frustrated

Here's an excerpt from my book Buck Naked. Referring to stripping ourselves buck naked and becoming who we really are, if we can get past all of the foolishness and burdens that have been given to us. Look at the obligations we are bombarded with daily.

Regarding holidays? It costs money and time to prepare for New Years', Valentine's Day, St. Patrick's Day, Easter, Mother's Day, Father's Day, 4th of July, Memorial Day, Labor Day, Halloween, Thanksgiving, and Christmas. Add to that list the birthdays, funerals, weddings, baby showers, flowers and get well cards for hospital visits, retirement parties, school graduations, special uniforms for school activities, conferences and workshops, store sales - buying designer clothing from people you'll never meet and who will not come to your rescue when your lights get turned off. Electric bill, gas bill, cable bill. God forbid that you have unruly children and in a bad relationship. Did I mention the use of cigarettes, drugs, and alcohol that rob our brains, whether we take a little or use a lot? A friend told me that he smokes two packs a day, and it's $7 a pack, which makes $14 a day to equal $434 a month x 12 months = $5,208 just on cigarettes to help kill you. How do you measure poison? Whether we use a little or a lot, it is all poisoning our brains. The bible speaks of constant wars and rumors of wars to come as well. Oh, you go to church too?

Adding to our stress levels are long lines in banks, long lines in supermarkets, long lines in gas stations, long lines in hospitals, long lines in social security offices, long lines in restaurants, traffic backed up on freeways, drive-by shootings, cheap bosses, employees dipping into our business, illnesses, medicines (especially worrying about the side effects), accidents, murders, crooked tax laws, rapes, wars, junk mail and the constant negative news on television. With cable television costing about $1,000 a year, you have 300 channels and often can't find anything decent to watch. There are also cell phone problems as they put out a new version every year that keeps you nervous because you have your whole life on it, as radiation runs through us all day long. God forbids technology crashes, and there are digital TV problems, as well as four or five remotes that you don't understand. Then you decide to get TIVO, and it doesn't work correctly. All of this, and then comes the COVID!

If you attend church, there is Sunday school, Sunday service, mid-week service, usher board meetings, deacon board meetings, church anniversaries, pastor's anniversaries, choir's anniversaries, pastor's aid, women's day, men's day, revivals, banquets, visiting other churches with the pastor and the church business meetings where arguments arise. Plus, Uncle Sam and his crooked tax laws in which there are thousands of laws within the tax itself. Payroll/income taxes, Property tax, Sales tax, Estate, and Gift tax. Who can keep up?

All of these things cost money, and you work to pay for them. The vacation was not mentioned anywhere on that list. There's nothing worse than going on a vacation, enjoying yourself, and returning to worry about how you are going to pay for it because you've "maxed out" your charge card. **WHEW! And they come to church to be beaten down and manipulated? You have a tube of dynamite sitting in front of you, waiting to explode, and then, unfortunately, they eventually die with no joy.**

Not being negative with the list, but it's time you face the facts. Is there any real-time to do what Jesus asks us to do? It looks like it's hard to fit him into our schedule. What happened to us visiting the sick, homeless, widows and those in jail? There is something wrong with this picture because the world has addicted us to foolishness. That's why when we do any one of the above, we have to tell everyone because it's a rarity and we're shocked we did it ourselves. However, there was a good feeling after we did it.

Matthew 24:1-14- 1 Jesus left the temple and was walking away when his disciples came up to him to call his attention to its buildings. **2**"Do you see all these things?" he asked. "Truly I tell you, not one stone here will be left on another; everyone will be thrown down."

3As Jesus was sitting on the Mount of Olives, the disciples came to him privately. "Tell us," they said, "when will this happen, and what will be the sign of your coming and of the end of the age?"

4Jesus answered: "Watch out that no one deceives you. **5**For many will come in my name, claiming, 'I am the Messiah,' and will deceive many

You will hear of wars and rumors of wars but see to it that you are not alarmed. Such things must happen, but the end is still to come. **7**Nation will rise against nation, and kingdom against kingdom. There will be famines and earthquakes in various places. **8**All these are the beginning of birth pains.

9"Then you will be handed over to be persecuted and put to death, and you will be hated by all nations because of me. **10At that time, many will turn away from the faith and will betray and hate each other**, **11**and many false prophets will appear and deceive many people. **12**Because of the increase of wickedness, the love of most will grow cold, **13**but the one who stands firm to the end will be saved. **14**And this gospel of the kingdom will be preached in the whole world as a testimony to all nations, and then the end will come.

We always hear of wars on the news, and soon the United States will face what some of the other countries have faced already for years. We already deal with our many street gangs arising, not to mention being fearful of police officers, not knowing if they feel trigger happy, or just wanting to intimidate a person. Not to mention all of the diseases in the world that is caused by pharmaceuticals and other causes. Our minds are always racing. After all of this and then we die, blessed be the name of the Lord!

Also, let us keep in mind that we want to be healed, but be healed to do what? Is it to just sit around and do nothing? If so, what good was the healing?

How many rare diseases are there?

- There are nearly 7,000 rare diseases. More than 25 million Americans have one rare disease. It may involve chronic illness, disability, and often premature death. Usually have no treatment or not a very effective treatment and frequently not diagnosed correctly.

Ecclesiastes 9:5
[5] For the living know that they will die;
But the dead know nothing,
And they have no more reward,
For the memory of them is forgotten.
[6] Also, their love, their hatred, and their envy have now perished;
Nevermore will they have a share
In anything done under the sun.
[7] Go, eat your bread with joy,
And drink your wine with a merry heart;
For God has already accepted your works.
[8] Let your garments always be white,
And let your head lack no oil.

Just think, if you were terminally ill for one year, you would not think about any of the things listed above. However, you are not sick and unable to pull away for a year to better yourself in a career. Why not? Because you've been indoctrinated into the world of chaos, and the government wants you to fill out a census form to make sure you're involved in the mess they've created. The Census is curious about where you're living now, so they may target chaos. Look at healthcare. Do you think the government cares about you and your illness that, more than likely, they caused?

Just to throw this in, what about the number of lawsuits going on to keep your mind going? Television is loaded down with lawyer commercials hunting down businesses acting as they care. Still, it's all about the money and a push of their pen, knowing that the lawyers will get the most money when it is all ended.   Welcome to the world of chaos!

Recap of Sunday Ideas

Once again, ways to get a person to return to your church?

1. Length of service- How long is this service? The larger part of it is just fluff. Unless the real anointing comes in, you should make your service in a shorter period, and you will be surprised at how it grows. 3 hrs of what?

2. Courtesy of ushers- What is their real attitude? They can cause you to lose members or visitors.
3. Seating- Fill up the front first. Let the latecomers sit in the back.
4. Sound system- Can they hear clearly. Make your system loud enough to listen clearly to what is being preached and avoid making people stay at home because they can't understand anyway. Some churches have the speakers just in the front, in which they should be all around.
5. Help Departments such as;
    ➤ Youth
    ➤ Housing
    ➤ Real Estate
    ➤ Employment
    ➤ Health
    ➤ Business classes
6. Weekly follow up of members and how they are doing. In the business world, salespeople have made much more money because of follow-up and care.
7. Music- The music should be both for the young and old. This new contemporary music doesn't move anyone but the choir itself, but what about the elderly and middle age? I always marvel when I go to a church that has become contemporary, and they pull out one of those old gospel songs, and the church gets motivated. Music has moved the elderly out, and they were the ones that financed the church initially.

8. The appearance of dress- regardless of how a person feels is alarming. I've noticed that many of the praise teams have a terrible look for their choice of clothing. People are focused on what they wear and not listening to what they sing. Sorry, but they all need to go back to robes. Robes have a glorious feeling, and it should be captured. Man looks at the outward appearance, so don't give him a reason to frown at something that doesn't look decent. People may look cute to themselves, but not to others.

9. Offering/ Obligations- How many of these do you have? For some reason, offerings bring down the church's anointing because of how some of them beg so hard. Some people come with an offering in mind, not knowing there will be a second or third offering, and the last one is called a Sacrificial Offering. As far as some people are concerned, the first offering was already a sacrifice for them to give. They were nibbling at their pockets. Now Corinthians 9:6-7 is thrown in; God loves a cheerful giver for guilt.

10. Are your sermons constantly beating them down? Where is the hope?

11. Cleanliness of church/ upkeep/restrooms

12. Parking. Is there someone to monitor parking

13. Why Sunday School? How about 15 minutes during the morning service. Those who want it in depth can go to Sunday School or Bible study. However, every Sunday morning service is a bible study. People are just tired.

How can you have 15,000 members and only 400 show up for bible study mid-week? Did the other 14,600 receive a revelation that the 400 didn't? Everyone should purchase the same bible, and you can tell them which page to turn to. By the time some find the name of the chapter, many will have finished reading the scripture. People know numbers. You can also have custom bibles made with added information about your church. I know that many use their phones, or scriptures can be put on the monitors. Some churches have all the words of the songs the choir is singing on the monitors. Sometimes you don't know what the choir is singing, and it also helps to sing along.

14. Drama department. Preparing 10 -15 min every Sunday

15. Dance dept. Praise dancers can also usher the choirs in if they march in—a beautiful site.

16. Church Bulletin- advertising members' businesses.

17. Welcome, Home Sunday- How many members have stopped coming to your church for whatever reason. Mail out letters or postcards in which you will get discounts for bulk mail. Stating that you are planning a great Sunday for them, and they will receive a gift as a token of love. There are all kinds of incentive programs and novelties that are a penny on a dollar. You can also make an email site that they will opt-in stating that they will come and their unique gift is

waiting for them. Of course, you don't pass out the gifts until after service. More than likely, their offering will be worth more than the gift you chose. There are incentive packages online. Don't you think they need an incentive? How many incentives have the world sold you on things that weren't worth it?

Also, plan a spectacular day without a lot of begging of offerings, but get to the point of service of why they are there, and they will automatically give. Sure, you may want to do extraordinary things that will take a little extra time, but it's all how you do it unless a high anointing is present try not to keep them more than an hour to an hour and a half. Realize these people love God, but they still want to get home to the home God gave them.

18. Why not have a mass choir day, and they march in like they use to. That was very beautiful. Those who can't march, allow them to sit in the choir stand in advance or stand to the side in the choir stand, and when their section comes, they automatically slide in.

19. You can also have a particular survey to fill out, stating what they like about the service on that day and what they didn't like. Nothing lengthy, and they can again turn in their survey to receive their gift. If the sheet were anonymous, they would tell you how they really felt, mostly if it was something negative, even though you didn't want to

hear it. Once again, one bad apple can spoil the whole bunch. What this person see at your church, maybe 50 others that saw it and didn't return.

20. I went to a Catholic Church once to visit, and I could not believe all of the things they did in an hour with a 25 to a 30-minute sermon, and it was communion day. They had three songs, one offering, one sermon, a few announcements, and communion. Wow! Nobody is rushing God here, but there is a valid point to be made, that people value their time. Can you imagine how many business people with high salaries and ideas you have lost because you're dragging out service with announcements or trying to brainwash people in the name of Jesus? Or trying to make people have what we call church? Some millionaires love God too. It's like having a 45-minute commercial before they get to the real reason why people come to church. People pay extra on their television and radio to delete commercials. I'm not saying that certain things aren't necessary, because if you don't tell them, how will they know?

   a. Just for my curiosity, I also went to another Catholic Church, and they didn't take an offering. I am not a Catholic, but I was on a mission to see what other denominations were doing and why some of them are so successful to a certain degree. However, before you entered this particular church, there was a wall with many slots and envelopes where people put their offerings before they entered in the sanctuary. The church was enormous. Jesus loves a cheerful giver. Usually, when offerings are called, a lot of people's facial appearance drop because they wonder what unique way this offering will be held to get more money. You go to church long enough you will know some of the games.

21. Get a real estate person or an investor who will talk to your congregation about paying for their house even for seven years. However, all real estate agents don't know how to do this.

22. Serving breakfast or dinner at church. You can sell breakfast if you like, but a good thing to do is ask those who want breakfast to pay in advance for the following week. That way, you will have an idea of how much to make with a little extra. If possible, you should pay the cooks. And for the record requires good personalities. "A bad personality can make good food taste bad."

23. Have a speaker come on Sunday morning who will explain the benefits of having Medicare or Medical. More than likely, the pastor will have a special meeting for the seniors to come out another day. Is he going to make calls? The church should be a source of information.

24. In the same way, also he took the cup after supper, saying, "This cup is the new covenant in my blood. **Do this, as often as you drink it, in remembrance of me**. 1Corinthians 11:25
Are they aware that they can have communion every day? **It says as often as you can do this,** not necessarily just the first Sunday. The way it looks, we only remember Jesus once a month, while the rest of the month, we remember ourselves. We should have an altar in our homes and have a communion set. Many of the Buddist build Gohonzon for their belief and chant.

Genesis 12:7
The Lord appeared to Abram and said, "To your descendants, I will give this land." So he built an altar there to the Lord who had appeared to him.

25. Why not purchase inexpensive communion sets and sell them to the congregation that they may have communion every day and also have it on the first Sunday if they choose.
26. Security. How is the security at your church? Are their armed servicemen that make members feel secure? Security is not just for the leaders. Things have changed, and we need more than prayer. Having no security is like you live in your private home, but you

leave the front door open all night and pray that no one will walk in. Trust no one but God. Times have changed.

27. Church badges. Why shouldn't every member have a name badge? Big business conventions do.

Chapter 6
Funerals and Weddings

Before I get into this section, I have found that funerals and weddings are the most expensive things in the church, and they are the most boring. Half the time, you want to sleep. May I repeat, they are the most boring events I have ever seen when they should be the most exciting events. The first thing people look for in a funeral is how the deceased look, who took it hard, and what kind of food for the repast, and can they get an obituary, and hopefully it's nice?

I must add that the average cost of an excellent obituary with card stock may run you anywhere from one to two dollars, depending on the number of pages. It is essential to have a nice one—all of the frills they put for a funeral and a not so good obituary. Funeral homes tend to soak up most of the money playing on compassion and the basic to classic. Funerals usually are a couple of songs, a sermonette, and a few words from friends, and yet this event may cost $10,000 or more or less.

Just think of all the creative things you can do from the dance, choir, praise, artist painting while the choir is singing, and so much more that you can present creatively. I guess I think this because I'm an artist, and I see the value in time and creativity. I never understood these four hours or more funerals, but I thought maybe God was in the casket. No offense, but people usually sit there out of respect, and they wanted to leave within two hours—the same as a wedding. What people anticipate in a wedding is how the bride looks, the cake, and the food. A couple of songs, they march down the aisle, vows, and an expensive dinner that the meat was cooked two days ago and just heated, but no creativity at all with still a high cost. I'm a playwright, and I can create either presentation at the drop of a hat, and it's only a gift given to me. That is the reason why weddings and funerals are nothing but a stage production. There's a plot, a stage, props, and there's a performance. You can't hire a funeral director or church committee to do your wedding if you want something custom and creative. Wedding planners are useful. However, some end up costing you a lot of money because they have to buy your creativity. After all, they don't necessarily have a great idea themselves.

Hire a play director or someone in the arts and watch the style; you'd be amazed because these people are artists. The only ones who are super excited at either of these events are getting paid for a repeated performance each time they can do blindfold. Often, there's money paid for the programs, the funeral itself, the minister, and a few other things. Why not have a choir there that will sing and not always for free if it can be afforded. What if you gave each choir member $25, and if it were 30 members, it would equal about $750. Trust me, they can afford it, but doing this sounds new to them. When have you heard someone leave a funeral saying it was fantastic?

You should look online at individual hidden funeral costs. I'm sure they showed you the deluxe package, making you feel guilty, but what did you do for the person while they were alive. Do you see the little petty things the funeral home will charge you? For example, a leak-proof coffin. Are you going back to dig someone up? It should be leak-proof any way, and they charge for services at different times of the day.

Sometimes I think most funerals should be held in the evening so that everyone can attend. Can you imagine if you took the funeral's total cost, how much people lost from taking off work, and for those who bought something new to wear? Look how much money was saved during COVID and how the handling of funerals. They were on the internet, or many did not travel due to the disease's capacity restriction or fear.

For much as spent on a funeral, it should be one of the most spectacular events. However, we spend the money on the casket and in the funeral home. Churches spend very little on just having a joyous service unless it's some sort of dignitary. Everyone is important, and if nothing more, they are the dignitary of their family, if not the community.

Ecclesiastes 7:1   A good name is better than fine perfume, and the day of death is better than the day of birth.

It's amazing how people have spent years in the church and can't get a decent funeral. But going back to my list of ideas, the church would have known what the person had before they were deceased. I went to a funeral, and this person had spent many years in the church and didn't have a decent flower arrangement. There was only one small flower arrangement by the casket, and there was a bouquet on the coffin itself. Perhaps the church thought the family had it figured out. However, if the bereavement department would have helped and gone over details, they would have known. Or let's give them the benefit of the doubt that the family didn't want any flowers and wanted the money donated to a cause. Who talked to the family and asked them did they have everything they needed? Better yet, what did they prepare for the services? I guess if we didn't think it was ashamed, we would each write out our complete service, and hopefully, someone would add to it and make it a little more elaborate at our funeral. Pre-need insurance everyone needs. Many people hate to talk about funeral arrangements before or after, but we all will leave here someday. The only person that won't be worried about arrangements is the one in the casket, previously hoping a responsible person fulfilled their arrangements. Some people do write out their service, but very few do. Another high cost can be the repast or serving food after the service. Is this for a select group or the entire church? This can be very expensive and time-consuming as well. I know this would shock you, but why not have a dinner that people buy tickets in advance? This can come along with entertainment. *(Think outside the box, it's much more space to be free).*

When we are born, we have nothing to show for our works, but when we pass away, others are left with a memory of the things we have done, whether good or bad. It reminds me of that favorite poem called The Dash. This relates to the dash between the time you were born and the time you were deceased. What type of life did the dash represent? It doesn't say specifically in the bible that we should mourn when they are born and rejoice when they pass away. This expression comes from the Buddhists.

Back to my topic, I never understood how the pianist got paid in the church, but the choir members didn't get anything, not even breakfast, especially at these large churches. The choir members have to come to church like the pianist and director, and on top of that, they ask the choir members to pay for their robes. Some churches ask choir members for monthly or weekly dues. Believe it or not, some of these dues add up, and the choir is assessed so much for the pastor's anniversary the money is given to him instead. Who is appreciated around here? I'm not sure. Why give it all to the funeral home? Get a different casket. I'm just thinking ahead of how some money is not used wisely.

Funerals

It's all understandable when death happens in the family or to a member of the church. Many times they come to the church for guidance or financial help. Much of this can be done early only if we'd do it. As said many times, it's better to have it and not need it than to need it and not have it. Perhaps one Sunday, you should have someone speak on these needs and what can occur if you don't have insurance, and if you don't, maybe cremation is the way.

I went to a seminar, and it stated that 75% of people are getting cremated these days. If that is true, watch how cremated prices start going up. Be careful that all the money is not spent on a funeral. Often, because a person is not thinking, they buy the most elaborate things and spend money on something that may not be necessary. Later, to find out that they are broke and still owe a bill. If you want to see the change of attitude in people and problems, you should have a funeral or a wedding.

Things will come up that you would never have thought. **I wondered how they have offerings for everything else, but they won't take one at a funeral or a wedding**. You never know what's going on in the family, and it's not to announce what they don't have or even if they do have. It's just a special blessing offering and leave it like that, and there's no need for a long announcement of why, because it will become a tradition. It's like it has become a tradition to pin money on the bride at the reception when you dance with her. It should be natural—just one of my unusual thoughts. Now let's talk about funerals.

1. First, to have sample copies of a will and see to it that each member has one. In some cases, people do not tell a person if they are a beneficiary to keep other thoughts or problems occurring.

    The wickedness of some families is that some feel they deserve something when a person is deceased. Of course, it is said that some people are worth more dead than alive, and the family wants a piece of the rock. So some people don't tell who the beneficiary is. Trust me, some people's families have had them murdered for the money.

2. You can also have a sample sheet of funeral arrangements of what type of service they would like and who to do what. This will save so much time. Someone who is over the funeral may not be thinking and nor will they have family support should they expire. These ideas can be mapped out from colors, songs, and other desires. This type of form can be renewed once a year if a person changes their mind about their service. Go over it on a Sunday morning and ask them to bring it back the next Sunday. As you see, I'm always for Sunday morning information because that's when most of the people are there.

3. Making sure that members have some type of small insurance or explain to them what happens and what burden they would put on the family if they don't? Can the church pay insurance for a member? Some burial insurance may be only $40 a month for some. The church can be the beneficiary; however, this member puts $100 a month in church. It sounds strange, but many people don't think about it even if they can afford it. Many people would not be able to retire if the government didn't take the money out first. Some races have become wealthy because they had good insurance policies on their loved ones, while others took that same money and spent it on lavish living and drugs.

Weddings

We know that this can be a special day for any bride or groom. However, it can be a nightmare if not done right, arranging from misunderstandings to a large bill full of payments after the wedding is over. If you have to charge a wedding, you don't need anything elaborate, but it can be just as creative and beautiful if you have a smart coordinator.

One of the most massive divorce problems is financial, and who needs to start one with a financial bill that you're still paying for a wedding you had four years ago if it last that long. Helping the bride and groom understand that marriage is a serious business and needs to be counseled individually and as a couple. I heard a psychiatrist had specific ways he used to counsel a couple that is getting married. He would ask each to give three reasons why they would get a divorce. After they wrote down or verbally answered the three reasons, and regardless of the reasons, he would say, "You're not ready to get married." Of course, they would say why, and he would say, "There shouldn't be a reason you should get a divorce; this is for better or worse." People should calm down regardless of all the responsibilities that are involved. Don't get the hype of what they see of the wedding on television or in books. People spend thousands on marriages and divorces a year. I'm not trying to make it scary, but I'm just trying not to sugar coat anything. For example, it was said, and I don't know the truth, but Joan Rivers spent more than 3 million dollars on her daughter Melissa's wedding, and she and her husband filed for divorce 2 ½ years later and had one son.

Run a list down the responsibility of marriage. Although the comparison is strange, I heard that you should get a dog if you want to test out to see if you're marriage material. If you can groom him, walk him, take him to the vet and feed him on time, you might be a candidate for marriage and children. I use to think of marriage was like living with your parents, but you're having sex, and it's worse if you do not have it at all. Other than that, all of the rules and questions are the same, such as "I've got to beat her home, Where have you been? Where are you going? Who is that? And yes, you still love your parents.

Contrary to what others believe, I feel marriages should be like a driver's license—renewed every four years. Can you imagine how much money the state would make, and of course, the lawyers would be quite angry because they wouldn't have too much to file, nor will they make as much money. It's over!

My Personal Pet Peeves

I know we are not living in a perfect world, and this is also understandable, and many times we pick up habits of other services and members, and I am not exempt; however, there are a few things that have disturbed me about the church.

1. Saying turn to your neighbor and say_____.
   Sometimes, it is redundant that I want to take my neighbor sitting next to me outdoors and talk.
2. Go to two or three people, shake their hand and welcome them and say_____. This is a nice gesture; however, after the right word of wisdom or anointed song, the service is paused to do this, which breaks up the service's flow. It's like eating a good dinner and the phone rings, and you have to stop and answer it. People often pick and choose whose hand they would like to shake and crossing over others,

leaving others feeling left out. After church, they would barely speak to them, and if you're waiting on a bus, they will pass you by, and some might even wave.

3. Churches that record video will allow the videographer to put the camera right in your face while you are praising God. We are human beings, and we tend to hold back on things when there's a camera in our face, let alone knowing we are videoed. Some people don't like pictures. Do you have celebrities at church? They may not want to be on video.

4. Service has started, and ushers are continually bringing people down to the front, trying to find them a seat. Very annoying. Fill up the front seats, and the latecomers sit in the back.

5. Some ushers stand in the middle isles, just waiting and looking for someone who needs help or a tissue. However, they are blocking the view of seeing the speaker. We can sit in a movie theatre for two hours straight and don't need an usher.

6. The sound system is not clear at all and sometimes too loud and other times too low. Speakers should be in the front and the back of the church. A beautiful church and a terrible sound system? That tells you where the importance was. Perhaps if people knew what you were saying, they'd probably invite someone else to hear it too. Speakers should be all around, not just in front.

Who is checking this stuff? Why have a large congregation in front of you, and they don't understand what you're saying? Very annoying.

P.S. Speaking of beautiful churches, something came to my mind. There's nothing wrong with a gorgeous church on the outside, but having the sanctuary plain is a good idea. Sometimes because of the chandeliers and beauty, people are so busy admiring them that they take their minds off the reason they are there. Go ahead and say, many years ago, the synagogues in the bible were beautiful; however, the difference was they took care of the people and their needs. Atmospheres change personalities the same as clothing. You feel different in a pair of jeans than in a suit. Such as I mentioned earlier about everyone wearing robes and being all on one accord. It's hard enough to live this life; who needs little distractions because it doesn't take much to correct it?

Chapter 7
How Much Does Going to Church Cost You?

I know we've been trained that we are going to church to serve the Lord, which he serves us big time in reality. We are told that going to church shows reverence, and this we should do every Sunday or even every day. Sometimes I get the feeling that serving the Lord can get very expensive the way it is done today, and some of us are still looking for a return on our investment, but we are also told not to give grudgingly as they put such harsh demands on us. I'm going to show analysis, and it's not for everyone, but just to give you an idea of what a person is spending, and I'm sure some are spending much more, and perhaps some are spending less. Let's use one family with two children. Put yours on a spreadsheet and look at it.

Husband, wife, a boy and a girl.

Cost of dressing each: I am not talking about designer clothing; it's even worse. This is spending for one week. (Did you save money during the pandemic for not going?) (What did you miss?)

Wife: $125 dress and accessories
Husband: $300 suit and accessories
Boy: $100
Girl: $100

Totaling $625 for that Sunday. Of course, these prices will vary with different families; some may only spend a total of $200 to 400 depending on how frugal they are in their spending. Are we talking about weekly or monthly? You choose. Approximately 6 hours total to get dressed.

It will take each 1 to 1 ½ hour to get dressed. Wouldn't it be nice to get paid for that hour and a half? Let's be modest and say you lived 25 miles away and gas cost $4.00 per gallon, and you get 25 miles per gallon, and your round trip would be $8.00 a Sunday. Next is your offering, and you and your family go to Sunday School. The total offering is $12, that's $5 each for Dad and Mom and $1 for each of the children.

Now let's consider the offering for 11 am Sunday. Some churches have a Benevolent offering before the primary offering; the approximate total the family gives is $6. Then there's the primary offering. Let's suppose they are tithers by choice, and both parents worked 40 hours each at $15 per hour totaling $1,200 per week, tithe equaling $120 for both, and they give the children $3 each equaling $6. We are not adding in the building fund offering, church anniversary, or pastor's anniversary, nor coming back for an evening program or the revival this week. None are wearing designer clothing. So, let's look at the numbers in chronological order. Of course, these prices vary.

Wife Clothing	$125
Husband/ Suit	$300
Boy's clothing	$100
Girl's clothing	$100
Gas	$8
Sunday School	$12
Benevolent Offering	$6
Tithe	$120
Children offering	$6
Totaling	**$777 (A magic number)**

Spend all that money for one Sunday to get fussed at because of what someone thinks you're not doing. Oh, I forgot, did you want to eat to take the family to dinner too? Mmmm, now I see why there's no out of town vacations because it's on the clothing rack and other church responsibilities. This just to make you think. Thank God, at least the pastor can go on vacation.

Try it one Sunday and add up everything that you are spending, and you will be surprised. Going to church can be pretty expensive, which is one reason why people don't believe in the Bougie Jesus. It's not that people always want a handout, but it's how the church has been built for years that make people come Sunday morning and frustrated by Sunday evening with all the obligations, etc.

They don't have time to build their homes because of the guilt of not going to church.

In the south, many churches have services only on the 1st and 3rd Sunday or the 2nd and 4th, which I thought was very interesting, giving family relaxation and freedom.

However, some pastors have two churches in many cases, which would equal fours week for them. I am aware that everything cost, but where and how we channel our monies is so important. Money is like a seed, and we want to plant it in good seed for a return. When people plant money in your church, what is the return?

After you have spent that much, what did the church give you? AARP at least gives you 10% discounts for about $16 a year. Does your church have a discount card?

Sunday is the most prejudiced day of the week because the church gangs have their "set" in which they are involved and go-to for the many denominations. I'm not Jewish or Jehovah's Witness, but I think church services should be held on Saturday, and you will have a beautiful Sunday off or close the church one Sunday a month and have internet service. Perhaps have church just one Saturday for tryouts and see how it works for you. They will be so relaxed for work on Monday. I am just throwing things out there. People are getting tired, and there will always be many live streaming services where people will become addicted to them. The future has a way of molding us into things we never thought about. Look how Uber has taken over taxis, Amazon has taken over retail stores, Apple/Spotify has taken over the music industry. Netflix/YouTube has taken over schools, micro-waves have taken over stoves, you can have your own online business or YouTube Channel, and you don't think the internet will not take over the churchgoers? Don't fool yourself. Many will be surprised at how much money and time they will save by not going. Churches need to be more concerned, which will not happen for some because they will love the interaction of live human beings; however, you have will to be doing something great to keep them coming. Before the Coronavirus, I saw a poster that showed a kid could go to school from first grade to the twelfth grade online. Whether people want to accept it or not, the computer age is taking over.

Some preachers have services in the south on the first and third Sunday, and others have second and fourth Sunday; it all depends. I'm sure something will click. If many leaders had counted up the cost of the edifice they have built, they wouldn't burden members to pay for it even though I understand that something has to be built or rented to hold them. It is a waste of the land-only holding service in a 5 million dollar building only on Sunday or Wednesday night prayer meeting. What' else can that space be used or rented for? God's Temple? Yea, right, Jesus turned over the tables at the temple, for they had made it a swap meet (Matthew 21:12). What if the sanctuary, dining hall, or life center would allow so many homeless to lay in there a couple of nights? Uh Oh! I've gone too far.

The city shelters allow some to spend a night or two and give them a cot. Indeed the church should do the same. I'm sure you would need a clean-up crew after they left. Only allowing them to bring what's on their back and a small bag for clean up; otherwise, you will find them bringing in lots of items, leaving them and you trying to find a place to discard them. Something I'm sure could work out. While they are there, you could find out what skills some of them have. If there would be a total disaster in the city such as 9/11, I guarantee you would not be thinking about who came in for shelter. The other situation would be if the government knew you were doing this; they may require certain things to be there and a specific type of insurance. Yes, it can be expensive, I'm sure. Look at those cities that have weather disasters, and they have to find shelter. Ask them how did they handle it? While they are in there, give them a sandwich, quick service, and mini-concert. Indeed one or two nights of the week can be done. Just another thought!!!!

Jesus entered the temple courts and drove out all who were buying and selling there. He overturned the tables of the money-changers and the benches of those selling doves. Today there are all types of sales, prayer lines, anniversaries, and any other sophisticated name you would like to call it. Of course, in the bible, people were required to sell their goods and bring them to the prophet, but what was the reason then? They were to spread things out evenly to those who didn't have them. I have stayed in a shelter myself for about three months; however, thank God I had a private room but a community bathroom. This organization was not from a church.

You can testify all day and tell the church how financially blessed you are, but they are coming for your money and not necessarily in love when you do. Instead of just giving or willing, little subtle things are being said to coerce you into giving. What was so funny about this incident I was sitting there, and my sister was beside me. As soon as the lady said it, I hunched my sister and said, watch this, and the following happened. A lady testifying and said that she and her husband had just paid off their house and free from any bills. Immediately after she had spoken, the pastor said, now she has more money to put in the kingdom.

Often, leaders use very high power testimonials to draw more people or convince them to give large offerings. It's a commercial, but we call it testimonials. God has never been ignorant of what is going on.

Everyone is not poor; however, they have struggled and sacrificed to get what they have and wish not to be swindled out of their money, not knowing what's happening. As said when people have achieved a lot: "You may see my glory, but you don't know my story." And in the same token, they are thanking God that they don't look like what they've been through, which could be more than you imagined. We can show an unwise Christian something about giving, and they will give every dime they have, and when the person is in need, all they are offered is prayer. People are sitting in the congregation all dressed up and may have $5 in their pocket. Anything could have happened to them, but we don't know because we don't call members and understand their situation. They could have faced a foreclosure system where the church could have stepped in and owned the house or helped them stay in it. Just because a person has lost everything or in a bad situation, they are not necessarily going to throw away the clothes they have bought previously, but are still looking good. People lose jobs every day, and things happen as well as people are being blessed tremendously financially.

Look at this. What if tithing was compared to what you were doing or volunteering? Example:
You were paid,
$15 hour times 8 hours a day = $12 X 4 week
$480   total

Tithes @10% of $480   = $48.00
You would have to work approximately 3 hours 15 to make $48.00 for tithes if that's your choice.

Hypothetically if you volunteered and helped someone freely for 3 hours and 15, you have tithed.

You could be volunteering working in the church restaurant or car wash, and they didn't have to pay you. But as you know that most churches don't own anything. Because of the stinginess of the mind, some people wouldn't volunteer or give anyway. God knows your heart, and all that matters if it's a good heart.

The following was a story that I was inspired to write.

He Knows Me
A short story by Stewart Marshall Gulley

Once upon a little time, there was a small town that lived a little boy. There was nothing about this little boy that stood out. Quiet, but he did look at you as though he was looking clean through you with his piercing eyes, but that was it. By the way, the little boy's name was Daniel. Well, like any other five-year-old, Daniel loved to run and play but very wise. He miraculously had the mind of a 60-year-old person.

But still, that was not unusual because older people always would babysit him, and as you know, most older adults love to talk. Now you must understand that although Daniel was only five years old, his reading and comprehension level was that of a 21-year-old. There was nothing unusual about that because his mother was a school teacher, and at the time of his birth, she was only 31 years old.

This one particular day, Daniel and his mother were in the basement emptying boxes. Many of the boxes had several books. So Daniel happened to stumble upon the Bible. Although he was very brilliant, Daniel had never been introduced to the Bible because his parents never took him to church. One of the reasons they didn't take him to church because their parents never took them to church either.

The closest they've gotten to church was when a big-time motivational speaker came in town discussing positive thinking, and he happened to mention God here and there, or it was a funeral or wedding, and that was about all the church they were going to get. Anyway, his mother saw him take the bible and placed it by the steps going up from the basement, but she said nothing about it. About an hour later, Daniel and his mother finished, and they went back upstairs, and Daniel picked up the bible on his way up.

As time would permit, Daniel would read that old dusty little Bible. He became so fascinated and thrilled when he learned that someone in the Bible had the same name as his, and this man ended up in the Lion's Den, and his God shut the lion's mouth that they would not eat him. Little Daniel said to himself, "Now that's what kind of God I want, he'll shut a lion's mouth for me." Oh, what an exciting story he thought that was.

Months went by, and Daniel's expression became a little peculiar. His behavior had gotten so strange that his mother asked his opinion on certain adult matters. And she would often catch herself, saying, "Why am I asking a five-year-old questions like this?" What was stranger than her asking the questions was the sound answers that seemed sensible that Daniel gave her. The school Daniel attended was only two short blocks away, and he would sometimes walk alone because he was so mature. Just before he would reach his school, he'd always past a convalescent home that was very large.

One afternoon after school was over, Daniel passed the convalescent home, and he stopped and peeked in the window. A little man about 85 years old saw him looking, and with a slight smile, the man waved at Daniel. Daniel returned the smile and the wave, and then he walked away. As he was walking, there was like a tiny voice in his head that told him to turn around, and so that's just what he did, and he went into the convalescent home. He walked to the front desk, and he asked if he could go to room 108.

He wanted that particular number because it was the number on the door he saw of the little man that waved to him. The nurse looked at him and said that he could not go in unless accompanied by an adult.

Daniel held his head down, and then he held it back up and said, "I read that God gives me anything I want, and I am asking God to let me see the man in room 108."

The nurse looked at him again and began to smile, and she said, "Young man, we usually don't do this, but you seem to be a brilliant little fella, and I'm going to go with you to room 108 for just a couple of minutes since it's that important to you." Daniel smiled and thanked her. The nurse walked him to the room, and the old man had one of the biggest smiles on him that the nurse has ever seen.

He beckoned Daniel to come to him with much conversation. Daniel had found out that the man he had been talking to for the last few minutes was his grandfather. You see, Daniel's mother had put her father in a convalescent home many years ago, but she did not visit him, and Daniel had no idea he was down the street. His mother wanted to keep her father close by, so the father got the care he needed, even though she did not visit him.

Daniel was a happy boy because he knew where his grandfather was and didn't have to wonder where he was every time the conversation came up. Being intelligent as he was, he explained to the nurse everything about his family. The nurse checked the records and found out that Daniel knew what he was talking about concerning his grandfather and who his guardian was. Daniel hugged his grandfather and told him that he would make it his duty to stop by the window every day and tell him hello. Of course, in times to come, Daniel made his way in and saw him, but Daniel kept it to himself and never told his parents what he found out.

One Tuesday morning, Daniel's mother noticed him carrying an extra coat in his backpack. Although it was an older coat, it was in good condition. That afternoon Daniel came home without the coat, and his mother said nothing, but she had a very solemn look on her face. She almost wanted to ask the question, "Honey did God move in this house?" She just kept the thought to herself. Daniel's mother usually would pack his lunch for school the night before.

Early one morning, around 1:30 am, to be exact, Daniel sneaked into the kitchen and made an extra sandwich, and he also packed a little extra bottle of orange juice. The slight unwrapping of the cheese awakened his mother, and she quietly tipped to the kitchen door, and she saw Daniel carefully tipping across the floor, being extra careful, trying not to make any noise.

His mother eased away with a puzzled look on her face, and she went back to bed, remembering Daniel talking about a little girl at school who never brought lunch. She wondered was he making a sandwich for her because he was definitely up to something. Finally, she went to sleep.

Time went by, and Daniel's father had a best friend named John. John had a son whose name was

Larry. Larry was only 16 years old, but he seemed to have been a troublemaker. He caused his parents all sorts of problems until, eventually, Larry ended up in juvenile detention. This detention home was like a real prison, but it was strictly for hard to handle juveniles. Larry's parents practically had given up on him because they knew nothing else they could do; they were tired. They didn't believe in corporal punishment, but Daniel remembered reading in the bible that you will spoil the child if you spare the rod. Strangely enough, Daniel had never gotten spanked because he hadn't done anything wrong yet, and if he did, he hadn't gotten caught.

Larry's parents had given him the best clothes, best DVDs, best bikes, and he was soon working on having the best of a small sports car should he graduate from school. Larry had gotten picked up for shoplifting about the tenth time, and the courts had had enough. One day Daniel asked his mother if she'd take him to see Larry.

She thought it was strange because Daniel only heard about Larry and didn't know him. Anyway, without question, his mother made arrangements for them to see Larry. Slowly walking through a small door came Larry to see Daniel and his mother. Larry had a bizarre look on his face because he wasn't sure who they were because he had only seen them once some time ago when Daniel was only a baby.

Daniel's mother explained who they were, and Larry said, "O.K., I got you, so you came to see the bad seed, huh?" Daniel's mother laughed, but Daniel remarked, "The bad seed? Then a seed has to be sowed, and after a while, you reap, so Larry, you have reaped what you have sown," said Daniel in a serious, calm voice. Daniel's mother's eyes opened wide because she never could get used to the point of what might come out of his mouth. Daniel and his mother ended up talking to Larry for an hour, and had you heard the conversation; you thought you were listening to three old adults.

They soon left, and Daniel's mother could not drive home fast enough to get on the phone to tell her friends the wisdom of her little Daniel. Little did she know that her little Daniel became fascinated with the Bible and had been reading it in the wee hours of the night ever since he found it in the basement as God was continuing giving him revelation and knowledge as he read.

The next evening Daniel and his mother and father were in a discussion at the dinner table, and it just so happen to be about God. His mother and father began to argue about who God was. His mother said, "I am God, and I was made in His image, and I have faith, and I don't have to go to any church and constantly hear all the God stories." Daniel couldn't take it anymore, and he yelled out, "Well, what do you think an image is a mother? Daniel continued to talk, "It's a likeness, I am an image of my Daddy, but I'm not my Daddy, because

I'm sure if you were 100% God, you would not be doing some of the things you do."

At that moment, there was silence, and his mother slowly held her head back up, and his father stared him straight in the eye and said, "What has gotten into you," he yelled, and Daniel looked his father in the eye and said, "God doesn't know you." His mother's eyes froze in focus, and his Dad stood straight up and slowly bent over to Daniel's face, and he grabbed him by the collar. Daniel looked as though he was choking as his father's nose was touching him, and sweat began to pop instantly from his father's head, and then his father said, "What did you say, boy?"

Although Daniel's father was much larger than he was, Daniel stood up slowly while gasping for air, and Daniel said, "No weapon formed against me shall prosper." Now, this would have been a good time for an earthquake, but Daniel's mother immediately jumped in and pulled her husband away and said to Daniel, "What do you mean God doesn't know us?" Daniel said, "Hold on," and he ran and got the Bible. His mother and father glanced at each other, and they both looked back at Daniel.

Daniel hurried back, and like a grown person, he licked his index finger and began to flip the pages in the Bible. He went straight to Matthew 25:42, and he began to read: For I was hungry, and you gave Me no food, I was thirsty, and you gave Me no drink; I was a stranger, and you did not take Me in, I was naked, and you did not clothe Me; I was sick and in prison, and you did not visit Me. Then they also will answer Him, saying, "Lord, when did we see you hungry or thirsty or a stranger or naked or sick or in prison and did not minister to You?" Then He will answer them, saying, "Assuredly I say to you since you did not do it to one of the least of these, you did not do it to Me.

Daniel paused for a moment, and then he said, "Mother and father, I love you, but that's why I said that God doesn't know you because I've not seen you do none of these for anyone. I've been trying to do things on my own. That's why I took the lunch, took the coat and gave it away and went to the juvenile prison to see Larry and I want to tell you something else, but I need to keep it a secret" He was referring to seeing his grandfather. Both of Daniel's parents became speechless as he slowly walked away with his head down.

Later that evening, Daniel went to his little desk and pulled out his favorite pen, and he tore one page out of his notebook, and he remembered a poem he had read that sound like what he has just gone through. He decided to copy the poem word for word, and this is what he wrote.

"It's All About God"
by Stewart Marshall Gulley

Have I done all I could?
Some things I won't and some things I should
I shake my head when I see those in need,
Some I can help, but all I can't feed,

Who will share my deepest sorrow?
God needs food, like a sandwich tomorrow
Sometimes God is in the hospital, and He starts
looking pale
I must go and visit Him because he doesn't feel
well
Sometimes God gets homeless, and he lives by
the boat
I know he gets cold, so I'll give him my coat
Sometimes God gets thirsty and can't go.
I will take this bottle; he likes orange juice
you know
And if God goes to prison, and no matter what he
did
I'll still come and visit, although I'm a kid
Whatever is in my power, and no matter how I
feel
I have to make sure that my God knows me and
that's for real
Regardless of our situation and sometimes things
get very hard
But it's not all about you; it's really all about
God

Faith is Not Always Easy

We have to step out on faith in our ministries.
"Anything that is not of faith is sin" (Rom. 14:23).
When I came across that scripture, it shocked me
because it was a form of sin other than the Ten
Commandments, plus others. [8] If we claim to be

without sin, we deceive ourselves and the truth is not in us. 1John 1:8

As said, without faith, it is impossible to please God. As far as I am concerned, without faith, it is impossible to please yourself as well. What have we been taught all of these years regarding what's in us? Using our gifts and talents should have been instilled in us. Romans 8:30, Moreover whom he did predestinate, them he also called: and whom He called, them He also justified: and whom He justified, them he also glorified. 2 Timothy 1:6-8: Therefore, I remind you to stir up the gift of God, which is in you through the laying on of my hands. For God has not given us a spirit of fear, but of power and love and a sound mind.

Understand that the devil goes to church too to discourage you. Where else will he go to find people who are looking for a better life?

Now there was a day when the sons of God came to present themselves before the LORD, and Satan also came among them. Job 1:6

There were signs of our gifts as a toddler, but our parents thought it was just something cute that we did, not knowing that the talent should have been nurtured. Who started that men should wear blue and women wear pink or Men can't cook, and women shouldn't try to build. There's a man in every woman and a woman in every man. And it took both male and female to make either one. You are who you are, and God has chosen what he has put in you. You have men that act feminine and women that act masculine, but it doesn't matter because male and female are in them both. One of them is more prominent. We don't know how this happens, but I focus on a person's gift that God has given them. As far as I'm concerned, we are all kin if we go by the story of Adam and Eve. They started this whole story, and when the man got a hold of it, everything changed. People spend their entire life seeking power and giving out rules.

If you think this book is something, try the whole Bible. It is the grace of God that has opened our eyes and given us the power to do His will. I don't think the bible is always such a loving book, such as today, people fought and killed all through the bible. I do like listening to the dramatized version of the bible on YouTube. It almost sounds like you are there. The Bible's danger is that very few know what's in it, and those who know still have questions unanswered. Many people have watched churchgoers and have seen a difference in them not doing what they say, making a person numb to life. However, some have seen an absolute difference in a person when they have been converted by God, which they will see the evidence in their life and makes them say, "There is a God."

Although the Bible has its controversies, it is still written by men. In the same breath, it states: Let God be true and every man a liar. (Romans 3:4). There are so many gaps and spaces in the bible that people use their imagination of what they think happened. Eat it like a fish dinner; you eat the meat and spit out the bones.

Many times, when scriptures are revealed that we've read, we feel funny initiating them because so few others are not. Once again, the harvest is great, but the laborers are few. There's always a space waiting to be filled with an excuse.

The ministry can be a dog-eat-dog world. It can be worse than the fight for who will be the next president of the United States. And the battle can be all in the name of Jesus regardless of who gets scarred. People fight over positions, and each rub each other's back. The real work is never done because of so much rubbing and kissing up to people, because of who they are. And if you are poor, the very ones you have lifted just might drag you to court. (James 2:6)

I haven't figured it out yet as to how that can happen. There are so many gifts that God has distributed, and many are sitting right there in the church already; the leaders are not aware because they are too busy trying to be the star of the show, not understanding that wise leaders use wise people.

Think of how many top record producers there are, and they use the artist to the max, yet the producer makes more than the artist. Once again, the producer makes more than the singer, but ultimately the singer is the star. Leaders are trying to be stars, and they haven't gotten the picture yet.

You are a leader, but you are also a producer, and the stars are in the audience.

The ministry can be a close-knit world. You can have pastors calling pastors to run revivals because they believe that they owe them. You know the system: you scratch my back, and I'll scratch yours. How many members do you have, so I will see if it's worth my coming?

You can have evangelists who are pastors, knowing they don't have the close love of a pastor; they just fell into the position because their fathers left them their churches. Every time you turn around, the pastor is out of town preaching somewhere else. I heard of a pastor being in the ministry for about two years, and the next thing I knew, she was stepping down and having a retirement program from the ministry. They hadn't been in anything long enough to retire. The scenarios can go on and on.

Whatever your position is in the church, do it wholeheartedly or get out of it. No one is making you stay. God may want you somewhere else, and you're there mumbling. Why are you miserable where you are? Should you be somewhere else. God is about peace, even though un-peaceful things happen. There are more positions outside of the church than for those fighting for positions in the church. Politics are in church as well.

If we are ever honest with ourselves and get in the right position, things will work out a little better.

I wrote a book called *"Stay In Your Lane for the Entrepreneur."* God knows who you are and is waiting for you to start or move over to your rightful place. Why do you think your spirit is so restless? Until we do what we are called to do, we will not be pleased. There's always a challenge. Why not let it be in what you love to do, and that's a job to have. Many members leave church miserable because they are only doing what the leaders tell them, but their heart is somewhere else seeking true happiness.

God has called me into several gifts. I thought I was losing my mind. One day, I consulted God about myself, and he told me that I was very wise but that I didn't know everything. He also said that not everyone would listen to the information that I would be giving. I asked him why that was, and he politely told me, "Now you see how I feel."

There were other times when my empathy would kick in, and I would see someone whose body had been damaged or afflicted, and it was like I could feel the pain in my legs. Once again, "Now you see how I feel."

I decided not to watch television for a month. And as far as television is concerned, I've only watched about 2 hours of news collectively in the last 35 years or so. Perhaps planted in my heart the scripture from Titus 3:2 saying, "Speak evil of no one." That's all the news does. The only thing I watched was on YouTube, and they were meditation-videos, cooking, How To's, and some

Netflix. However, during this month, I was only to listen to videos that had meditation music and not any affirmations. All I wanted was the instrumental music and to hear myself thinking and only my voice. What's so funny about listening to God quietly is that his voice sounds like yours. I was continually writing notes of things that were coming to me or what I needed to do in life. The funny thing about it after the 30 days was up. I had six full pages of notes. I then told God that He had given me a lot to do. He consulted back and said, "No, you are just that far behind." The message I got was that we have more time to do things than we think, but we're not doing them; we are only thinking about doing them, which makes us tired. As said, some people are so far behind that they think they are first!

Later on, I got a revelation about my not knowing everything and relaxed. God reveals things as needed. He will allow you to go through stuff for your learning. Whether you liked it or not, have you ever disliked a teacher? But they taught you the things you did not know, and you didn't appreciate it until you got older, the same as our parents.

You never know the trials and things you will go through when God is training you. If you asked God to help you and teach you, see that he chooses the lesson. Many years ago, after living in California, I had moved to Mississippi, which was almost a nightmare. I had never seen so many uncaring and selfish people, but I kept things to myself.

I went through trial after trial, and God finally gave me a revelation. He knew I had to be trained well, so he sent me to a place that could do it. It's just like coming out of medical school; you have to do your internship somewhere. What better place could it be than in the hospital in the worst place in the city with the most traumas?

That way, you can experience some of everything. Now I thank God for the "internship" in this city; I've learned that each trial and place has a reason and serves a purpose. "And we know that all things work together for good to them that love God, to them who are called according to his purpose" (Rom. 8:28).

I once got so fed up with a church that I told God I would never join another one, and if he weren't going to be my pastor, I just wouldn't have one! It sounds like I was pretty mad, huh? I stayed out for over ten years or more, not realizing God was training me hands-on. I have to admit that I felt so free without any church obligations.

It has to be approximately 35 years from the calling, and boy, has my brain been tired. God had to allow me to go through many things so that I would have something to say. Many people would say that I was running, but what they didn't know was that God was giving me something to run with, and when I kept seeing the foolishness in the church in all denominations, I then said, "This is it." I've learned to address a cause and figure out how to solve it if a person would listen. (Ecclesiastes 9:13-16). Wisdom is better than strength.

It is so amazing that from the beginning of the call, He told me that suits and ties would not be my wardrobe, nor would there be many to call on me to speak because of what I knew. After that beginning message and revelation from God, I just kept on doing good, working with children, and using the gifts God gave me. I was not to push speaking engagement or any such thing. God told me that he'd do it.

"And when God does it, he does all things well!" (Mark 7:37). Although there are many other gifts in the body of Christ, such as the ministry of help, I have found the five-fold ministry to be quite significant. When they are in order, they will help guide all of the other gifts God has placed in the church. You can pull a church congregation together the hard way or the easy way. You choose!

I later got a revelation of the things God taught me. How was I going to teach churches if I stayed out of them? I slowly returned, but it's not like I had before when there was pressure to go or feeling damned if I didn't show up. Unfortunately, many of the mature and elderly have stopped going because they thought there was nothing there for them anymore. Look at most churches; still, a faithful few are going. Did "Church Gentrification" happen?

<u>Concerning Spiritual Gifts</u>

1 Corinthians 12:1-31

1. Now, about the gifts of the Spirit, brothers, and sisters, I do not want you to be uninformed.

2. You know that when you were pagans, somehow or other, you were influenced and led astray to mute idols.

3. Therefore, I want you to know that no one who is speaking by the Spirit of God says, "Jesus be cursed," and no one can say, "Jesus is Lord," except by the Holy Spirit.

4. There are different kinds of gifts, but the same Spirit distributes them.

5. There are different kinds of service, but the same Lord.

6. There are different kinds of working, but it is the same God at work in all of them and everyone.

7. Now, to each one, the manifestation of the Spirit is given for the common good.

8. To one, there is given through the Spirit a message of wisdom, to another a message of knowledge using the same Spirit,

9. To another faith by the same Spirit, to another gift of healing by that same Spirit,

10. To another miraculous power, to another prophecy, to another distinguishing between spirits, to another speaking in different kinds of tongues, and to still another the interpretation of tongues.

11. All these are the work of the same Spirit, and he distributes them to each one, just as he determines.

Unity and Diversity in the Body

12. Just as a body, though one, has many parts, but all its many parts form one body, so it is with Christ.

13. For we were all baptized by one Spirit to form one body—whether Jews or Gentiles, slave or free—and we were all given the one Spirit to drink.

14. Even so, the body is not made up of one part but of many.

15. Now, if the foot should say, "Because I am not a hand, I do not belong to the body," it would not for that reason stop being part of the body.

16 And if the ear should say, "Because I am not an eye, I do not belong to the body," it would not for that reason stop being part of the body.

17. If the whole body were an eye, where would the sense of hearing be? If the whole body were an ear, where would the sense of smell be?

18. But in fact, God has placed the parts in the body, every one of them, just as he wanted them to be.

19. If they were all one part, where would the body be?

20. As it is, there are many parts, but one body.

21. The eye cannot say to the hand, "I don't need you!" And the head cannot say to the feet, "I don't need you!"

22. On the contrary, those parts of the body that seem to be weaker are indispensable,

23. And the parts that we think are less honorable we treat with special honor. And the parts that are un-presentable are treated with special modesty,

24. While our presentable parts need no special treatment. But God has put the body together, giving greater honor to the parts that lacked it,

25. so that there should be no division in the body, but that its parts should have equal concern for each other.

26 If one part suffers, every part suffers with it; if one part is honored, every part rejoices with it.

27. Now you are the body of Christ, and each one of you is a part of it.

28. And God has placed in the church first of all apostles, second prophets, third teachers, then miracles, then gifts of healing, those who help others, the gift of leadership, and different kinds of tongues.

29. Are all apostles? Are all prophets? Are all teachers? Do all work miracles?

30. Do all have gifts of healing? Do all speak in tongues? Do all interpret?

31. Now eagerly desire the greater gifts. And yet I will show you the most excellent way.

No one likes order today at all; everyone has their way. It started at age 21, but now its toddlers and teenagers tell the parents what they will and will not do. Because society says children are little adults, and they feel they rule—such a sad mistake. As sure as we live, however, there is an order to everything, and we are all under someone's authority. The authority can be (1) spiritual, which is God; (2) domestic, which has to do with the rules and regulations within your household; (3) governmental, which causes us to obey the laws of the land—or else be fined or jailed.

All of it reflects God because he ordains it all. "Let every soul be subject unto higher powers, for there is no power but of God, the powers that be are ordained of God. Whosoever, therefore, resists the power, resists the ordinance of God: and they that resist shall receive to themselves damnation" (Rom. 13:1). What if you have a corrupt government? Or perhaps the bible was written by the government to control people knowing they would not be able to fulfill the rules to make money. So many crooked laws and signs you don't understand, such as parking. Making you think? Huh

Where there is unity, there is strength. Not real unity is the biggest problem in the church, which consequently starts with the name of the denomination. Satan has divided the minds mentally, and it's hard to pull them together on one accord. The chief desire of the apostolic church of today should be the following;

They Had Everything in Common

Now the full number of those who believed were of one heart and soul, and no one said that any of the things that belonged to him was his own, but they had everything in common. Acts 4:32

What do you or your church have that the others don't? The world has its corporate discounts and so forth, and what does the church have? More than likely, nothing but prayer lines and offerings. If it weren't for welfare, people would be messed up.

I believe that churches should take the apostles doctrine at its word and start all over again. Of course, with all of these now liberated people, there would only be a few trying it and hoping others will adapt. Of course, people will call it a cult. What it says, do; just try it. If they take chapter by chapter of the church-conduct books—such as Corinthians, Ephesians, Titus, and Acts—what does a person have to lose but his or her mind?

"Let this mind be in you, which was also in Christ Jesus" (Phil. 2:5). So, maybe we should lose our minds and get the mind of Christ. So as he thinks in his heart, so is he. (Proverb 23:7) God knows if we are sincere in our trying. After all, it is He that has made us and not we ourselves. (Psalms 100:3). **Isaiah 43:7-** *Even* **every one that is called by my name: for I have created him for my glory; I have formed him; yea, I have made him.**

The church world knows too much about God to act the way they do, but we all like to run our mouths. We think we sound good to one another as we let each other know all the scriptures we've learned and how many members our church has, but the man outside the church is still looking for results and looking for a real reason to come back in.

1 Corinthians 13:2

[1]Though I speak with the tongues of men and angels and have not charity, I have become *as* sounding brass or a tinkling cymbal. [2]And though I have *the gift of* prophecy, and understand all mysteries, and all knowledge; and though I have all faith so that I could remove mountains, and have not charity, I am nothing. [3]And though I bestow all my goods to feed *the poor*, and though I give my body to be burned, and have not charity, it profits me nothing. [4]Charity suffers long, *and* is kind; charity envies not; charity vaunts, not itself, is not puffed up, [5]Doth not behave itself unseemly, seeks not her own, is not easily provoked, thinks no evil.

When you are being taught how to love, it is very challenging. You will often have to bite your tongue and say nothing and allow God to handle the situation. Vengeance is mine, and I will repay, says the Lord. Romans 12:17

If it weren't for welfare, the Salvation Army, and shelters, many more people would be out in the streets. The sad thing about it, that many out there were once churchgoers. I do recall someone telling me about a city that doesn't have any homeless on the streets because they are taken care of by the churches and the welfare system. Nevertheless, where was the church when all of these things were going on or first started? I know many of us want to fuss about handouts, but the Bible stated that the poor would always be with us and who else would need a handout but them? Statistics indicate that the average person is two paychecks from poverty; therefore, there is still a space to give. Thanksgiving and Christmas, of course, is one good day, but what about the other 363? Once again, if it weren't for welfare, many people in the church would be starving as well.

I remember when God was giving me a test. He told me to take a roll of quarters, which was $10. Anytime someone would ask me for a quarter, I was to give it to them. I started looking for people to provide a quarter to, hoping someone would ask me. The key was that they had to "ask" me for the money. I was to do this for a whole month. It also helped me from turning my head or nose up at someone if they asked. Anyway, after a month, I had $6.00 left to spend for myself. That was shocking to me because it gave me peace of mind when they approached me. After all, I knew I was to provide them with a quarter. Now I just do it naturally. Although it was only $4 for the whole month, I think of how we will leave more than $4 for a waitress's tip. (You ever had a waitress tell you, "I know you're going to leave me a good tip?") lol. I have!

It makes me feel better now if I just go ahead and do it. I will say, "Who am I going to bless with a quarter today?" That way, it is quicker to give the quarter and hear a thank you than to shake my head no, knowing there is a quarter in my pocket. Sure, you would say, "All they are going to do with it is buy themselves a drink." We always judge. Even the drunks have to eat food sometimes.

If we start some people over again and give them the word of God, there should be a change. Remember the saying, "If you feed a man a fish dinner, he will only eat that day, but if you teach him how to fish, he will eat every day." Homeless people are still gifted, and besides feeding them, I think someone should ask what their gifts are and direct them to a source if they know of one. I remember back in the 80's I had a Skidrow Community Choir. I worked in Beverly Hills, but I would come down to Skidrow and rehearse at a church. And by the way, they could sing. I eventually stopped the choir due to other obligations, but it remains on my mind.

1 J o h n   3 : 1 7

"But whoso has this world's good, and sees his brother have a need and shuts up his bowels *of compassion* from him, how dwells the love of God in him?"

Can you imagine these next statistics? They will never get the exact number I'm sure. Take a look at the following. There are approximately 134,000 homeless in California. I'm sure this number is shocking, and there will be some statistical reports that will break these numbers down and says something else. Who's sitting back and counting? However, it started with a few somewhere in California, and who decided to turn their heads and let the numbers grow regardless of what it is? They saw it coming and did nothing. If you saw the true pictures of California, you might be afraid to come.

134, 000   Homeless
22,176   Churches
58 Counties in California.
(Rounded off numbers)

Let's only take 134,000 Homeless = 134,000
10% of the 22,176 Churches = 2,217

Now divide 2,217 into 134,000 = 60 homeless That's each church taking care of approximately 60 homeless each. Of course, this would be much less if 20% did it and each housed 30. People are always talking about the 20/80 rule.

This task would be building housing units, and if you understood real estate, you would get as many units as you could, which will build equity. You would also get government assistance, section 8, food stamps, and church assistance to nurture homeless people to find their gifts and needs and not make them lazy, such as those who are not homeless and lazy. Indeed, there are some mental cases involved, but the government will assist in that as well. Hopefully, they will, I should say, because during President Ronald Reagan's reign, they shut down the mental hospitals in 1981, and many became homeless. Some of this problem is the reason many homeless people are on the street today. In 1955 there were 560,000 mental patients in hospitals. Read the full report at "KQED.org," topic- Did the Emptying of Mental Hospitals Contribute to Homelessness?." Now you see why the harvest is great, but the laborers are few. The United States is much crueler than you think. Why should you have to vote for better housing, better schools, and healthcare? You would think the United States would want it. However, it's only united for a certain group of people. Today you see the negative results, and it's not over.

My close friends did not know about me because I learned first-hand what it was like to be homeless. I never told them, and when I saw them, I always had a smile on my face because I knew that what I was going through was temporary. I once had to live on skid row in Los Angeles for about three months. Prayer and faith brought me out. Another time I stayed in a shelter in Atlanta for about a week, and one more time, I slept in a church, eating just donuts in Pomona, CA. Everyone homeless does not want to be homeless. I was determined to make something of myself. Some people couldn't take my experiences and probably would instead commit suicide, especially if they asked for help and couldn't get it.

Just for the record, approximately there are 45,000 people a year commit suicide. Just think, had 450 churches been on the ball, each could have had an extra 100 members had they checked and ministered adequately and checked on them. "Who knows, 100 calls in time could have saved 100."

Everyone that has a need or needs prayer doesn't report to the church. If people were checking on a person and a person confiding in them, they would tell them what's going on. No, there are times that you can't help every situation yourself, but you may have a piece of information that you can lead them to other sources.

People always use the slogan "A closed mouth doesn't get fed," however, some have opened their mouths and become broken-hearted because of how the church or interviewer treated them. Now too embarrassed and hurt to say anything, so back to the streets they go to rest where they can. Who else can hurt you worse than the church and a friend?

SUICIDE
General Statistics (USA)

Suicide is the 10th leading cause of death in the US for all ages. (CDC)

Every day, approximately 123 Americans die by suicide. (CDC)

There is one death by suicide in the US every 12 minutes. (CDC)

Depression affects 20-25% of Americans ages 18+ in a given year. (CDC)

Suicide takes the lives of over 44,965 Americans every year. (CDC)

The highest suicide rates in the US are among Whites, American Indians, and Alaska Natives.

Only half of all Americans experiencing an episode of major depression receive treatment. (NAMI)

80% -90% of people that seek treatment for depression are treated successfully using therapy and medication. (TADS study)

An estimated quarter-million people each year become suicide survivors (AAS).

There is one suicide for every estimated 25 suicide attempts. (CDC)

There is one suicide for every estimated four suicide attempts in the elderly. (CDC)...Info from Save.org

So while we are shouting, praising God, dressing to impress, and manipulating huge offerings, there are people committing suicide due to the lack of love or help.

YOU HAVE TO START SOMEWHERE!!!!!

The church reminds me of the gym. If everyone who has **joined** the gym decided to go, you would not get in it. If everyone who had once gone to church would have stayed in it, just about all churches would have been full; however, people have become wise as well as frustrated. Dropping off an offering doesn't mean that you are getting spiritually helped; it's almost like the saying throwing your money down the drain.

Just because a church grows, it doesn't mean the members will stay there. Remember that bad weeds grow as well. It's just like living in the United States, where millions of people are not being fed properly or healthy due to all the chemicals they put in foods. Processed foods are destroying us, and the scientist knows it. People have been booted out or killed because they found cures for certain diseases. It's all about the money. The pharmacist has taken old home remedies, put fancy names on them, and charges a lot of money.

Everyone has their reason for leaving a church. Some people don't like large churches; however, they weren't there from the beginning when the church was small. You can't help that a church grows because people are continually looking for an answer, and they are hoping to find it in church. Whatever the reason may be, some churches do not grow. In the same token, the Lord knows how much you can bear. That reminds me of a little story where a homeless lady had lots of bags that she was slowly carrying. She got to the corner and was trying to cross the streets with them. A young muscular guy decided he would help her. He took many of the bags and crossed the streets as he still struggled. When he got to the other side, he dropped dead. The moral of the story is that the homeless lady was used to carrying that load, and he wasn't, even though he appeared to be strong and healthy. God knew how much he could bear.

Many so-called Christians today act like they are almost embarrassed that they know God. If we are ashamed of Jesus, he will be ashamed of us before the Father (Mark.8:38). Some are afraid to bow their heads in public to pray over their food. There's a trend being repeated that there is no rapture, no Jesus, and no hell. But as said, let every man be persuaded by his mind (Romans 14:5). Don't' get shocked!

The mind is the controlling center of the whole body. It's like a 16 wheeler truck. What goes on with the steering wheel (mind) will maneuver all of that truck directing it to a proper delivery or bad. The mind can think any and everything regardless of how vulgar. When you see dramatic, freaky and dangerous movies, realize that someone's mind is on film, and it will remain subconsciously in the viewer's mind. We can think of things that are horrible and wonder how could this be in our minds? Some think it and do it regardless of the outcome of who it hurts. As said:

2 Corinthians 10:5

"Casting down imaginations, and every high thing that exalts itself against the knowledge of God, and bringing into captivity every thought to the obedience of Christ;" As Paul says in the bible, knowing that we all struggle the same as he:

Romans 7:18-20

[18] I know that good itself does not dwell in me, that is, in my sinful nature. For I have the desire to do what is good, but I cannot carry it out.
[19] I do not do the good I want to do, but the evil I do not want to do—this I keep on doing. [20] Now, if I do what I do not want to do, it is no longer I who do it, but it is sin living in me that does it.

Is this like the church today? The things they should do, they do not do, but the things they shouldn't do, they do!

I heard a joke that a lot of people were told to accept Jesus. However, there was a group that was just thinking about it. The devil came and told them that they didn't have to believe in Jesus right now, but they have plenty of time! Don't fool yourself.

If you confess with your mouth, "Jesus is Lord," and believe in your heart that God raised Him from the dead, you will be saved. Do it now, in case you haven't.

I didn't want to get involved in the ministry because of what it represented, and all of the said negative things, and I didn't want to be labeled. The ministry seemed like a sophisticated gang collecting large sums of money, and may the best denomination win. I will never forget back in the '80s, and a young female bus driver was driving the bus. I knew her and I happened to get on her bus. The first thing she said was, "Hi Stewart. I heard you were called in the ministry that is so good because that's such a lucrative business." Strangely enough, she was not joking when she said it; I dropped my head and said to myself, "I wondered who told her about me, and she wasn't a churchgoer." She felt it was a profitable money-making business.

I recall the first message I spoke about 35 years ago entitled "Packing Up and Getting Ready to Go," taken from Matthew 24:40. What was so strange about it that no one knew it was my first message, nor did Pastor Eldoris Bonner, but she was just open like that. I happen to visit her church, A very inspiring and anointed lady. She and I were talking after service, and the discussion came up about me being a minister. She quickly said that she wanted me to preach next Sunday. Well, the daring and adventurous person I was, I said, "Sure." I didn't want to tell anyone that it was my first sermon because I didn't want anyone to start judging me and telling me how I did. As God would have it, I lit the church up, and it was an exciting noisy service if you know what I mean. I even recorded it. After service, I went home to hear myself on the tape. As soon as I stepped on my front step, God said to me, "You see, anybody can preach, but the problem is getting people to do the work." I was stunned. Not only that, when I played the tape, there was nothing on it. What a day! Unfortunately, many years had gone by, and Pastor Bonner passed away.

Many people are so embarrassed that they go to church and what it has represented, let alone the things their church does that they disagree with come Sunday morning. They won't tell anyone about their church or invite them to it because they don't want to be asked the question, "Why do you go here?" Furthermore, why do you come home every Sunday angry at what went on at church that day? And you wonder why the person you told won't go. People are beginning to wise up and sick of the games. I'll repeat it, "What is your church doing for you and vice versa? Once again, AARP will at least get you a discount on stuff, and it only costs about $16 a year. If the pastor had been pastoring 16 years, he'd ask for $16 or $160 for his anniversary. I'm not fussing, but I'm just letting you know some of the creative tactics.

You give your church probably over a hundred dollars a month, and what do you get besides another obligation of something they want you to fund. If you sincerely needed something, you'd have to go through a bunch of red tapes, and it's not that you go to church to get something material from it. Even if it was just information you needed. Everyone doesn't need something, but at least you know it's available, just like car insurance. You haven't had a wreck, but just in case you do, the insurance was available. What if the money you put in the church would have been invested like stock? You'd be a happy person and would be able to help others in need. Go ahead and say that your money was invested in Jesus. Did he need it? Uh, oh, I've just said too much. Ok, let's just say the church needed it for all of its expenses.

However, what you may need would have been known if each member had gotten a call once a week. Many would probably say they are fine, but just the fact you cared would make the real difference. However, the lazy church will automate everything because they don't want to hear it. I believe you can discern a user if you talk to them.

Back to speaking of prayer, I'll never forget the time when my wife was babysitting about four children. Their lunch had not been prepared yet, so my wife passed out a cracker to each. One of the little girls bowed her head and said her prayers over the one cracker. Another girl watched her and asked, "Why are you praying now? That's just a cracker?" It was so funny because of how it was said. Unfortunately, my wife, Deloris, passed away in 2005. The incident reminds me of a scripture that reads: "In everything give thanks for this is the will of Christ Jesus concerning you" (1 Thess. 5:18).

You know, people like statistics and numbers, but I heard that there were over 160 million Christians in the world. Now that's an astronomical figure for the Christians for the world to be so weak.

It's almost frightening. Men are so busy fussing about women in the ministry, had they stopped rubbing shoulders and do the work of the Lord, maybe it never would have happened if that's the way they think. I don't know; however, God will never leave us without a witness, whether it's male or female, and he is pouring out his Spirit on all. Many female pastors are rising, but we must remember they are still the weaker vessel, regardless of the position (1 Pet. 3:7), even though it refers to how husbands treat their wives. That's another topic because when a woman gets upset regardless of her position, everything changes. Many women do not get along with one another, even though women groups are continually rising. You will see the fury! Proverbs 21:19 - It is better to dwell in the wilderness than with a contentious and an angry woman.

This is not a message to bash women of any sort, it's just a fact, and very few do not fall in this line, only because they practice not to be of the norm. Many women groups are rising, and you know as well as I do that women only get along with each other for a while. There's always a Princess Anna that wants to see things her way and a Cruella de Vil that stirs up strife. Even though women are the majority in the churches, much would not get done if it weren't for them, so pastors cater to them. However, since so much is catered to women and the pastor makes a mistake and fails one, know that the word will get around, and the majority of them will leave that church, and they will talk about forgiveness later. It's almost like saying putting all your eggs in one basket. Men are not so quick to follow some pastors because some men see things quite differently.

Today, there is much talk about women being as equal as men, but when something happens, they want to fall back into the woman's weak mode and feel entitled to special treatment. Fair is fair, whether it is for the male or female.

Our television shows always have an angry woman who carries the plot, which develops many people's attitudes that continuously watch these shows. These types of personalities continue off the TV. As we know, when a woman comes on the scene, all of the rules change out of respect. They know this. I never understood how there are special men's meetings, and a woman is sitting there, which might be someone's wife. The men will say to themselves, "What is she doing here?" If a special session should be for women, then let the women run it, same as for a man.

There are things you want to say but you won't because the opposite sex is there. Same as a parent that brings their young child to the meeting. There are things the speaker may not say because of their presence. That one person can change a whole message.

Every time we turn around, there's a new feminist group, but the war would be if there were as many male groups rising. So men are becoming fearful of women, which shouldn't be so. But because of how some women are taught and the schemes of lawyers in divorces and friends, it makes men wanting to be alone, and perhaps the women feel the same way. The competition would not be about getting things done, but what team has the most power, that there would be no time to make any more children. Many men will do just what their significant other wants, only to keep an argument down; they will let the woman get by without saying anything, whether it is right or wrong. The wheel with the loudest noise gets the oil. We need each other. That one chromosome has made a big difference. Males have one chromosome, and females have two. Another story!

Thank God some women are stepping out, but they will always need a man, just as a man will still need a woman. God will always have a ram in the bush. A woman was made to be a helpmate to the man. However, she can help build him up or help tear him down. Help is help, whatever way the pendulum is swinging. She is needed to help the man in the ministry, especially if he appears to have gone astray. There's nothing like an extra set of eyes.

The pastor may be a woman, but there's a man on the inside whose name is Jesus Christ. I can't worry about what God told the woman who is in the ministry. I'm too busy trying to get myself together with what He is telling me. If she's reading the same book that I'm reading, we all have our work cut out for us. People are so busy fighting over positions and titles that nothing that makes sense is getting done. It reminds me of the school system; the last thing our system thinks about is the children. It is a priority, but not the way you think it should be; as long as the government can keep them ignorant and candidates for prison, everything will go forward as planned.

One of the main reasons churches are having a difficult time is TVs, radios, and telephones. The devil wants to promote unrighteousness and does it by sight and through the airwaves, but what he meant for the harm you can use for your good. Call someone on the telephone and bless him or her today.

We have been taught as children not to talk with strangers. Today the stranger has moved into the house through the television and computer. The strangers on TV that you or your child may never meet teach you every day through repetition.

Millions of books are being made from the Bible, but the Bible itself will never lose its power. The Holy Ghost is waiting for many to receive, but it will not force himself on any. Ask, and it shall be given, seek, and you will find, knock, and it will be opened to you. Matthew:7:7.

Some people may never read the Bible, and they can only see it through another person's walk. However, those who have read it will understand it through their walk with Christ. Not always an easy walk, but it's a pleasant walk. The only letter of recommendation you need is yourself. You yourselves are our letter, written on our hearts, known and read by everyone. You show that you are a letter from Christ, the result of our ministry, written not with ink but with the Spirit of the living God, not on tablets of stone but tablets of human hearts.   (2 Corinthians 3:2)

1 Peter 3:17 [17] **For it is better to suffer for doing good if that should be God's will, than for doing evil.**

If we were all to write a resume on where we've been and what we've done, it would surely be devastating. The main thing that should be on it now is the objective "To be filled with the Holy Ghost and to work for the Lord while it's day; when night comes, no man can work (John.9:4)." While we are living, we should do what we can. Although we didn't ask to be here, we might as well make the best of it.

I recall seeing a movie long ago called Baby Boy, and in it, one of the actors said in his distress, "Lord, show me the way, and if you don't show me the way, forgive me for being lost."

God will tear us down before he builds us up. He knows all about the foolishness we've been taught and manipulations we've been part of, whether it was financial or for the show, but yet many have gotten saved.

For since in the wisdom of God, the world through its wisdom did not know him, God was pleased through the foolishness of what was preached to save those who believe.
(1Corinthians 1:21)

He just wants us to have some good roots before he starts blessing. Now that's a sure foundation. "Verily, verily I say unto you, Except a corn of wheat fall into the ground and die, it abides alone: but if it dies, it brings forth much fruit (John.12:24)"

Unless we die in our thinking, we cannot be fruitful in our doings.

Churches should keep in mind that many people have settled for the television ministries for their spiritual word because there are much confusion and favoritism in the local church. By watching church on television, a person doesn't have to listen or sit through all of the politics and preliminaries of church proto-call. Nowadays, everything is about the convenience of home. Did the Coronavirus pandemic start retraining others to have church service at home? So what is your church giving you that makes you want to leave home and be there in person? I know many churches use Hebrew: 10:25 to pressure people about coming to church. It says: Forsaking not the assembling of others as some have.

However, Matthew 18:20 says: Where there are two or three gathered in my name there I am with them.

Eventually, people will become like David when they wanted to stone him, and he had to **encourage himself in the Lord or, like Paul said, "I think myself happy." This was when they tried to persecute Paul (Acts 26:2).**

Although the Bible does not directly say that the children will become weaker but wiser, it is a fact. Technology is moving faster than ever, and it feeds our children. Therefore, the church has to wise up or be overthrown by the upcoming young generation with no sense of respect. But as said in the scripture, regardless of what's going on in your church or otherwise, we must work out our own salvation. Philippians 2:12-16 "Therefore, my beloved, as you have always obeyed, not as in my presence only, but now much more in my absence, work out your own salvation with fear and trembling; for it is God who works in you both to will and to do for His good pleasure.

If I had to update that scripture as words working today, such as the artist Patti Labelle's song "I Got a New Attitude."

I think about the comedian Robin Williams, had he encouraged himself or gotten a new attitude about life, he would still possibly be here. In this case, we have a comedian that has made many people laugh, but he goes home depressed and commits suicide by hanging, and he was worth more than 50 million dollars. So you thought money was everything?

Some people have stopped going to church in a split second for some reason. It's like they had a quick car wreck and refuse to go to the doctor because the doctor's problems are greater than his. Some people may stop going after reading the Bible and become angry because they may feel their church is not doing anything that the Bible says and not willing to try.

Due to the Coronavirus, there may only be two or three in their houses, praying as they were in a church.

We can only speculate about the trillions of dollars this virus has caused and the thousands of deaths and loss of jobs forcing people to be home and pray. Some just might get used to it and don't miss the church. The closing of malls, churches, businesses, restaurants, amusement parks, and so much more. Can you imagine the loss of income of those who were getting paid under the table? The money loss in parking lots in the thousands as well, because people are home. I've seen parking for $20 and $30. What about the loss of offering at church? Especially on Easter as this pandemic goes through holidays, and people are staying home.

As said long ago, "You don't miss your water until your well runs dry."

What about law enforcement? They can't give as many crooked or unfair tickets right now because many people are not out. I'm sure when this is over, they will be issuing tickets for the least little thing, hoping you don't appear in court to fight it. Years ago, I got a $163 ticket for eating shelled peanuts on the ramp waiting for the subway here in Los Angeles. I'm almost afraid to eat peanut butter now. Lol. Even when this pandemic is over, I must remind you that we are guaranteed to have an epidemic of something else that will cause people to panic in years to come. Over 18,000 have died because of the coronavirus, and I'm sure the numbers will get higher before it stops. The United States has been blessed knowing that third world countries live with this stuff every day from contaminated water, no shelter, diseases, no food, and shootings in front of them from their government and terrorist groups. Of course, we know more things than the coronavirus is killing people.

Church members should be reminded of Matthew 6:6

But when you pray, go into your room and shut the door, and pray to your Father who is in secret.

And your Father who sees in secret will reward you. This time could be your relationship with God.

TV ministries run their large conferences because home is not taking care of business. But what viewers fail to realize that these large ministries will not be there to meet their needs personally. Large television ministries will send you a computerized letter about everything but your problem because the needs are so high from many of the listeners. They barely have time to pull out your check. If time permitted and expenses were affordable, they would only suggest you seeking your local church. Uh, oh! Well, that's why you left the local church.

Sending them an offering is still beneficial because they have ministered to you as though you attended a nearby service, and it is expensive for them to be on the air. Remember, Satan is Prince of the air, and he's not going to let them get by cheap.

Hopefully, this small book has helped you. Simply writing it has helped me. If my message reaches just one of you, the angels will be rejoicing for one more soul to Christ whose eyes have been opened.

The heart *is* deceitful above all *things* and desperately wicked: who can know it?

About Your Father's Business

Luke 2:41-52- Now His parents went to Jerusalem every year at the Feast of the Passover.

⁴² And when He was twelve years old, they went up to Jerusalem according to the custom of the Feast.

⁴³ And when they had fulfilled the days, as they returned, the child Jesus tarried behind in Jerusalem; and Joseph and His mother knew not of it.

⁴⁴ But they, supposing Him to have been in the company, went a day's journey; and they sought Him among their kinsfolk and acquaintances.

⁴⁵ And when they found Him not, they turned back again to Jerusalem, seeking Him.

⁴⁶ And it came to pass that after three days, they found Him in the temple, sitting in the midst of the doctors, both hearing them and asking them questions.

⁴⁷ And all who heard Him were astonished at His understanding and answers.

⁴⁸ And when they saw Him, they were amazed, and His mother said unto Him, "Son, why hast Thou thus dealt with us? Behold, Thy father and I have sought Thee sorrowing."

⁴⁹ And He said unto them, "How is it that ye sought Me? Knew ye not that I must be about My Father's business?"

⁵⁰ And they understood not the saying which He spoke unto them.

⁵¹ And He went down with them and came to Nazareth, and was subject unto them. But His mother kept all these things in her heart.

⁵² And Jesus increased in wisdom and stature, and in favor with God and man.

Although Jesus was in the temple seeking wisdom, he did something with what he learned. Many of us go to church to hear a good word and to be seen, so we can at least say we went to church. We are to be about our Father's business and do something that he has given us in our hearts; otherwise, we are nothing. The scripture says occupy until I come. (Luke 19:13). We are to be doing something and not just sitting around watching television or running to every church program we hear. What are you doing personally that God has given you? We often say it repeatedly that we are going to start a business or work with an organization and never do it. Before we know it 10 more years have gone by. Or we say we're going to college for a certain degree. Afterwhich you think about it and say that the degree will take five years and you are now 45 and in 5 years you will be 50. How old will you be in five years if you don't get the degree? We are full of excuses from fear, laziness, or someone holding you back. Even if you started and then stopped. The question now is, you were running so well, who hindered you? Galatians 5:7

Chapter 8
My Mission

If you've gotten this far, you have done well, and hopefully, you haven't skipped anything. Because the same page you may have neglected indeed could have been the answer you needed.

There comes a time when you find a rare and significantly different person, and when they appear, it seems like something is wrong. It's nothing wrong it's just over 50 years of hidden wisdom about to be revealed about the church and the blessings and consequences for going. The goose that laid the Golden Egg hid it in the church and never explained why. It was pretty and gold on the outside, but the inside stunk of rotten eggs. Many times we say, "If I knew then what I knew now, I would have done things differently. Well, unfortunately, we did know. Someone older told us, but we didn't listen, and now our world is in a mess. It's like looking at the Good, the Bad, and Ugly under the sacred cross. We've made mistakes perpetually and continue until there is no more.

The wisdom given to me is trying to prevent the falling away of the church as much as possible, but when you show you don't care, don't expect anyone to be hanging around very long. After staying out for more than ten years, I came back in shock at what I saw. My conviction came from the words of God, "Stewart, for as much as you have learned, how are you going to help the church if you stay out of it? After visiting many denominations and organizations as an adult, I found out that techniques and wording were different, but the desire for the results was the same. "Offering, Gift, Sacrifice, For the Lord, Pray about it and any other title needed money is at the end, which is highly required, but not how you think. Rest assure if confusion is in your church. Don't feel lonely; it's everywhere, so welcome home. Your answer is here! I don't claim to know it all, but I know quite a bit and still learning, but I chose never to speak outwardly about it over all of these years.

We are always learning. One day we will wake up and find out that we have become old students!

I'm like everyone else, and we all know in part, and perhaps your part will help my part become wiser and likewise. 1Corinthians 13:9-For we know in part, and we prophesy in part, but when that which is perfect comes, then that which is in part shall be done away.

After you're "saved," these are the five things they want to know very cunningly.

1. How much do you give financially, or how much money do you make?
2. What can you do for the church free? Talents, gifts, or skills
3. Who are you sleeping with? Are you married, single, straight, gay, or free?
4. Do you believe in the same religion as they do?

5. Possibly, what church did you come from?

After these questions are answered to their desire, you will be acknowledged, and it's a great possibility you will get somewhere in today's church.

A Warning against Hypocrisy
Matthew 23

23 Then Jesus said to the crowds and to his disciples: **2** "The teachers of the law and the Pharisees sit in Moses' seat.

3 So you must be careful to do everything they tell you. But do not do what they do, for they do not practice what they preach.

4 They tie up heavy, cumbersome loads and put them on other people's shoulders, but they themselves are not willing to lift a finger to move them.

5 "Everything they do is done for people to see: They make their phylacteries wide and the tassels on their garments long;

6 they love the place of honor at banquets and the most important seats in the synagogues;

7 they love to be greeted with respect in the marketplaces and called 'Rabbi' by others.

8 "But you are not to be called 'Rabbi,' for you have one Teacher, and you are all brothers.

9 And do not call anyone on earth 'father,' for you have one Father, and he is in heaven.

10 Nor are you to be called instructors, for you have one Instructor, the Messiah.

11 The greatest among you will be your servant.

12 For those who exalt themselves will be humbled, and those who humble themselves will be exalted.

Does a lot of this sound like what's going on today? However, it was going on thousands of years ago, and once again, there's nothing new under the sun. When you began to recognize the traits, it's not for you to become judgmental but wise in your doings when it comes to church or any person that wishes your time and money. Some of us are casting our pearls before the swine. "Do not give dogs what is sacred; do not throw your pearls to pigs. If you do, they may trample them under their feet and turn and tear you to pieces. (Matthew 7:6). In other words, don't give what you have to someone who doesn't care or value what you give, whether it be money or time.

Seven Woes on the Teachers of the Law and the Pharisees (Matthew 23 Cont'd)

13 "Woe to you, teachers of the law and Pharisees, you hypocrites! You shut the door of the kingdom of heaven in people's faces. You yourselves do not enter, nor will you let those enter who are trying to.

14 Woe unto you, scribes and Pharisees, hypocrites! for ye devour widows' houses, and for a pretense make long prayer: therefore ye shall receive the greater damnation.

15 *"Woe to you, teachers of the law and Pharisees, you hypocrites! You travel over land and sea to* *win a single convert, and when you have succeeded, you make them twice as much a child of hell as you are.*

16 "Woe to you, blind guides! You say, 'If anyone swears by the temple, it means nothing; but anyone who swears by the gold of the temple is bound by that oath.'

17 You blind fools! Which is greater: the gold or the temple that makes the gold sacred?

18 You also say, 'If anyone swears by the altar, it means nothing; but anyone who swears by the gift on the altar is bound by that oath.'

19 You blind men! Which is greater: the gift or the altar that makes the gift sacred?

20 Therefore, anyone who swears by the altar swears by it and by everything on it.

21 And anyone who swears by the temple swears by it and by the one who dwells in it.

22 And anyone who swears by heaven swears by God's throne and by the one who sits on it.

23 "Woe to you, teachers of the law and Pharisees, you hypocrites! You give a tenth of your spices—mint, dill and cumin. But you have neglected the more important matters of the law—justice, mercy, and faithfulness. You should have practiced the latter without neglecting the former.

24 You blind guides! You strain out a gnat but swallow a camel.

25 *"Woe to you, teachers of the law and Pharisees, you hypocrites! You clean the outside of the cup and dish, but inside they are full of greed and self-indulgence.*

26 Blind Pharisee! First, clean the inside of the cup and dish, and then the outside also will be clean.

27 "Woe to you, teachers of the law and Pharisees, you hypocrites! You are like whitewashed tombs, which look beautiful on the outside but on the inside are full of the bones of the dead and everything unclean.

28 In the same way, on the outside you appear to people as righteous but on the inside you are full of hypocrisy and wickedness.

29 "Woe to you, teachers of the law and Pharisees, you hypocrites! You build tombs for the prophets and decorate the graves of the righteous.

30 And you say, 'If we had lived in the days of our ancestors, we would not have taken part with them in shedding the blood of the prophets.'

31 So you testify against yourselves that you are the descendants of those who murdered the prophets.

32 Go ahead, then, and complete what your ancestors started!

33 "You snakes! You brood of vipers! How will you escape being condemned to hell?

34 Therefore, I am sending you prophets and sages and teachers. Some of them you will kill and crucify; others you will flog in your synagogues and pursue from town to town.

35 And so upon you will come all the righteous blood that has been shed on earth, from the blood of righteous Abel to the blood of Zechariah, son of Berekiah, whom you murdered between the temple and the altar.

36 Truly I tell you, all this will come on this generation.

37 "Jerusalem, Jerusalem, you who kill the prophets and stone those sent to you, how often I have longed to gather your children together, as a hen gathers her chicks under her wings, and you were not willing.

38 Look, your house is left to you desolate.

39 For I tell you, you will not see me again until you say, 'Blessed is he who comes in the name of the Lord.'"

The Holy Spirit Comes at Pentecost

ACTS 2

1 When the day of Pentecost came, they were all together in one place.

2 Suddenly a sound like the blowing of a violent wind came from heaven and filled the whole house where they were sitting.

3 They saw what seemed to be tongues of fire that separated and came to rest on each of them.

4 All of them were filled with the Holy Spirit and began to speak in other tongues as the Spirit enabled them.

5 Now there were staying in Jerusalem God-fearing Jews from every nation under heaven.

6 When they heard this sound, a crowd came together in bewilderment, because each one heard their own language being spoken.

7 Utterly amazed, they asked: "Aren't all these who are speaking Galileans?

8 Then how is it that each of us hears them in our native language?

9 Parthians, Medes and Elamites; residents of Mesopotamia, Judea and Cappadocia, Pontus and Asia,

10 Phrygia and Pamphylia, Egypt and the parts of Libya near Cyrene; visitors from Rome

11 (both Jews and converts to Judaism); Cretans and Arabs—we hear them declaring the wonders of God in our own tongues!"

12 Amazed and perplexed, they asked one another, "What does this mean?"

13 Some, however, made fun of them and said, "They have had too much wine."

Peter Addresses the Crowd

14 Then Peter stood up with the Eleven, raised his voice and addressed the crowd: "Fellow Jews and all of you who live in Jerusalem, let me explain this to you; listen carefully to what I say.

15 These people are not drunk, as you suppose. It's only nine in the morning!

16 No, this is what was spoken by the prophet Joel:

17 "In the last days, God says, I will pour out my Spirit on all people. Your sons and daughters will prophesy, your young men will see visions; your old men will dream dreams.

18 Even on my servants, both men and women, I will pour out my Spirit in those days, and they will prophesy.

19 I will show wonders in the heavens above and signs on the earth below, blood and fire and billows of smoke.

20 The sun will be turned to darkness and the moon to blood before the coming of the great and glorious day of the Lord.

21 And everyone who calls on the name of the Lord will be saved.'

22 "Fellow Israelites, listen to this: Jesus of Nazareth was a man accredited by God to you by miracles, wonders and signs, which God did among you through him, as you yourselves know.

23 This man was handed over to you by God's deliberate plan and foreknowledge; and you, with the help of wicked men, put him to death by nailing him to the cross.

24 But God raised him from the dead, freeing him from the agony of death because it was impossible for death to keep its hold on him.

25 David said about him: " 'I saw the Lord always before me. Because he is at my right hand, I will not be shaken.

26 Therefore my heart is glad, and my tongue rejoices; my body also will rest in hope,

27 because you will not abandon me to the realm of the dead; you will not let your holy one see decay.

28 You have made known to me the paths of life; you will fill me with joy in your presence.'

29 "Fellow Israelites, I can tell you confidently that the patriarch David died and was buried and his tomb is here to this day.

30 But he was a prophet and knew that God had promised him on oath that he would place one of his descendants on his throne.

31 Seeing what was to come, he spoke of the resurrection of the Messiah, that he was not abandoned to the realm of the dead, nor did his body see decay.

32 God has raised this Jesus to life, and we are all witnesses of it.

33 Exalted to the right hand of God, he has received from the Father the promised Holy Spirit and has poured out what you now see and hear.

34 For David did not ascend to heaven, and yet he said, "'The Lord said to my Lord: "Sit at my right hand

35 until I make your enemies a footstool for your feet."'

36 "Therefore let all Israel be assured of this: God has made this Jesus, whom you crucified, both Lord and Messiah."

37 When the people heard this, they were cut to the heart and said to Peter and the other apostles, "Brothers, what shall we do?"

38 Peter replied, "Repent and be baptized, every one of you, in the name of Jesus Christ for the forgiveness of your sins. And you will receive the gift of the Holy Spirit.

39 The promise is for you and your children and for all who are far off—for all whom the Lord our God will call."

40 With many other words, he warned them; and he pleaded with them, "Save yourselves from this corrupt generation."

41 Those who accepted his message were baptized, and about three thousand were added to their number that day.

The Fellowship of the Believers

42 They devoted themselves to the apostles' teaching and to fellowship, to the breaking of bread and to prayer.

43 Everyone was filled with awe at the many wonders and signs performed by the apostles.

44 All the believers were together and had everything in common.

45 They sold property and possessions to give to anyone who had need.

46 Every day they continued to meet together in the temple courts. They broke bread in their homes and ate together with glad and sincere hearts,

47 praising God and enjoying the favor of all the people. And the Lord added to the church daily those who were being saved.

How are those being added to your church? Concerts? Programs? Anniversaries?

Or perhaps your method should be turned around and do as the apostles that were looking for the needs of the people!

21 days and then what?
Daniel 10:2

In those days, I, Daniel, was mourning for three weeks. I ate no delicacies, no meat or wine entered my mouth, nor did I anoint myself at all, for the full three weeks. Then he [the angel Gabriel] said to me, "Fear not, Daniel, for from the first day that you set your heart to understand and humbled yourself before your God, your words have been heard, and I have come because of your words. The prince of the kingdom of Persia withstood me twenty-one days, but Michael, one of the chief princes, came to help me, for I was left there with the kings of Persia,

As soon as Daniel started praying, Gabriel was dispatched with his answer. However, the demons in charge of Persia withstood Gabriel for those three weeks until the arch-angel Michael came to assist Gabriel.

Many theories have come out of the scripture as far as what can happen in 21 days. We have the 21 Day Daniel fast, which is a vegetarian diet. However, neurologist says that anything we do for 21 days reshifts the brain and you can create a new habit in what you're doing. This very well can be real. Some people started smoking and drinking and any other addiction and thought it was cute and just fun. After so many days, it became a habit and now hard to break. Now they are losing jobs, family, houses, and appearance. This can happen with anything, whether good or bad, and it depends on whose eyes we're looking through. Every good or bad habit starts with the first day of initiation. Can you imagine what kind of significant change there would be if this is true if the church tried some new ideas for 21 days and what the outcome could be? God would hear the prayers from the very first day, knowing that we ask for forgiveness because we did things wrong and desire to learn and do better. Of course, all types of people would try to interfere and say that it will not work or hinder the process and have the attitude of Persia's demons. If our prayers and thoughts are sincere, God will make our enemy our footstool.

Also, look at the damage the coronavirus has done. For example, people staying away from church for 21 days. How many groups of 21 days are there in a year. That habit can be so bad that some people may never go back to church. However, let us look at the positive side and believe that God will stretch our ideas to uplift one another and show that we care through this book. As said, There's nothing that will beat a failure but a try

I remember when I started becoming a Vegan, and after 21 days, I kept going, and I did it for eight months with no meat, etc. I finally started back eating a little meat only because I mentally got tired of figuring out what to eat that didn't have meat in it and it still tastes good. Or you went somewhere and you had to become very picky, or the host had to prepare something special for you, and a lot of it was left because everyone wasn't Vegan. Who knows, I may try it again, but right now, some good fried chicken and pork chops are delicious.

Conclusion

"Let us hear the conclusion of the whole matter: Fear God, and keep his commandments; for this is the whole duty of man" (Eccles. 12:13).

When the people cry out to Jesus, something has to happen. People just need someone to care, and in these last days, God will send someone who does. Will it be you? For men shall become lovers of themselves, covetous, boasters, proud, blasphemers, disobedient to parents, unthankful, unholy. 2Timothy 3:2). In other words, it's about them and not about you. Selfishness is growing by the mounds.

WARNING: Caring takes a little extra time, and you might not have it to spare.

Have we become like the church of the Laodiceans?

"I know your works that you are neither cold nor hot. I wish you were cold or hot. So, because you are lukewarm and neither hot nor cold, I will vomit you out of my mouth.

.Because you say, 'I am rich, and have gotten riches, and have need of nothing;' and don't know that you are the wretched one, miserable, poor, blind, and naked; (Rev.3:15-17)

*Some of us are blind and we think we see.

> Satan, who is the god of this world, has blinded the minds of those who don't believe. They are unable to see the glorious light of the Good News. They don't understand this message about the glory of Christ, who is the exact likeness of God (2Cor.4:4).

Moral of the Day

> Good advice is only useful if you use it, other than that it's just noise!

If you could get half of the people "saved" and filled with the Holy Ghost that's already going to your church regularly, you'd be doing something.

Don't be scared. John 6:44 – No one can come to me unless the Father who sent me draws them. And I will raise them up at the last day.

The Spirit is always drawing us with light; you did not read this book by accident. The Holy Ghost may have to start with the leader. But if they don't ask for it or desire it, they won't get it. Being saved merely means accepting Christ and showing love for others, as he has demonstrated for us. But being saved is like the cake, and the Holy Ghost is the frosting. Pound cake is good, but there's nothing like a yellow cake with chocolate cream cheese frosting. The Holy Ghost only makes you wiser. I think what's so amazing to me about all of it, which is so simple, is that the astute or intelligent leaders don't go near it?

2 Timothy 3 : 7

"Ever learning and never able to come to the knowledge of the truth."

Matthew 7:9- Which of you, if his son asks for bread, will give him a stone? Matthew 7:11 So if you who are evil know how to give good gifts to your children, how much more will your Father in heaven give good things to those who ask Him!

Why am I talking about this? Only because your eyes will be open. If you have been speaking your natural language all of these years and this miracle happen to you, I'm sure you would want everyone to have it, but of course, many will reject it but may soon come to the knowledge of it later. It won't make you perfect it will just make you aware of the supernatural world we live in and how awesome God will be in your personal life. Just think about it, there are billions of people on the earth, and none of us are exactly alike, nor do we have the same fingerprints. How supernatural is that? Tear down that stony heart and listen to me, please. Will everyone receive it?

I can hear someone saying now, "Well, it doesn't take all of that." All I can say is suit yourself. It took me 35 years to come to the knowledge of it. And no, don't expect your leader to make you get it. Your leader may not even mention it to you. It's personal, and people are still receiving it, and it's mentioned in the same Bible that you're carrying. Of course, your leader will look at you strangely if you receive it and tell him about it. Or may have a slight smile and say, "Well, that's good for you."

Although it will be the beginning of the new birth and you're a babe. Once again, you will crawl before you walk. But thank God, at least you were born again.

Christians need to KNOW they have power and not think they have it. I guess it's like having a car. You have the keys to drive it, but you won't. You will have the power to deal with situations that will come in your life. None of us are exempt, but it's how we mentally deal with the things that will come.

They will be a witness unto Jerusalem and Judaea, and in Samaria, and unto the uttermost part of the earth (Acts.1:8). And especially in your own hometown. Having spiritual power will not make you perfect, but make you more aware of what is in you and will give you the strength to do what you were called to do. Your best friend will not push you as God will. In having our power, we must realize that God has the last word. **How many people have we prayed for, and they still passed away,** even though it is said that we have the power to raise the dead? That's a shocking statement isn't it? We learn as we live.

We don't talk about death enough as though we have become very fearful, but there's no way we can escape. Same as sex. People hate to talk about it, but how else in the world did you get here? The only time we are talking about death is at a funeral; otherwise, it is a negative subject as though it is not going to happen. People talk so much positive that they have forgotten some of the reality of life. If death is negative, how in the world will we see Jesus. Going to heaven suppose to be a better place, and what could be more positive than that? The following artist have these songs on YouTube, and when you listen to them, they will make you think:

Can't Run

Lee Williams & the Spiritual QC's

CHORUS

You can't run, You can't hide

There's no need, No need to try

You Don't know when or how he's coming

You just can't get by, help me tell 'em

VERSE 1

Oh devil is like a policeman

Traveling through this land, he's serving

A death notice to every woman and man

You're gonna need a lawyer, if I were you that's the

next thing I would do

Just as sure as you're sitting here tonight one day
he's got a warrant for you, but you know what

VERSE 2

Jesus, is a lawyer, one who never lost a case, If I
were you, I get lawyer Jesus

I wouldn't wait, I would make haste

This is something you can't get around, no matter
what you do

Just as sure as you can hear my voice today, one
day he's got a warrant for you

But you know what

VERSE 3

He'll take babies from his mother's breast

He'll take the rich man and everybody else

Take mothers, daughters, father and son

Sometimes he won't stop 'til he got that last one

Get Your House in Order

Dottie Peoples

Get your house in order
Oh do it today
Get your house in order
Oh do it right away
For Jesus is coming
No man knows where or when
Get your house in order
For he's coming back again
Let me tell you something
You know there's earthquakes
Hurricanes
Famine and disease
Can't you see my Lord's talking to you
You better take heed
Get your house in order
Oh do it today
Get your house in order
Oh do it right away
For Jesus is coming

No man knows where or when

Get your house in order

For he's coming back again

One more thing

You know there's so many

Homeless people

In this world today

But my God got plenty of houses and land

If you give him your life today

Get your house in order

Oh do it today

Get your house in order

Oh do it right away

For Jesus is coming

No man knows where or when

Get your house in order

For he's coming back again

For he's coming back again

(Get your house in order)

For he's coming back again

(Oh) For he's coming

(Oh he's coming) For he's coming
(He's coming back again)
For he's coming back again

Your days are numbered, regardless of how great
you think you are.

James 4:14 - Why you do not even know what will

happen tomorrow. What is your life? You are a mist

that appears for a little while and then vanishes.

Job 14:5 -A person's days are determined; you

have decreed the number of his months and have set

limits he cannot exceed.

Psalm 44:22 -Yea, for thy sake are we killed
all the day long; we are counted as sheep for the
slaughter.

Famous people you may never have met.

Are any of the following people still here? Even though they had the best doctors and the highest bishops in authority to pray. They have had hands laid on them and have passed out under the power of the Holy Ghost, and they are still gone. Are they still here? Regardless of the reason or age, we must leave here.

Michael Jackson- 50- Cardiac arrest

Mother Teresa- 87- Cardiac arrest

Kobe Bryant- 41- Helicopter crash

James Cleveland- 59 - heart - respiratory

Billy Graham -99- Natural causes

Muhammad Ali-74- Septic shock

Sun Myung Moon-92- Pneumonia

Kathryn Kuhlman-68- a heart condition

Aretha Franklin- 76- Pancreatic cancer

Martin Luther King- 39- Assassination

Socrates-71- forced suicide

Steve Jobs-56- Respiratory arrest

Wayne Dyer-75- Heart attack

Albert Einstein-76-abdominal, aneurism

Stephen in the bible-29- stoned to death

Moses-120- as commanded by God

Samson-80- collapsing of pillars

Jesus-crucified -33- But he got up with all power
in his hands!

and the list goes on forever.

Regardless of how we leave here, the scriptures say that we should occupy until he comes. (Luke 19:13). Meaning we should be doing something and occupying our time using the gifts and knowledge he has given us until he comes for us.

How Much Time Do You Have?

Television Statistics

Dec 5, 2018 — **Children** ages 2 to 5 **watched TV** for more than 32 hours a week. **Kids** ages 6 to 8 spent 28 hours per week in front of the tube. The **average child** will **watch** 8,000 murders on **TV** before finishing elementary school.

According to the A.C. Nielsen Co., the **average** American **watches** more than 4 hours of **TV each** day (or 28 hours/week, or 2 months of nonstop **TV-watching per year**). In **a** 65-**year** life, that **person will** have spent 9 **years** glued to the tube.

A study by AAA, the average American spends 17,600 minutes in their car every **year**.

Some people are so busy that they don't have time to pray, and they can do that in their mind, but it's too occupied.

How much of your time is helping others and doing what you are supposed to do? We will all be shocked at how much we don't do. We are only busy in our minds and not doing the work.

CHECKLIST

Remind them of Matthew 10:25

I have come to set a man against his father, a daughter against her mother, and a daughter-in-law against her mother-in-law. Your enemies will be right in your own household!' In other words, there are enough problems in your own family, and many choose to mind other people's business instead of taking care of their own. (1 Peter 4:15) But let none of you suffer as a murderer, or as a thief or as an evildoer or as a busybody in other men's matters.

1 Corinthians 13:2 Context

As read earlier, here's the chapter once again for emphasis on what love is all about.

[1]Though I speak with the tongues of men and of angels and have not charity, I have become *as* sounding brass or a tinkling cymbal. [2]**And though I have** *the gift of* **prophecy, and understand all mysteries, and all knowledge; and though I have all faith so that I could remove mountains, and have not charity, I am nothing.** [3]And though I bestow all my goods to feed *the poor* and though I give my body to be burned, and have not charity, it profits me nothing. [4]Charity suffers long, *and* is kind; charity envies not; charity, not itself, is not puffed up, [5]Does not behave itself unseemly, seeks not her own, is not easily provoked, thinks no evil;

Although scripture is meaningful, it takes time to learn how to love and understand how we should live. It is not an overnight course. Of course, we cannot become pushovers, but we know when we should have to stand up for what's right and fair and move on. God also speaks to you the same as he does your leader. Is it God telling you both something different.? How can two walk together, except they agreed? Amos 3:3. It's like a fight where one person wants to go left and the other wants to go right. Same as a marriage headed for divorce. Every leader is not a true leader, and every church member is not a faithful follower.

If some of the following questions are answered on the Confidential Information Sheet, there should be fewer problems. However, in every family, when death arises, look for the devil to raise his head and speak about what he wants and how he feels. If the church would show its love in advance by asking questions, it should eliminate some problems.

Two of the most significant places where there is turmoil for some reason are funerals and weddings. Full of last-minute decisions, accidents, or someone not agreeing on something. If some things are written in advance, the church's administrative part would have a little idea of what is expected or who to contact.

Things you should know about every member.
Confidential information

1. Name
2. Address
3. Phone number
4. Where they work
5. What kind of work they do?
6. Do they have insurance? If not, can the church purchase insurance for them and be the beneficiary? It would benefit the church, making sure everyone is insured.
7. Who are their beneficiaries?
8. If none, would they like the church to be the beneficiary? Beneficiaries can be changed anytime.
9. Emergency number. Name, address, phone
10. Do they have a will?

11. They can make a will and can include the church if they wish, and can be changed any time. How do you think the Catholic Church has become so wealthy?
12. Would they like to write out what they would like to occur at their funeral instructions? Funeral wishes.
13. What five people need to be notified, should something happen?
14. What talent or gift does the member have?
15. What would they like to happen for themselves?
16. They should have certain personal information hidden in their homes with all names and passwords to individual accounts.

17. At least one person should know where it is, and it should not be opened unless an emergency. If a lot of this is not done, especially when the money is involved, know that the government would love to take it.

Recap of Information and Questions

18. Do you have a good choir that can record every year or a soloist that you can produce? Do you have auditions for your choir members? Do you recommend private voice lessons? Singing is not everyone's gift. Those who can't sing throw the other members off and leave gaps in the sound. You can have a choir stand of 40 members, and only 20 of them can sing.
19. Do you have specialized usher training? Get the ROTC to train them.

20. Do you have a suggestion box?
21. Do you have ads in the back of your program for the members of your church that has businesses, and do they offer discounts because they attend your church? Up to date picture.
22. Perhaps you want to print out a phone directory of businesses and special events coming every year.

You must understand that the church is a personal business that represents God. People will eventually get tired of the same old stuff and move on. McDonald's Hamburger has a school to teach their franchises. Just because you have the money to purchases a franchise, you have to be qualified to run a business their way. One person can mess up and represent all McDonald's. What do you think has happened to pastors, and how hurt members feel about all of them? McDonald's requires an application and a minimum of $500,000 in liquid assets + $45,000 Franchise fee and construction-related expenses. There are more than 37,000 restaurants. Be unaware that McDonald's is basically interested in real estate; hamburgers are just a bonus. That's another story.

How many churches are running the same way and the same beliefs? And you wonder why many people don't go? There is no consistency. And many use the same Bible, but they use it as they please and create what they think is best. No, it's not an easy book to follow due to the many controversies. There are so many different thoughts and so many empty spaces in years to various events. What happened in between?

23. Do you have a system for people to get rides home?

24. Does your member desire marriage? If so, do you think there should be some severe counseling, not only together but one on one, and if you discern something, you may choose to say something or not?

Personally, although I had been married twice, had I been counseled the first time properly, I probably would not have gotten married. But who is to say that you're not ready? Some people's attitudes are, "Just like I got married, and I can do the same by getting a divorce."

25. A photograph of the church member

The Rude Awakening

Has it ever crossed your mind that a person can read the Bible and take everything literally whether or not they studied further or even went to bible study for years? Just learning for themselves and getting their own revelation about life that they considered not going to church. They may feel that leaders do not make it easy for them to attend by back-lashing and to put large obligations and burdens on them as they beat them down about sin Rom. 3:23. We all have sinned. Teach me how to live through this crooked economy!

Now after punishing them about the sin and frustrating them, who is doing the work of the Lord, with him knowing that our righteousness is as filthy rags: (Isaiah 64:6)

Scriptures that may want churchgoers to stay home and worship God for themselves.

1. Hebrew 10:25 -Forsake not the assembling of others- It didn't say it had to be a big crowd organized religion. It was just uniting with others of the same faith.
2. Matthew 18:20-Whether 2 or 3 or gathered in his name, there he is in the midst. Once again, it didn't say it had to be a large crowd
3. 1 Samuel 16:7-Man looks at the outward appearance, and God looks at the heart. - It didn't say you had to go to church to prove anything to God; He already knows your heart when you went. All clothes are not appropriate for church, and some will take the focus off of God.
   Jeremiah 17:9 - The heart *is* deceitful above all *things*, and desperately wicked: who can know it?
4. Hebrews 10:16 -He has automatically put his laws in our hearts and minds whether we went to church or not.
   Acts 2:17 "'And in the last days, it shall be, God declares, that I will pour out my Spirit on ALL flesh, and your sons and your daughters shall prophesy, and your young men shall see visions, and your old men shall dream dreams. (Do you have to be at church for God to pour his Spirit out on you?)

5. **"But whoso hath this world's good, and sees his brother have a need and shuts up his bowels** *of compassion* **from him, how dwells the love of God in him? 1John3:17** (Can you have compassion for others and help them without going to church, knowing that the love of God is in you?)

Some are feeding the homeless, giving clothing, visiting the prison and the sick. We can do that on our own, if we'd do it. I'm talking about myself as well because none of us are exempt from helping someone. There will come a time that we will need the same help.

It would probably be more appreciated if we did that than sitting up in a church for 2 or 3 hours wondering why we are there or wish service would soon be over so we can go home and eat.

This is not to discourage anyone from going to church; however, are any of these things set up in a church that we are sanctioned to do or part of the church ministry? I know the first thing a person would say, "Well, our church has the Sick Committee." That's nice, but what about you? Although the Jehovah's Witnesses stand on the corner every week, they are doing their hours of ministry, however, how many sick or homeless do they help or visit instead of standing on the corn corner? We are all guilty. At least they are making a presence. Most people hate to see them come knocking on their doors on Saturday when trying to relax or take care of chores.

There's not anything to do after the church but eat. If anything, that should be the day the hospital, jails are full. Of course, anytime during the week is just as good. And you still will tend to your family after spending that one hour with someone. Whether you do it once a week or once a month, it's your decision and not to make you a slave to it. If we had been taught that earlier in life, it would have been a natural thing to do.

Due to this pandemic, the excuse we have now is that we can't visit anyone. Perhaps churches to start a penpal group to hospitals and friends and mail a card or gift to someone in the hospital. It works for those in prison. There is always a way if we think and ask for wisdom. The surprise would be if they received something from an organization that they knew nothing about but realized they cared.

When we are brought up in something, it will make it easy as an adult. What if we were brought up as a teenager to go to the convalescent home once a month for two hours? So many people just drop their loved ones off, and no one sees them. If we were taught how to care like we were taught to go to church every Sunday, the convalescent homes would be full every week. It didn't say we had to know the person that we visited. Just like the story you read earlier, "He Knows Me."

There are so many reasons that memberships are declining, and leaders ignore the signs. People are telling them bit by bit. However, the line you will hear all the time is, "We're still learning." Some basic things need to be addressed because the church should know better. How are the educated going to stay or revisit your church, and you're begging for money like it's an auction? Of course, it's much more than that, but as you know, the biggest complaints you hear are offerings and long service full of hoopla. When I was a cosmetology instructor, I told the students that there are two things you need to learn in the hair business, and that's not to cut a person's hair too short if they don't want it and don't keep them in the salon all day. After then, you may grow a profitable business with a few skills.

You could have had a millionaire visit your church or a person that may soon become one, but they didn't see any sincerity to give. As said by many, if you know better, you do better. However, that statement sounds nice, but it is not necessarily true. Many people learn better to do certain things, but they won't.

As mentioned earlier, how amazing it was to me when I went to a nice size Catholic service, and within one hour, they did a lot, and service was dismissed. At the same time, other churches will take them 3 hours to deal with the sales pitches or try to make a person shout when there's no anointing present. Do leaders realize people have jobs and families?

This is so true because I had been part of several denominations, and when all the hoopla is over, you can become depressed about the obligation you are taxed at the end of the service and how long they kept you. There's a difference between the anointing and the appointing.

People want to go home. They are not trying to rush church, but so much is going on in service is not necessary. They wish they would have stayed home or come to church late. 3 hours of what? How many people visit and do not return? If they could get out that day, you are guaranteed not to see them again. Some extra people may show up on Easter or Mother's Day but may not return until next year. Yes, you have a faithful few that remain, and when they become old, they don't come either because the service is too long or it doesn't seem like church anymore. Not to mention all of the ailments they may have. They may sit an hour, but 3? Once again, not trying to rush God here, but give me the cake, and you can keep the frosting. Maybe that's the Catholic Spirit in me, although I'm not Catholic. Every denomination (Gang) has some good and bad traits.

This is a strange thought. Long ago in the Old Testament, people had to present a lamb for sacrifice for their sins, and they had to go to the priest for confession. That was done away. Next in the New Testament, you hear the scripture, "How can you hear without a preacher?" That was interrupted by the coronavirus, so people had to read and believe God on their own if they didn't have internet service. To top this next phase off, the Bible says that he will pour out his Spirit amongst all flesh. My question is: Is each phase of rituals being phased out that people can go to God themselves because leaders have become so wicked?

How Long is Your Service?

These times are not written in stone but have you ever considered this.

First of all, do you start the service on time, which can begin a negative feeling if you don't? I have a book called "It Started at 2:00, Not 2:15." Great information regarding being late for anything. The following are estimates of breaking down a service.

Songs	15 minutes	(3 Songs 5 min ea)
Offering	15 minutes	
3 Prayers	10 minutes	
Sermon	30 minutes	
Announcements	10 minutes	

That's approximately 1 hour and 20 minutes. What in the world is going on for about 3 hours? I understand should the anointing occur; however, you can't force people to have what some call church. Let them leave on a high and not wear them out, and then you want them to come back for evening service? My God! Same as these choir anniversaries. You invite ten choirs and each sing for about 10 minutes and some sing more.

Well, that's 100 minutes there, which does not include all of the talking in between or even a funeral where you have ten ministers attend, and they all have something to say. Everyone wants to be in the program. Who are we trying to impress? Trust me that people are only sitting there out of respect and want to go home. A four-hour funeral? Many have wanted to go home two hours ago.

Take into consideration the prodigal son in how he threw all of his money away, but then one day he woke up and came back home. (Luke 15: 11-32) If your members wake up before you give special attention to things that would benefit them, they may stop coming to church at all because they see no benefit. People come to the Lord for a reason, so why are they coming to you, blocking the space to get to him? Are you an extension of God's hand? The Bible says that there will be a great falling away from the church for many reasons. Will some of this be part of it? (2Thesselonians 2:3) "Let no one deceive you by any means; for that day will not come unless the falling away comes first. Know that the son of perdition will exalt himself.

Of course, some leaders want you to praise them like they are God, and many times, this ministry does not grow or began to decline for various reasons besides leaders exalting themselves. People see more than you think, but they are waiting for the right moment to dismiss themselves from attending. If you don't believe you think there's a falling away of members, check your church roster. They may be on the role but not in the seat.

AN AMAZING DREAM

Here is something to think about. We all have dreams. Am I right?

Acts 2:17 " 'In the last days, God says, I will pour out my Spirit on all people. Your sons and daughters will prophesy, your young men will see visions; your old men will dream dreams.

Genesis 1:27

So God created man in his own image, in the image of God, he created them; male and female he created them.

The thought: What if we dream because God dreams and we were made in his image? And what if the world is just a dream of God's? We have good and bad dreams, and the world acts out terror and good and beautiful things. Look at the horror in movies that we watch or produce, and it all starts in the mind. But it's just a movie. Now let's say that when God wakes up, the world will be no more. Such as when we wake up from our earthly dreams. Mmmmmm!

It's incredible how many of us believe in Jesus, and still, there are lots of problems. Can you imagine what the world would be like if none of us believed in him? It's like having no stop signs ever.

When is Your Enough Enough?

There was an elderly couple that had been married for over 60 years. After 60 years, the wife filed for a divorce. When they went to court, the judge asked, "Ma'am, why after 60 years of marriage, have you decided to get a divorce.? She replied, "Your honor, enough, is just enough!

My point: When is the church going to say there's enough foolishness and change things around, but switch back to how they are supposed to be and once was? We have all of this technology and have gotten worse. Who made the church 100 % contemporary? It started somewhere. We all like fads, and some trends don't last, and you will see the effects of them. McDonald's had the craze of starting a cheeseburger, and others followed. However, even though McDonald's added many things on the menu, they did not forget how to make the original burger, and it is still their signature sandwich. We have added so much to the church in certain areas we forgot why we came together.

Some people laugh at me and think I'm half crazy, but the other half is even worse. Lol. Peace!

We are to inform ourselves of some everyday life information. However, we get caught up in studying and never do what we were meant to do. God pulled me out of one of the most prominent bible colleges because it seemed like students were more interested in what grade they were going to get from the instructor and so on. We can read about swimming all day long, but until you put the book down and jump in the water, you will never be able to swim. We are forever learning and never coming to the truth of things. 2Timothy 3:7

The church needs the guts of Rosa Parks and the drive of Harriett Tubman. A made-up mind for what is right can get you a long way, and it can be perpetual. They didn't have to vote; they didn't have television or the internet. They just stuck together and did what they did. Today we vote and find out all kinds of things are wrong with the machines. But the golden rule has been, whoever has the gold RULES!

Hopefully, this book has opened your eyes to what we all need to do and consider. I'm sure many more ideas will come to your mind that you will implement. Even if you initiate a few of the suggestions, more than likely, your congregation will grow, and you will see happier members, and they will be glad to be part of your ministry.

"Don't hurt the church, encourage it, and you can only do it with real love."

You don't have to fake it until you make it; you just have to do it until you're true to it.

Stewart Marshall Gulley

Prayer and Affirmations
What's the point?

We can pray all day long and use affirmations, but there is work to be done after each. Saying I'm going to paint the wall is not going to happen unless I pick up the brush and start painting. The prayer should be, Lord, help me pick up that brush and attempt to do it. Some people feel just because they say something it's going to happen immediately. Yes, it may happen, but your slow actions will slow up the process. Many prayers have been written or said, but if you don't know how to pray; the greatest prayer there is has everything you need to ask God, and it's the Lord's Prayer;

The Lord's Prayer

Matthew 6:5-13 -And when thou prayest, thou shalt not be as the hypocrites are: for they love to pray standing in the synagogues and in the corners of the streets, that they may be seen of men. Verily I say unto you, they have their reward.

[6] But thou, when thou prayest, enter into thy closet, and when thou hast shut thy door, pray to thy Father which is in secret; and thy Father which seeth in secret shall reward thee openly.

[7] But when ye pray, use not vain repetitions, as the heathen do: for they think that they shall be heard for their much speaking.

[8] Be not ye therefore like unto them: for your Father knoweth what things ye have need of, before ye ask him.

[9] After this manner therefore pray ye: Our Father which art in heaven, Hallowed be thy name.

[10] Thy kingdom come, Thy will be done in earth, as it is in heaven.

[11] Give us this day our daily bread.

[12] And forgive us our debts, as we forgive our debtors.

[13] And lead us not into temptation, but deliver us from evil: For thine is the kingdom, and the power, and the glory, for ever. Amen.

.

We ask to do God's will and his kingdom to come in our hearts. We ask him to feed us every day. We pray to forgive those who have sinned against us and forgiveness of those we have sinned towards. We pray to lead us not into tempting to do wrong things and deliver us from the evil things that work. It is a prayer in a nutshell. Many of us ask for material things, but God knows what we need.

These things are done day by day and have to stay in our minds. It is not an overnight fix. We can attend church and hear something said that is wrong, but we must focus on what God has told us individually and move on. Saying good affirmations is like a shovel. It is to dig out all of the wrongs we've been taught and fill that space with good thoughts. As mentioned, "How do you eat an elephant? One bite at a time." And eventually, he will be eaten up.

Just because you say something one day doesn't always mean it will happen on the same day. Putting a kernel of corn in the ground on Sunday will not sprout up on Monday. It will take weeks of nurturing and watering, and so does prayers and affirmations. I know some people have these long prayers and maybe from their heart's sincerity, but action needs to follow the prayer. Whether you have the extended version or the short version like the Lord's Prayer, something needs to be said. Of course, he already knows what you need, but perhaps he just wants to hear it come out of your mouth. After all, he has given you a full 24 hours, so what is a one or two-minute prayer of thankfulness and asking the one who made us? Day by day, new mercies we see and the mercies we had yesterday are gone. What type of mercy will work today?

Lamentations 3:22-23

[22] Because of the LORD's great love, we are not consumed,   for his compassions never fail.
[23] They are new every morning;
great is your faithfulness.

Although the Lord's Prayer is the essential prayer, I have this affirmation next to the mirror in my bathroom:

Everything I touch or do will be successful, for all things are working out for my good. I have no fear.

I draw good health, success, harmony, peace, love, and financial blessings to help myself and others.

I love me, and this is how God has made me. When I love myself, I love God. When I love others, I love God all the more.

Good morning! This is God. I will be handling all of your problems today. I will not need your advice. I will not need your suggestions. The only thing I will need from you is your cooperation. So, relax and have a great day! *END*

Whatsoever your hand finds to do, do it with your might; for there is no work, nor device, nor knowledge, nor wisdom, in the grave, where you go. Ecclesiastes 9:10

Matthew 24:14, "And this gospel of the kingdom will be proclaimed throughout the whole world as a testimony to all nations, and then the end will come."

Jesus has just talked about all kinds of terrible things that will happen that will point to the end of time. Accept him today! Has the internet made it easier and quicker for everyone to hear the word before the end? We've gone from the Pony Express to the Internet Express, and the speed is updated continuously.

Now that you have read this book in its entirety know that with much wisdom comes much sorrow. Ecclesiastes 1:18

Proverbs 3:13- Happy is the man who finds wisdom, and the man who gains understanding.

1 Peter 2:9--But ye *are* a chosen generation, a royal priesthood, a holy nation, **a peculiar people**; that ye should show forth the praises of him who hath called you out of darkness into his marvelous light:

Joshua 1:9- Have I not commanded you? Be strong and courageous. Do not be afraid; do not be discouraged, for the Lord, your God will be with you where you may go!

The Fight for Survival

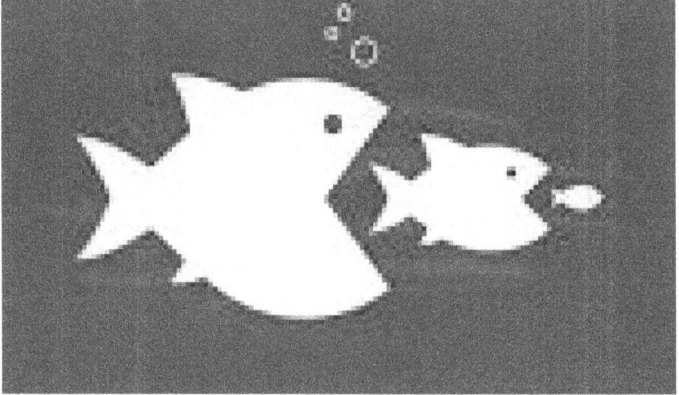

We fight for survival every day, not realizing that God is always in control. Why do many of us mention God and don't believe him? Knowing that He has made us and not we ourselves, we are the sheep of His pasture. Psalm 100:3

Luke 12:25 -Who of you by worrying **can add a single hour** to your life? Since you cannot do this very little thing, why do you worry about the rest? "

We all struggle with believing and surviving, and regardless of how hard we pray, we can't add a day, and it would take a lot of unbelief to take a day away, referring to suicide. As the scripture says, we must work while day; when night comes, no man can work. Meaning while we are living and breathing, we must work while it is daylight in our lives. And whatever our hands find to do, we must do it with all of our might, because there is no more doing when we leave here. Ecclesiastes 9:10

Such as the fish in the water, each one is looking for survival. The fishes in the water are looking for water, not realizing they are in the water. Such as we are looking for something special and the special thing is already in us. All we have to do is reach inside our hearts and go for it. We must stir up the gift that is within us. 2 Timothy 1:6-7

[6] Wherefore I put thee in remembrance that thou stir up the gift of God, which is in thee by the putting on of my hands.

[7] For God hath not given us the spirit of fear, but of power, and of love, and of a sound mind.

As we fight for survival we need to realize that the punches we will receive will be less if would work on doing what is right and what we are called to do. So many are in the wrong position.

As Peter said in Acts 2:40- With many other words he testified, and he urged them, Save yourselves from this corrupt generation." Those who embraced his message were baptized, and about three thousand were added to the believers that day.

Ecclesiastes 10:7

I have **seen** slaves on horseback, while princes

go on **foot** like slaves.

Is this what people think of church?

K.E. Martin

The Yes and No of Life

Somewhere in life, we have developed a pattern between yes, no, and maybe. It's like asking a person to come to church this Saturday and asking them to help feed the homeless, and the answer may be: "Let me check on something, and maybe I can make it, but I'm not for sure." Asking the same person: "Come to church this Saturday, and they are giving away $100 gift cards to our members-only. Do you think you can make it?" "Yes, I can. I will be there early."

Regardless of what the bible says we are to do, we get to a point in life that we choose what we will and will not do, and most of the time, we can do it only if it is convenient for us, someone made us feel guilty, or there is a benefit. Sacrificing doing something with a bad attitude can be very annoying to others. Why bring the whole team down if you don't want to be there?

Colossians 3:23-

And whatever you do, do it heartily, as to the Lord and not to men, knowing that from the Lord you will receive the reward of the inheritance; for you serve the Lord Christ.

Matthew 5:37

But let your word 'yes be 'yes,' and your 'no be 'no.' Anything more than this is from the evil one.

James 5:12.
"But above all things, my brethren, swear not, neither by heaven, neither by the earth, neither by any other oath: but let your yea be yea; and your nay, nay; lest ye fall into condemnation.

"Maybe" keeps people on edge, not knowing what you will do and not always a pleasant feeling.

Revelation 3:14-17

14 And unto the angel of the church of the Laodiceans write; These things saith the Amen, the faithful and true witness, the beginning of the creation of God;
15 I know thy works, that thou art neither cold nor hot: I would thou were cold or hot.
16 So then because thou art lukewarm, and neither cold nor hot, I will spit thee out of my mouth.
17 Because thou sayest, I am rich, and increased with goods, and have need of nothing; and knowest not that thou art wretched, and miserable, and poor, and blind, and naked:

Will we say yes, no or maybe to the will of God?

Yes, if you're going to do it (Hot)
No, you're not going to do it (Cold)
Maybe it is lukewarm (I haven't decided yet)

There's a difference between the word maybe
and may be. In other words, you may be coming or
maybe not, which leaves a person wondering. It all
depends on where the space is in the word "maybe"

If you said yes and didn't do it. You lied
If you said maybe, it keeps me on edge,
wondering if you're going to do it.
If you said No, and end up doing it, I could get
upset because if I had known you were going to do
it, I could have saved money or time.

The Loose Garment

For years I would hear the expression that you to
wear the world as a loose garment, and I was
looking for the bible scripture to relate to it. I
couldn't find anything directly to say that.
However, some scriptures have been paraphrased
about it. My understanding is that the expression
came from **Francis of Assisi**, the 13th-century saint
whose spiritual awakening took him from boozing
in silks as a rich party boy to preaching the Gospel
in rags. There will be a change when there is a
conversion in your life, and people will know it.
Wearing the world as a loose garment means being
able to let something go freely. If a garment is too
tight, it is tough to get out of to the point you need
someone to help you relieve yourself from it. Same
as material things and relationships. We are so close

to those things that we almost want to commit suicide if they are gone. It is not that you aren't to care, but those things are not your world. Look at Job in the bible. He lost everything, and God gave him double for his trouble. Most of us can't get double because we are holding too tight and not considering God and not remembering everything belongs to him, and it's not ours. The earth is the Lord's and the fullness thereof. Psalm 24:24

² For he hath founded it upon the seas, and established it upon the floods.

³ Who shall ascend into the hill of the LORD? or who shall stand in his holy place?

⁴ He that hath clean hands, and a pure heart; who hath not lifted up his soul unto vanity, nor sworn deceitfully.

⁵ He shall receive the blessing from the LORD and righteousness from the God of his salvation.

⁶ This is the generation of them that seek him, that seek thy face, O Jacob. Selah.

⁷ Lift up your heads, O ye gates; and be ye lift up, ye everlasting doors; and the King of glory shall come in.

⁸ Who is this King of glory? The LORD strong and mighty, the LORD mighty in battle.

I know many of us can quote many scriptures, but if we can remember them, they will bring peace to the soul. I mentioned earlier how I gave up a beautiful salon, a Pizza Hut converted, and I had to let it go because God told me I was a writer. I did let it go and have written over 20 books, and some are still being published. It wasn't about the salon, but it was about God. Yes, in that type of business, you can minister to your customers and began to justify while you are still there, and it is your primary income. It was my primary income, and I had a house note and no money in the bank except for specific mandatory bills. I let it go, even though I paid the house note with a charge card for a year, and then I sold the house. No, I didn't get money from selling the home because I broke even and wanted to free myself. I knew I had to let everything go. However, when God is ready to elevate you, you have to be prepared to move by faith. Yes, it has been a fight, but I just trust God anyway.

If your garment of life is too tight, you need to loosen it to free yourself and move forward to what God has been trying to draw you to do. After you get that next house, car or garment, next husband or wife, boyfriend or girlfriend and then what? The eyes are never satisfied. Proverbs 27:20.

If people don't receive what you do, just shake the dust off your feet and keep moving. Remember, Jesus' own did not receive him, and he kept going.

Just think, if he hadn't, what would the world look like today?

John 1:11- He came unto His own, and His own received Him not. But as many as received Him, to them gave He the power to become the sons of God, even to those who believe in His name.

Matthew 10:14 -And whosoever shall not receive you, nor hear your words, when ye depart out of that house or city, shake off the dust of your feet.

(Version A)

Luke 12:48 But he that knew not, and did commit things worthy of stripes, shall be beaten with few stripes. For unto whomsoever much is given, of him shall be much required: and to whom men have committed much, of him they will ask the more.

(Version B Paraphrased)

Luke 12:48-But anyone who is not aware that he is doing wrong will be punished only lightly. Much is required from those to whom much is given, for their responsibility is greater

Don't just hang in there; it's time to swing forward!

Cartoon Prophecy

It's incredible how we watch television or go to the movies and feel that we are just watching something to get excited about, not realizing much of this stuff will come true or things very familiar to it. I've always said that we all think of all sorts of things, whether good or bad. However, some people will do what comes to their mind, and others will not think about it again. People predict things, not even knowing that's what they are doing. Prophecy doesn't always come directly from the church, such as the music artist Prince. In 1982 his song 1999 said that we should dance like it's 1999, and it was only 1982. We danced past 1999 and Prince passed away in 2016, and his music is continually played.

Many remember the Jetsons that was created in 1962 by William Hanna and Joseph Barbera.

The original animator artist was Bob Singer. Later it was about 15 animators. We laughed and thought it was just a fantasy or something weird. George Jetson works three hours a day and three days a week for his short, tyrannical boss named Cosmo G. Spacely, owner of the company Spacely Space Sprockets. Typical episodes involve Mr. Spacely firing and rehiring George Jetson or promoting and demoting him. Mr. Spacely has a competitor, H. G. Cogswell, owner of the rival company Cogswell Cogs. The Jetson family lives in Orbit City. George commutes to work in an aero car that resembles a flying saucer that takes him all over the city.

Look how much of that stuff is true today, from the flying planes, robots, and appliances that will work for us, and all we have to do is turn them on. In some cases, we don't have to turn them on, we can program things, and they will start at a specific time without us being at home.

That was the prediction in the **Jetsons** cartoon tv show 1962, which was set in 2062, precisely almost 60 years from 2021. The time will come that we'll be driving around in flying cars and doing things electronically. Some people will feel that they will not have to depend on one another, while the church will be holding 3-day fasts, all-night prayer, prayer lines, strange offerings, video cell phones and gossiping. Beware, let's not be ignorant of Satan's devices. Technology serves its purpose if we use it correctly. However, Satan has access to the same tools. Is anyone educating the church?

Luke 16-8

And the lord commended the unjust steward because he had done wisely: for the children of this world are in their generation wiser than the children of light.

2 Corinthians 2:11

Lest Satan should get an advantage of us: for we are not

ignorant of his devices.

The Beatitudes

Matthew 5

5 And seeing the multitudes, He went up on a mountain, and when He was seated His disciples came to Him. [2] Then He opened His mouth and taught them, saying:

The **beatitudes,** statements of characteristics and blessing, are part of the Sermon on the Mount that Jesus spoke and is recorded in Matthew. Each beatitude looks at different circumstances of life and how all Christians are blessed through their faith. Through these 8 Beatitudes, Jesus teaches virtues and values in life that will result in blessings and rewards. These beatitudes are not singled out for specific people - they are blessings applicable to all Christians.

These Scriptures will encourage you and give you hope as you face each day, knowing that you are called blessed! No matter your age, job, or family role, if you apply the beatitudes to your life, you will experience a joyful, fulfilled life! You can read the full Bible passage below where the words of Jesus are recorded; however, here is a short summary.

The 8 Beatitudes and Their Meaning

1. Blessed are the poor in spirit, for theirs is the kingdom of heaven

The poor in spirit are those who feel a deep sense of spiritual destitution and comprehend their nothingness before God. The kingdom of heaven is theirs because they seek it, and therefore find and abide in it. To this virtue is opposed the pride of the Pharisee, which caused him to thank God that he was not like other men and to despise and reject the kingdom of heaven. There must be emptiness before there can be fullness, and so poverty of spirit precedes riches and grace in the kingdom of God.

2. Blessed are they that mourn: for they shall be comforted.

The blessing is not upon all that mourn but upon those who mourn in reference to sin. They shall be comforted by the discovery and appropriation of God's pardon. But all mourning is traced directly or indirectly to sin. We may take it, therefore, that in its widest sense, the beatitude covers all those who are led by mourning to a discerning of sin, and who so deplore its effects and consequences in the world as to yearn for and seek the deliverance which is in Christ.

3. Blessed are the meek: for they shall inherit the earth

The humble would receive far greater than the arrogant and prideful. Not only do the meek enjoy more of life on earth because of their ability to be content, but they will possess and enjoy the earth after Jesus' return and triumphal entry.

4. Blessed are they who hunger and thirst after righteousness: for they shall be filled.

Because of Christ, we can cling to the promise of everlasting righteousness in heaven. While we are called to live like Christ, we also have forgiveness of sin.

5. Blessed are the merciful: for they shall obtain mercy.

Mercy is an active virtue that Christians can show to each other because we have been given mercy ourselves. Since God has forgiven our offenses, we should forgive others and show mercy.

6. Blessed are the pure in heart: for they shall see God.

The pure in heart are those who are free from evil desires and purposes. They can see and experience God's presence because they are free from self-righteousness and arrogance.

7. Blessed are the peacemakers: for they shall be called sons of God.

The term includes all who make peace between men, whether as individuals or as communities. It includes even those who worthily endeavor to make peace, though they fail of success. They shall be called God's children because he is the God of peace who sent His own Son as the Prince of Peace.

8. Blessed are they that have been persecuted for righteousness' sake: for theirs is the kingdom of heaven.

Those who suffer because of their loyalty to the kingdom of heaven are blessed by being bound more closely to that kingdom for which they suffer.

Biblestudytools.com

Special DVDs You Should See

While many churches have what we call "church," things are going on in the world that they don't know about—the following videos I have found very informative. However, when it comes to news, how do we know which part is real unless we were there. As far as that statement is concerned, we can feel that way about the Bible, but yet we believe. Some of the suggested videos are on YouTube, while others you may have to order, but they will be well worth it. Some of these videos can be a Sunday Morning Service. Educate your people. Don't make them come out on Wednesday when you already have a captive audience.

Let me also add that two of the DVD's were on infowars.com by Alex Jones. However, the media discredit him about a lot of information. The only thing I have said about a lie that part of it may be true, but which part?
Infowars.com

1. **The Obama Deception** by Alex Jones-Infowars.com
2. **Alex Jones Movie (2009) Fall of the Republic** Full movie 2:24:19 – YouTube.com
3. **Loose Change/ 911**. - YouTube/
4. **Fish Out of Water**- Gay Issues -DVD
5. **What the Health** – Food illnesses - YouTube
6. **The Most Powerful Strategy for Healing People and the Planet**- Michael Klaper-YouTube

7. **Plant-Strong & Healthy Living-**Rip Esseltyn –YouTube
8. **Plant Pure Nation-** A Must-See Documentary– YouTube
9. **Stop Eating Poison** Dr. John McDougall-YouTube
10. **From Babylon to America-The Prophecy Movie (A MUST SEE VIDEO, YOU WILL LEARN THINGS THAT CHURCH DOESN'T TALK ABOUT!)**

Let food be thy medicine!- Hippocrates

The doctor of the future will no longer treat the human frame with drugs but rather will cure and prevent disease with nutrition.

Thomas Edison

Find movies about finances, credit, and anything that has to do with everyday life. The way of fools seems right to them, but the wise listen to advice Proverbs 12:15

About the Author

Stewart Marshall Gulley spent most of his life in California, although born in Akron, Ohio, and graduating from Weequahic High School in Newark, New Jersey.

He has spent many years in church and realized it could be very uplifting and destroying due to habits passed down that had nothing to do with God. In the congregation, observing was his favorite seat, but God had another plan, ministering from the pulpit, and he found that both sides were a challenge because of what he saw. He no way claims to be a bible scholar or perfect and can only remember half of the bible scriptures at any given time. Still, God told him in advance that he would not be able to fully remember them because it was not all about who can remember the most bible verses and seem to be knowledgeable. Stewart just wanted to go to church and ignore things going on, but that would not just happen. His eyes opened, and what he saw bothered him for years. Understanding that members would not say anything because they felt it was wrong to talk about the church, but they spoke the same language when they discussed things they didn't like. He wrote the manuscript for this book 20 years ago but did not have it published. God spoke to him and said it's time to release it with the added knowledge accumulated over the past 20 years.

Early in life, being a pastor was not his gift, but it was a unique ministry that he had. Many say he missed his calling and should have been a comedian, but there was a deeper side they didn't know.

He has directed several youth organizations; and vibrantly attended many churches, regardless of their denomination. Founder of H.i.Y.O.B.Y – Helping in Your Own Back Yard. Although his modesty keeps him from elaborating on the 20 plus schools he has attended, but to name a few such as an artist, real estate agent, playwright, auctioneer, cosmetology instructor, ministry, cooking school, fashion design school, mortgage school as well as a coach and substitute teacher for several years and so much more. A man whose talents exceed the norm. The reason for so many schools was because he didn't see much on television that he liked. He thinks the news is full of lies and garbage, and he has only watched approximately 2 hours of news collectively in the last 35 years. Bad news in the morning and bad news at night, who could live that way?

He has never been evicted and fulfilled all leases but has moved more than 50 times. He had not owned a car in over 30 years but could maneuver and do everything he needed in business without bugging people; public transportation was his best friend. He left the driving to the driver so that he could concentrate on his next goal. He was called a gypsy, and he laughed because to him, it was a gypsy with a divine purpose.

All he knew when it was time to move, it was just time to move. It was God's way of showing love and laughter to others through Stewart wherever he moved. When you become restless where you are, there is a time for something to happen. He has lived in several states, has been a part of nine different denominations, was married twice, divorced twice, two children, and has written over 20 books. As he sometimes says: "You may see my glory, but you don't know my story."

To him, all of these things are not bragging; it is something that he did that took the place of television. He has something to talk about regarding church and believes that God will give every man his just reward (Rev, 22:12). Even though many once knew Christ and trying to denounce him, it would be better for them not to have known the way of righteousness than having known it, to turn away from the holy commandment handed on to them. (2Peter 2:21)

Without a second thought, he believes that the love of many has grown wax cold, whether they are in church or not. He doesn't think that the saying "What you don't know can't hurt you" is entirely wrong. Instead, he'd say, "What you do know but don't do will hurt you and others even more." Churches have thousands of members that go home unfulfilled, but they sing and rejoice due to their atmosphere.

He believes that we can all learn from one another, and he questions those who think they already know everything. We know in part and prophesy in part, but that which is perfect comes, then that which is in part shall be done away. (1Corinthians 13:9)."

The Greatest of These Is Love. "And now these three remain faith, hope, and love. But the greatest of these is love" (1 Corinthians 13:13).

"But above all these things put on love, which is the bond of perfection. (Colossians 3:14)

The Old Testament teaches you. The New Testament reaches you. The Future Testament, you'll be there living it and praising God in person.

Regardless of our trials or how we see life,

Ecclesiastes 7:8
The end of a matter is better than its beginning, and patience is better than pride.

Don't be fooled; God didn't heal you, save you, protect or even allow you to retire for you not to be doing something to better the world around you!

A Final Thought!

The following we may not want to hear or read because we are always told to think positive. However, when reality steps in positivity has to bow down. Look at all of the signs and the stuff we see going on every day. And this was prophesied before we were born. Is prophecy coming true?

Matthew: 24- And Jesus went out, and departed from the temple: and his disciples came to *him* for to show him the buildings of the temple. ² And Jesus said unto them, See ye not all these things? Verily I say unto you; There shall not be left here one stone upon another, that shall not be thrown down.

³ And as he sat upon the mount of Olives, the disciples came unto him privately, saying, Tell us, when shall these things be? And what *shall be* the sign of thy coming, and of the end of the world? ⁴ And Jesus answered and said unto them, Take heed that no man deceive you. ⁵ For many shall come in my name, saying, I am Christ; and shall deceive many. ⁶ **And ye shall hear of wars and rumors of wars:** see that ye be not troubled: for all *these things* must come to pass, but the end is

not yet. ^{7} For nation shall rise against nation, and kingdom against kingdom: and there shall be famines, and pestilences, and earthquakes, in divers places. ^{8} All these *are* the beginning of sorrows.

^{9} Then shall they deliver you up to be afflicted, and shall kill you: and ye shall be hated of all nations for my name's sake. ^{10} And then shall many be offended, and shall betray one another, and shall hate one another. ^{11} And many false prophets shall rise, and shall deceive many. ^{12} And because iniquity shall abound, the love of many shall wax cold. ^{13} But he that shall endure unto the end, the same shall be saved. ^{14} And this gospel of the kingdom shall be preached in all the world for a witness unto all nations; and then shall the end come.

^{34} "Do not think that I came to bring peace on earth. I did not come to bring peace but a sword. ^{35} For I have come to 'set[1] a man against his father, a daughter against her mother, and a daughter-in-law against her mother-in-law'; ^{36} and 'a **man's enemies** *will be* **those of his** *own* **household.'** ^{37} He who loves father or mother more than Me is not worthy of Me. And he who loves son or daughter more than Me is not worthy of Me. [38] And he who does not take his cross and follow after Me is not worthy of Me. [39] He who finds his life will lose it, and he who loses his life for My sake will find it.

Love one another while we can!

Romans 13:8 -Owe no man anything, but to

love one another, for he that loveth another hath

fulfilled the law.

Romans 12:2-Do not be conformed to this age, but be

transformed **by the renewing of your mind**, so that you

may discern what is the good, pleasing, and perfect will

of God.

John 16:33-I have told you these things, so that in

me you may have peace. In this world you will have

trouble. But take heart! I have overcome the

world."

Other Books by Stewart Marshall Gulley

- How to Get Over a Past Relationship Faster Than You Think: 2 ½ Hours to Freedom
- Stay in Your Own Lane for the Entrepreneur Book, Workshop and Course
- Buck Naked- Stripping yourself naked and becoming who you really are.
- It started at 2:00, Not 2:15 – for people who are consistently late
- Who in the Hell is They?- For people who don't reach their goal because of what THEY said.
- Church, The Falling Empire – Church structure
- Eric the Last Child – Mystery novel for adults
- Love Should Have Brought You Home Last Night- Novelette
- High Heels, Bad Feet- Novelette
- The Elephant and the Mouse – Children's Book
- His Eye Is on the Sparrow – Children's Book
- The Witch that Got a Miracle- Children's Book
- Words from the 21st Century Shakespearean Poet
- The Elephant and the Mouse-Children's book
- The Birthday Party to Which Nobody Came- Children's book
- The Lizard and the Frog- Children's Book

<u>Forth-coming books</u>

- Hear No Evil, See No Evil, Speak No Evil: A Guide for Parents, Grandparents, and Stepparents
- Baby, You Make Me Smile
  (Twenty-five short stories with lesson plans)
- Honey Drops from the Lips, Over 8000 original Quotes
- Everyday Life (Over 250 Poems)
- If You Thought Columbine Was Something, You Haven't Seen Anything Yet- The U.S. School System
- Adam is Eve Out to Get You?-A book every man and young boy should read.
- Over 8,000 Quotes

Also, other educational children's books are coming.

<u>Speaking Engagements</u>

Stewart is available for guest speaking, inspirational, colleges, motivational and spiritual engagements.

Contact

www. stewartmarshallgulley.com

P.O. Box 2063 Los Angeles, California 90078

Email: Stemagu7@aol.com

Free Download:

**The 5 Things that will help you're your
ministry be different right away**

www.stewartmarshallgulley.com

323-570-4735

*To the young at heart, you'll
never understand old age until you
get there!*

Stewart Marshall Gulley